B'NAI B'RITH

B'NAI
B'RITH

The story of a covenant

by Edward E. Grusd

APPLETON-CENTURY

NEW YORK

*It is not thy duty to complete
the work, but neither art thou
free to desist from it.*

Rabbi Tarfon,
in *Ethics of the Fathers,*
THE TALMUD

Preface

The story of B'nai B'rith must cheer all of those who prize man's concern for his fellow man. In its 123rd year, B'nai B'rith stands as an outstanding social achievement in which high idealistic vision is combined with great practical vigor. In a phrase, B'nai B'rith's history shows that there is only as much sky over our heads as land under our feet.

B'nai B'rith began as a fraternal organization. Its founding members numbered twelve; its treasury held $60. It took upon itself the work of promoting their highest interests and those of humanity. This B'nai B'rith has done—and has become an agency of great service, not just to the Jewish community, but to all Americans and to the world. Its workers are its 340,000 men and women in its 1,350 lodges and 900 chapters, and the tens of thousands more belonging to its affiliates for young men and women.

To read this laudable history is to review some of the most sublime moments in history—and some of the most agonizing. The terrible pogroms of eastern Europe, which B'nai B'rith sought to ease, remind us—if we need reminding—of man's capacity for brutality and cruelty to his fellow man.

A recent newspaper article describing the lives of the 815 remaining Jews in Berlin tells us further of the fiery hell of Hitler's terror. And it is instructive to know how grudgingly even the minor forms of man's prejudices yield to reason. As late as 1908, the author tells us, the Associated Press was identifying individuals charged with crimes as Jews. It was in response to such as this that Sigmund Livingston suggested formation of a National Caricature Committee. Such a group was founded as the Anti-Defamation League; and the ADL's unceasing efforts to protect civil rights and civil liberties has truly made it a guardian of the American dream.

As B'nai B'rith grew, so did its recognition and its accomplishments. William Howard Taft was the first president to appear in person and to address B'nai B'rith. In 1897 Theodore Herzl summoned the first Zionist Congress to Switzerland as a preliminary step toward a Jewish homeland in the Middle East. This step was not universally welcomed by the members of B'nai B'rith; but the terrors of oppression in Europe eventually persuaded the doubters. And the bravery and tenacity of Israel persuaded others who doubted other things.

During 1947–1948 I was a correspondent for a Boston newspaper, covering the war in Palestine. The energy, sacrifice, and idealism of the Jewish settler-fighters led me promptly to forecast that a homeland would be successfully won—although at the time the Israeli military situation was unfavorable. In this connection Mr. Grusd, the author, tells in his straightforward and clear narrative an interesting episode involving a secret visit by Chaim Weizmann to the White House which was followed shortly thereafter by United States recognition of Israel independence.

No aspect of man's civilizing influence has been left untouched by B'nai B'rith—culture, education, youth care, and the larger historical consequences of individual, corporate, and governmental actions.

And in these numerous activities B'nai B'rith stood beyond Jewish life. In a pluralistic society such as ours in the United States, its causes have not been merely "Jewish causes." They have been the causes of us all. Because where injustice exists—in the form of barbed wire or a locker-room slur—there we are all hurt; wherever it is endangered we are all endangered; but where freedom and justice exist, we are all enlarged.

Three hundred and fifty years ago another intrepid group, the Puritans, stood on a ship's deck and heard John Winthrop say: "We must consider that we shall be as a city set upon a hill, and the eyes of all people will be upon us."

The Puritans were in the middle of the Atlantic when they shared that vision of the city upon the hill. And we are still in the middle of our journey. As long as millions of Americans suffer indignity and punishment and deprivation because of their color, their poverty, their race, or their religion, we know that we are only halfway to our goal, a city and a country in which the promises of our Constitution are at last fulfilled for all Americans.

For that honor and justice we must all stand—and we must all work. And this means this informed history of B'nai B'rith is a beginning—not a finished product. There will be other occasions for pride and anguish in the years of struggle ahead. B'nai B'rith will surely be in the forefront of that struggle for justice and equality, as they have led us so often in the past.

Robert F. Kennedy

Foreword

Those whose responsibility it is to interpret B'nai B'rith
to the public have a formidable task: to telescope into
a few expressions the many diverse facets, long history,
and significant traditions and evolving goals of an organization which, from small beginnings, has grown into
a vast enterprise of nearly a half million men, women,
and young people in forty-four countries. It has become
so complex in its structure and activities that most of its
members—to say nothing of others—have only a limited
knowledge of its achievements, purposes, and scope.

This book, the first full-length history of B'nai B'rith,

fills a long-felt need. The dramatic story is here to read; it tells of the spirit and pattern of the organization, its persistent quest for Jewish unity, its constant (and sometimes romantic) striving to do more and more, its flexibility that enabled it to stay contemporary, meeting the changing needs of the changing generations. Reading it, leisurely, is likely to be an entertaining as well as educational experience.

For this volume is no chauvinistic salute. B'nai B'rith has always been a very human institution, and the author presents it objectively, with all its strengths and weaknesses, its successes and failures. Nor is this a dry "reading of the minutes," but a lively account of a unique movement in American and Jewish life, set in the context of its times. Edward E. Grusd is particularly qualified for the historian's task he achieves so ably in these pages. He has served B'nai B'rith as editor of *The National Jewish Monthly* for more than a generation, having joined its staff in 1928, and is today its senior member, in point of service. He has been a close observer of and a very intimate participant in the story of B'nai B'rith during its most explosive era of growth and creative service.

Whether or not man learns anything from history is a moot question; yet he can be inspired or depressed by it. Traditionally, Jews have been inspired by their history, and B'nai B'rith is a small part of that millennial saga. The author, in his final passage, declares, "The story of B'nai B'rith had a beginning, but it has no end. Or, more accurately, it has no end that can be foreseen." Our generation is fortunate that the founders of B'nai B'rith built better than they knew, and that we have today the organization and the experience to help make our hopes for a better future come true. In a very real sense, therefore, this book is a prologue to what is yet to be.

Dr. William A. Wexler
President, B'nai B'rith

Savannah, Georgia
March 1, 1966

Contents

A prefatory statement

It is astonishing that this is the first full-length history of B'nai B'rith. After all, it is not only America's largest, oldest, and most representative national Jewish organization, but also the nation's oldest native-born major service organization. The Masons and Odd Fellows are, of course, much older, and have been here much longer, but they were founded overseas; B'nai B'rith was born in America, in 1843. It is thus 37 years older than the Salvation Army, 38 years older than the American Red Cross, 39 years older than the Knights of Columbus, 47 years older than the Daughters of the American Revolution, and more than 70 years older than the Kiwanis, Lions, or American Legion.

Moreover, B'nai B'rith has always been history-conscious. It was scarcely 25 years old when the demand was first voiced that its history be written, and that demand was repeated periodically for a century. At times, the organization even appropriated money for the project, but for one reason or another it was never undertaken. And this present work is a private one, neither commissioned nor financed by the Order.

This is all the more strange because it has always been a very human institution. Its history need not be a dry accumulation of names, dates, and facts, but an account of interesting events, personalities, and ideas. Indeed, it can be seen as a story—a tale that winds its way through nearly 125 of the 190 years of American independence. Nor is it esoteric; although its name is Hebrew—meaning Sons of the Covenant—and although it is a Jewish organization, dedicated to the welfare and creative survival of the Jewish people, it is known (at least nominally) to every American Jew and to millions of Gentiles through the mass media.

Its story must necessarily include many pedestrian facts, but it is also quickened with the charm of the Victorian era, with many expressions of unconscious humor, with a variety of colorful people, with absorbing examples of organizational foibles and achievements, with dramatic factional struggles, and with all the fascination of any organism born and reared in the American horse-and-buggy age which has survived into the era of jet planes and atomic energy. It is a part of Jewish history, and a part of Americana.

And all this is overlaid with the fact that since its birth, despite the basic changes in the world, its fundamental principles and *raison d'être* remain the same, although its forms and expressions now would be unrecognizable to the founders.

It was a grave responsibility to undertake to tell its story objectively, without absurdly boasting of its achievements after the fashion of organizations, without getting its weaknesses out of focus, and withal doing it justice in spite of the fact that many details had to be omitted in order to make this book manageable. What made it possible, even almost easy, is the fact that B'nai B'rith is unique. There are hundreds of fine Jewish organizations, but none resembles the Order in the slightest degree. It has a character and personality all its own.

This is the story of that unique institution, and how it was born and struggled and grew and changed and contributed to the Jewish people and through them to all people, ever since John Tyler lived in the White House.

1
.

The background

When I was in high school I used to take a long walk
with my father almost every Sunday morning. He would
point out certain streets, buildings, private homes, and
vacant lots and tell me their history, and who lived in
some of the houses. He had come to the city in 1889, a
poor immigrant boy from Riga, but he had a vast curi-
osity about people and places and a zest for the simple
pleasures he could afford, like walking, and seeing new
things, and telling others about them. In this way he became a storehouse of information about his immediate
environment.

Our favorite walk was through the expensive section where most of the wealthy Jews lived at that time. The hushed, tree-shaded streets were lined with aristocratic mansions, each set far back on an acre of manicured lawn and protected by high walls or fences. My father had once dreamed of living in this area himself but had long since awakened to a very different kind of reality.

One Sunday we stopped in front of one of the richest estates. The three-story house of dark brick with white stone trim was set back at least a hundred feet, and the lawn was protected from passers-by by an iron spike fence six feet tall. Flower beds flashed vivid colors in the morning sun, and the quiet was so intense that the chirping of birds in the tall elm trees was piercing. Behind the mansion, in front of a two-car garage, a man in overalls was washing a black Pierce-Arrow.

We peered through the bars of the fence. When I looked at my father I saw that he was staring at me.

"Do you know who lives here?" he whispered, but did not wait for an answer. "One of the richest men in town. He owns a big factory, with maybe five hundred people working for him. And this isn't his only home; he's got another one in Florida, for winter." He paused, then added: "A German Jew, of course."

There was awe in his voice, but I must have appeared unimpressed, because he sighed.

"I was just thinking. You could have a house like this, some day. Don't laugh; I mean it. Me, I couldn't. I'm a foreigner, with no money. I speak broken English, and I had no education. Besides, I'm a Russian Jew. But you! You were born in America, you speak perfect English, you're smart in school, you're going to college, you're not bad-looking, you play football like a *goy*, you already make a pretty good public speech, you'll become a doctor or a lawyer—when you grow up you'll be as good as any German Jew. It's not like when I first came over from the old country—then the German Jews wouldn't give the time of day to people like us. But things are changing. There are millions of Russian Jews in this country now, and their children are beginning to go to college, to make money, and become somebody. But the German Jews are dying out. There aren't enough German young men for their daughters to marry. When they see a fine, American-born boy like you—a doctor or a lawyer, who speaks perfect English—they're not going to turn up their noses like they used to, just because his father came from Russia."

He glanced wistfully through the fence again.

"The old man who owns all this is over seventy now. He's retired, and his son runs the factory. The son has an only child." He regarded me solemnly. "A girl . . . about your age. She goes to private school."

I stared at him, aghast. He smiled.

"Who knows? This is America. Who knows?"

This little episode occurred seventy-five years after B'nai B'rith was founded, yet the two events are related, although only distantly. The immigrant from Russia and the man who owned the factory were divided, then, by a deep gulf which was, however, bridgeable, but it was a gulf that widened back through American Jewish history to 1843, when it divided many more groups than Germans and Russians, and seemed unbridgeable. That gulf, yawning wide in the 1840's, was the reason B'nai B'rith came into being.

Why 1843? Why not 1743, or 1643? In 1643 there were no Jews in the colonies, and in 1743 the problem did not exist because the few who were there were a homogeneous group—practically all Sephardim, descendants of the great Jewish community that was exiled from Spain in 1492. The survivors of that historic tragedy scattered to many places, including Brazil. In that country they lived in peace while it was controlled by the Netherlands, but when Portugal triumphed there, the persecution of the Inquisition followed, and the Wandering Jew took up his journey again. Several shiploads left Recife in 1654, headed for Holland, to escape the terror. But one of the vessels was captured on the high seas by a French privateer, and after the passengers had been robbed of everything they were put ashore at Dutch New Amsterdam.

When these twenty-three men, women, and children landed on the lower tip of Manhattan Island—penniless, bewildered, forsaken—they were treated to a taste of contemporary Christian charity as practiced by the God-fearing, churchgoing, Bible-reading Dutch burghers headed by peg-legged Governor Peter Stuyvesant. They were ordered to leave by the next ship. The thrifty Dutch colonists wanted no beggars around, living off the community. It was then that the little band of newcomers formulated a policy which was to influence Jewish life in America for the next three centuries: they informed Governor Stuyvesant and the Dutch West Indies Company that Jews would never become a public charge. They were then grudgingly permitted to remain, thus becoming, in 1654, the first Jewish community in America.

That community grew slowly, as did the colonial population in general, even after the British replaced the Dutch in 1664, when New Amsterdam became New York. By 1776, although hundreds were fighting in George Washington's armies, there were fewer than three thousand Jews in the newly independent United

States, and most of them were Sephardim. After the Revolution, however, there was a steady trickle of Jews from central and eastern Europe, the Ashkenazim, whose ancestors had not come from Spain, but the Sephardim remained the dominant element. They were religious traditionalists, aristocratic and proud of their ancient lineage, which dated back to the golden age of Spain. Even in colonial America they were among the aristocracy, with the already ancient date of 1654 as the time of their beginning, and they looked down upon their Ashkenazic brethren not only because they were newcomers, ignorant of the language and customs of the land, but because they worshiped differently in their synagogues, and because they were mostly poor and humble. Nevertheless they permitted a few of them, here and there, to join their congregations, although they never really accepted them, and the Ashkenazim usually broke away and formed their own congregations as immigration from central Europe continued.

As the nineteenth century got under way, the number of Ashkenazim slowly increased, while the number of Sephardim remained constant and later even decreased, since all their traditional religious observances did not save some of their children from intermarriage and assimilation. As time went on, something of the same process occurred among the so-called German Jews after they had been here for a generation or two and had acquired property and social ambitions. Sol Liptzin, in his *Generation of Decision*, points out that one of the reasons for the rapid assimilation of Jews into the American culture during the early part of the nineteenth century was because most Americans still cherished the romantic notions about Jews that were handed down to them by their colonial ancestors. The intellectuals,

poets, and clergymen, who shaped public opinion from
their ivory towers high above the grubby world of trade
and business, "still saw about the head of every Jew an
afterglow of Sinai, and their imagination was still
deeply stirred by the Hebrew tongue, the exotic Jewish
rituals, and the continuity of Jewish existence since the
beginning of time."

Actually the afterglow of Sinai was very dim around
the heads of most of the Ashkenazim who landed in
New York during the first half of the nineteenth century.
They came by families or in small groups from Germany
and Austria, Bohemia and Hungary, Russia and other
lands. They came to escape religious, economic, and
social discrimination, as well as poverty; they had heard
that America was a land of opportunity and freedom.
Obviously the "best elements" did not come, for they,
being well educated, were relatively well off, with a
stake in the status quo.

The ones who did brave the unknown were, therefore,
for the most part, what European oppression for centuries had made of them: poor and uneducated, ignorant
and superstitious, along with a sprinkling of skilled
craftsmen and ambitious entrepreneurs. By the early
1840's the Jews from central and eastern Europe out-
numbered the Sephardim.

That's when the caldron of Jewish life in America began to seethe. There were only about fifteen thousand
Jews in the entire country, with perhaps two-thirds of
them in New York City, and they constituted a micro-
scopic minority of the population. Moreover, they were
"different." They brought over with them from the old
country their own languages, customs, mores, religious
distinctiveness, prejudices, superstitions, even certain
habits of dress. They were an urban people and America

was largely a rural society. Generations of oppression, discrimination, and segregation in Europe had conditioned them psychologically and vocationally: they had been forbidden to own land, to live where they pleased, to attend universities, to engage in almost every means of earning a livelihood except in moneylending, shopkeeping, certain trades, and a number of marginal occupations.

Today Americans are a congress of peoples from all parts of the world. But in the early 1840's most of them were Protestants of British origin, and the miniscule Jewish group was even more conspicuously different by sheer constrast.

Cities were small. The government, headed by President John Tyler, was unimportant in the daily lives of the people. Life meant struggle, as always, but in those days it was less a struggle against human competitors than a fight to conquer the wilderness, push back the frontier, and build new things.

At the same time the seeds of bigotry and disunity lay deep in the otherwise rich American soil, and indeed they had been sprouting sporadically since the very beginnings of the American colonies—with witch hunts and the exile of Roger Williams from Massachusetts and cruelty against all nonconformists. Now those seeds were growing again. Most white people accepted Negro slavery as a time-honored institution, and although its abolition was becoming an issue, few dreamed that it was to tear the nation apart in less than twenty years. Protestant anti-Catholicism had long been a constant factor, but by the 1840's it was directed less against Catholics as such than against "popery" and "the dirty Irish." The word anti-Semitism was unknown (it was not coined until 1879, in a pamphlet published, significantly, in Germany), but it existed in fact, although not virulently, and it was accompanied by a comparatively small measure of discrimination.

There were rich people and poor, of course, but in general the gulf between them was not uncrossable, as it was in Europe. Alexis de Tocqueville wrote that "nothing struck me more forcibly than the general equality of conditions," which he called "the fundamental fact from which all others seem to be derived."

The Jews, too, among themselves, enjoyed a "general equality of conditions." There were a few wealthy families among them, but overwhelmingly they were workers, artisans, craftsmen, and shopkeepers. And like the rest of the population, they carried within themselves the seeds of strife and disunity.

It is difficult to explain Jews to Gentiles, because Jewishness is more than merely religion. Most Jews love their people, support their institutions generously, even prefer to live among themselves. But when it comes to differences in religious rituals, traditional customs, approaches to Jewish problems—even pronunciation of Yiddish—Jews can earn anew their ancient reputation as a stiff-necked people.

These passionate traits were more in evidence in the 1840's than they are today, and were rendered even more complex by the immigrant character of the Jewish community. The Jews in Germany had considered *die Ostjuden* (eastern European Jews) beneath their contempt. The *Ostjuden* not only scorned the "assimilated" German Jews, but one Jewish community often feuded with the ways of another in the same country, only a few miles away. To the Hungarian Jews, those in Russia were inferior, and vice versa, and so it was throughout Europe. Each *shtetl* (small Jewish community) had social and religious customs different from the others, often in only minor degree. They all believed in *Kol Yisrael Chaverim* (all Jews are brethren), but any whose practices differed from theirs were wrong—and in extreme cases were scarcely considered Jews at all!

When these people came to the United States, they brought their quarrels with them, and they nurtured them in the ghettos on the lower East Side of Manhattan. So fierce and passionate was the disunity that in some cases the marriage of a German Jew and a Polish Jewess was regarded as heretical as a marriage between a Jew and a Christian.

Each little group formed its own synagogue congregation, to which "outsiders" were not welcome, and to which those outsiders wouldn't have dreamed of going even if implored to. The hostility sometimes extended to the grave, with some groups establishing cemeteries solely for "their own." They organized a welter of educational, health, and charitable agencies: societies for orphan care and societies to help the sick, societies for burying the dead, societies for collecting dowries for poor brides, and societies to make interest-free loans. But each was sponsored by and limited to a clique. It would have been unthinkable to suggest that they all get together (even without giving up their own beliefs) to create a first-rate Jewish educational system, an outstanding hospital, or a high-quality social agency, to serve the needs of all. What! Work together with those ignorant Chassidim . . . those fanatics from Silesia . . . those peasants from the Ukraine . . . those stuck-up German Jews . . . those cold-hearted Sephardim with their *yiches*? (pride of ancestry). Never!

So deep and numerous were the divisions among New York's ten thousand Jews in 1840 that it took one of the most sensational *causes célèbres* of the nineteenth century to bring even a semblance of united action among them—and even that was too little and too late. Early that year, the head of a Franciscan monastery in Damascus, Syria, disappeared. The monks at once accused "the Jews" of murdering him to use his blood for ritual purposes—one of the anti-Jewish libels revived from the Middle Ages. Leading Jews were arrested and tortured, and sixty Jewish children were locked up and left to starve until some of their frantic parents "confessed"— only to repudiate such confessions later. The world press played up the story, and "the Damascus Affair" became a global issue.

The Jews of Great Britain and France, who were organizationally united, protested the ghastly injustice and roused their Christian countrymen and governments to protest. But in the United States separate actions were taken in each of the large cities, and separate meetings were held within those cities.

In New York, the Jews tardily agreed to a united protest meeting to appeal to the Federal Government to intervene. But Shearith Israel, the leading congregation, refused to participate because "no benefit can come from such a course." The session therefore took place at Bnai Jeshurun, an Ashkenazic congregation. A resolution was passed calling on President Martin Van Buren for diplomatic intervention with Syria. Ironically and embarrassingly, the Secretary of State informed the New York committee, as well as sponsors of similar meetings elsewhere, that the United States had already intervened—and successfully, as it turned out—before any of the protest meetings had been held!

The following year, as a direct result of the Damascus Affair, Rabbi Isaac Leeser of Philadelphia, the leading

Orthodox spokesman, tried to organize a representative Jewish body, but failed. He failed again in 1855, when he and Rabbi Isaac M. Wise, the leading Reform spokesman, joined forces in an effort to unite their rabbinical colleagues against Swiss anti-Semitism; the rabbis became too embroiled in doctrinal squabbles.

Then came the Mortara Case in 1858. Papal police kidnapped a small Jewish boy, Edgar Mortara, in Bologna, Italy, and had him reared as a Catholic (he later became a priest), on the grounds that he had been secretly baptized as an infant by an illiterate servant girl. This affair horrified and aroused Jews everywhere and actually led, in 1859, to the formation of the Board of Delegates of American Israelites. Even then, Jewish unity was far from perfect, since the Reform movement and the two prestigious Sephardic congregations in New York and Philadelphia refused to join. The Board had a good record of united action in a few cases, but it ended its existence in the 1870's, when the Union of American Hebrew Congregations was formed.

2

■

The very beginning

B'nai B'rith was founded on October 13, 1843, for the expressed purpose of ending, or at least reducing, the chaos and anarchy in Jewish life—or, as one of the founders put it, of "uniting and elevating the Sons of Abraham."

There were twelve founders, all in their twenties or thirties. All had been born in Germany, and had come to New York in the late 1820's or 1830's. All lived on the lower East Side, where most of them, at the time, were petty shopkeepers. The majority had not known one another in Germany, and only a few were acquainted before 1843.

Those few included Henry Jones, Isaac Rosenbourg, William Renau, and Reuben Rodacher. They met, apparently, because they were members of the Free Masons or Odd Fellows, as well as of several secret benevolent societies. They developed the habit of gathering frequently at Rosenbourg's little jewelry workshop and retail store at 450 Grand Street. The chief topic of conversation was, as Rosenbourg later described it, "the deplorable condition of the Jews in this, our newly adopted country."

The condition was deplorable not only because of the disunity and chaos within the Jewish community, but also because the animosities engendered by the warring congregations and organizations spilled over into the personal lives of the people. In a city as small as New York was in 1843, expressions of venomous discord could not be concealed from the general public, which looked with contempt at the scandalous spectacle. The fact that most of the Jews were recent immigrants of the poorer class—with characteristics which native Americans considered outlandish—combined with the ever-present latent anti-Semitism, did not improve what today we would call their image.

These and other considerations deeply concerned the serious young men who met in the jewelry store on Grand Street. By early autumn of 1843 they decided that an organization must be formed—of such a nature, and with such a program, that Jews of all shades of opinion, and of whatever origin, would join it and work together for a common purpose. It was a fantastic idea. How could people so at loggerheads that groups refused

to speak to one another be brought into one organization?

There is a legend, which is occasionally mentioned to
this day, that B'nai B'rith was founded because in 1843
Jews were barred from membership in the Masonic orders and the Odd Fellows. Obviously, that was not the
case, since several of the Order's founders were themselves members of those organizations. We have frag-
ments of memoirs written by Jones, Rosenbourg, and
Renau, as well as by others who joined B'nai B'rith soon
after it was founded, which leave no doubt about this.

Incidentally, these memoirs were written years later,
after the Order had achieved considerable success and
prestige. They all agree on the point about the Masons
and Odd Fellows, but disagree as to who should be considered the one who first actually proposed a new kind
of Jewish organization. Each nominated himself.

Jones wrote that Renau and Rodacher had called upon
him and asked if he would be interested in forming an
Odd Fellows lodge composed exclusively of Jews, since
some of their people had been refused admission to Odd
Fellows lodges. Jones replied that the Odd Fellows made
no religious distinctions, and that he was opposed to a
Jewish lodge of that Order, but that if Rodacher would
introduce him to "twelve respectable men," he would
help found an entirely Jewish organization which would,
"with the help of God, be the means of uniting the Israelites in America." (In those days, the words "Israelite" and "Hebrew" were considered more genteel than
the word "Jew.")

But Renau's memoir declared that Jones had come to
him, saying the Masons and Odd Fellows were discriminating against Jews and that they should get together
and form a Jewish lodge of one of those organizations.

Renau explained that the two orders did not discriminate, except against individuals, and that he suggested "a new Order with the principal aim of uniting and elevating the Sons of Abraham." The others "joyfully agreed."

Rosenbourg wrote that Renau had brought Jones to *him*, to discuss "the deplorable conditions" of Jews in New York, and that the three of them decided "to start a society like the Masons and Odd Fellows . . . capable of captivating the imagination." He, too, remarked that "the fact that some Jews were rejected in some lodges" of the Masons and Odd Fellows "did not concern the rest."

Who were the twelve men who founded B'nai B'rith, and what gave them the vision lacking in most of their contemporaries? Unfortunately, they left few records, and little is known of their backgrounds. Reuben Rodacher, Henry Kling, and Isaac Dittenhoefer all came to the United States on the same ship in 1836, although it is not known whether they first met aboard or had known one another in Germany. Rodacher, born in Hesse in 1805, a self-educated man active in synagogue affairs in New York during the 1840's and 1850's, was the oldest of the founders. He died in 1886.

All that is known of Kling and Dittenhoefer is that the first was in the paper business in New York during the 1840's, and the latter had a dry-goods store on the East Side during that decade. It is especially unfortunate that so little is known about Dittenhoefer, who died in 1860, because he became the first President of B'nai B'rith.

Jonas Hecht had the title of Reverend because he was the *chazan* (cantor) of New York's Temple Anshe Chesed during the 1840's. Henry Jones was secretary of the congregation, and the two were fast friends. Rev. Jonas Hecht later became cantor of a synagogue in Norfolk, Virginia, and outlived all his colleagues. Born in 1806, he died in 1899 at the age of ninety-three, and he was thus the first of many thousands of men who were affiliated with B'nai B'rith for more than half a century.

Valentine Koon was born in Stuttgart in 1810 and died in 1890. In the 1840's he operated a shoe store on Greenwich Street, but afterward went into the real estate and construction business, with considerable success. It was his firm which constructed the B'nai B'rith Home for the Aged at Yonkers in the 1880's. He was a fervent advocate of the Union cause, and in 1860 he was one of the New York State electors who cast the ballot for Abraham Lincoln.

William Renau first tried his hand at barbering in New York, then opened a cigar store on the East Side. He was one of the founders of New York's Temple Emanu-El. Early in 1850 he moved to Cincinnati, where he became prominent in politics, served as a magistrate, and was elected to several terms on the city council. He died there at the age of seventy-nine.

Isaac Rosenbourg, as we have seen, had a jewelry store on the East Side; his sister was the wife of Reuben Rodacher.

Hirsch Heineman had a trimmings shop, and Michael Schwab a dry-goods store. No information is available about Samuel Schaefer and Henry Anspacher.

Henry Jones was later officially designated as the chief founder of B'nai B'rith, and happily more is known about him than about any of the others. Born in Hamburg as Heinrich Jonas on December 22, 1811, he reached New York in 1829, and almost immediately became active in the Jewish community. He was a mechanic, and earned a modest living from his small shop. He married a woman ten years his senior, and although they had no children of their own, they adopted two. Long a member of Congregation Anshe Chesed, the city's third-oldest synagogue, he served as its secretary during part of the 1830's and 1840's and as such was known as "the power behind the throne" in the congregation. He was obviously a man of excellent Jewish background; his published constitution of the congregation is now a valuable historical document.

Together with Rev. Jonas Hecht, he was administrator of, and a teacher in, Anshe Chesed's Hebrew school, considered the best in New York at the time. Later, he was also on the board of directors of Temple Emanu-El. He was one of the leading spirits in B'nai B'rith from its founding until his death on February 16, 1866, and in addition to serving as the Order's first secretary and its second president, he was a chief organizer of its Maimonides Library Association, the remarkable institution that became New York's Jewish cultural center during the second half of the nineteenth century. Thanks to his leadership, B'nai B'rith's dedication to programs of cultural and educational content never wavered from the very beginning.

These, then, were the men who founded the Order. A curious mixture of apparently ordinary shopkeepers and intellectuals, they were united by a genuine love of Judaism which inspired them, from small beginnings, to build better than they knew.

After their many sessions of excited discussion and planning, the twelve met at Sinsheimer's Café, at 60 Essex Street, on October 13, 1843, and voted to form an organization. The minutes of that meeting, written in old-fashioned pointed German script, occupy the first page of a large, leather-bound minute-book, the only artifact which has survived from those days, and which reposes in the archives of B'nai B'rith in Washington, D.C.

Here is a translation of those minutes—and a more prosaic expression of a group of passionate idealists is difficult to imagine:

> New York, October 13, 1843. Today several men decided to form a society for the purpose of supporting its members in the event of illness and other untoward events. This society should be formed in such a manner that branches can be established in other cities. Henry Jones was elected president pro tem in order to present a plan for such a society. Thereafter, Messrs. Jonas Hecht, Schwab, Rosenbourg, Heineman, and Anspacher were designated a committee to prepare a constitution and by-laws. Messrs. Heineman, Cohn [Koon], and Jonas [sic] were to arrange everything necessary for installation. It was decided that each man would give an advance of $5 to cover meeting expenses, which would be refunded. Adjourned to the following Sunday.

Not a word about promoting the ideals of Judaism, serving humanity, uniting the anarchic Jewish community, or education, philanthropy, honor, patriotism, or any of the other virtues—all of which were among the motives of the founders. Perhaps they preferred to wait until these purposes could be formally phrased in a constitutional preamble—as was done the following week. At any rate, B'nai B'rith began its life with a dozen members and a treasury of sixty dollars which, however, was only a loan.

At the second meeting, on October 21, Henry Jones and William Renau submitted the draft of a constitution and by-laws, together with a ritual for the initiation of new members, and they were all adopted. Interestingly, at this second meeting, two names were considered for the organization. The first was Bundes Bruder (League of Brothers), obviously suggested because all the founders were from Germany. But it did not ring true to their purpose; it had no Jewish connotation. Apparently they liked the initials, though, because before the meeting ended they adopted B'nai B'rith as the name of the organization.

B'nai B'rith is Hebrew for Sons of the Covenant, and the covenant that God made with Abraham, the first Jew, and afterward renewed with Moses, is the central and deathless theme and constitution of Judaism.

This Covenant is repeated several times in the Bible, notably in Deuteronomy 5:1–3: "And Moses called unto all Israel, and said unto them . . . The Lord our God made a covenant with us in Horeb. The Lord made not this covenant with our fathers, but with us, even us, who are all of us here alive this day." And again, in Isaiah 59:21: "As for me, this is my covenant with them, saith the Lord; My Spirit that is upon thee, and my words which I have put in thy mouth, shall not depart out of thy mouth, nor out of the mouth of thy seed, nor out of the mouth of thy seed's seed, saith the Lord, from henceforth and forever."

And at that second meeting, or soon after, the founders adopted the menorah—the seven-branched candelabrum—as B'nai B'rith's symbol, not only because the original menorah stood in the ancient Temple in Jerusalem, but because it is the symbol of light.

Since other secret orders of the day had lengthier and more flamboyant titles, the founders decided that their organization's full name should be Independent Order of B'nai B'rith. A motto was also chosen: *Wohlthätigkeit,*

Bruderliebe, und Eintracht—Benevolence, Brotherly Love, and Harmony—and it remains the Order's motto now.

The Constitution had a Preamble which is still in use, although over the years it was amended a number of times before the original was restored:

> B'nai B'rith has taken upon itself the mission of uniting Israelites in the work of promoting their highest interests and those of humanity; of developing and elevating the mental and moral character of the people of our faith; of inculcating the purest principles of philanthropy, honor, and patriotism; of supporting science and art; alleviating the wants of the victims of persecution; providing for, protecting, and assisting the widow and orphan on the broadest principles of humanity.

The only change in this language today is that "Israelites" is replaced by "people of the Jewish faith." The fact that this Preamble, so inspiring and in tune with the needs of mid-nineteenth-century America, is still retained by B'nai B'rith, is anomalous. Except for the first few phrases, it no longer expresses either the spirit of our times, nor the needs of modern Jews, nor the program and purposes of the Order. Yet no serious consideration has been given to amending it during this century, probably because of the crushing weight of tradition and the sacrosanctity of words formulated by the founding fathers.

The Constitution created a supreme ruling body, called the Constitution Grand Lodge (CGL), which alone had the authority to issue and revoke charters for local lodges, frame laws binding upon all, confer degrees, and act as a final court in all disputes. It was to consist of the twelve founders plus the past presidents of all local lodges. In other words, the pioneers set up a ruling body the majority of which was to consist of past presidents of lodges that did not yet exist!

In line with their desire to have a Hebrew name for the group, they also chose Hebrew titles for their officers. The president was called the Grand Nasi Abh; the vice president, Grand Aleph; the secretary, Grand Sopher, etc. The ritual was similarly florid. It consisted of six degrees which imparted the aims and purposes of the Order, each illustrated by examples from Jewish history, thus imparting knowledge sadly lacking in most of the new members.

Messrs. Jones and Renau had been industrious, because they also came up with a whole arsenal of regalias and outward signs for each of the degrees and for each of the CGL and local lodge officers, as well as signs, grips, and passwords for the general membership.

The Constitution created a strictly fraternal agency, which B'nai B'rith remained throughout the nineteenth century. It set up a number of committees, and also a general committee to arrange for the installation of new lodges and to act on urgent questions between the quarterly meetings of the CGL, with the August session designated as the annual meeting, when Constitutional amendments would be considered. To receive a lodge charter, twenty-five "Israelites" had to send in a petition and pay the expense of a CGL committee visit to determine if the group was worthy. Each lodge had to collect dues from all its members, and an additional amount for a widows' and orphans' fund. Exclusive of that fund, each lodge had to remit 10 percent of its receipts to the CGL, and pay twenty dollars for its charter. The Constitution designated New York City as the permanent seat of the CGL, and it was to remain there until 1910.

With all these and many other matters decided, the twelve generals set about recruiting an army. Each undertook to propose at least one man worthy of meeting the high membership standards of the Order.

The Masonic Home, at the corner of Oliver and Henry Streets, was rented for two dollars a night, and on November 12, at 8 P.M., the first meeting of the first B'nai B'rith lodge was called to order by Henry Jones as temporary chairman. It was named New York Lodge No. 1, and it is still flourishing. It was impressively installed, with all the founders of the Order present, not only as the supreme ruling body, but as members of the lodge. Full of solemnity, they conducted for the first time the imposing ceremonies prescribed by the ritual, which presumably captivated the imagination of all present.

Isaac Dittenhoefer was elected the first regular president of the lodge, with Reuben Rodacher as vice president, Isaac Rosenbourg as treasurer, and Henry Jones as secretary.

The new group grew fairly rapidly. At each meeting there were from 20 to 25 applications for membership, although an average of four out of every ten were blackballed. And lo! the bold B'nai B'rith theory that Jews could be united was vindicated; the early members included Sephardim and Ashkenazim, although the latter were in the overwhelming majority, and the German language was used for years in the first few lodges. It was not until many years later, however, that the organization succeeded—an absolutely unique achievement —in bringing together in the same lodge room the German and the Russian, the Pole and the Hungarian, the Litvak and the Galician, the Orthodox and the Reform, and all the other elements of the warring tribes.

All fraternal bodies of the time were secret ones. Each

new B'nai B'rith member was admonished "to hear, to
see, and to keep silent." This aura of mystery intrigued
them and welded them more closely together in a solemn brotherhood. They visited sick brethren, followed
the deceased to the grave, and were concerned about the
welfare of the widows and orphans. The lodge code of
ethics and morality was a stern one and applied not
only at the meetings but in private life. Any infraction
of the laws of morality as accepted in that era—to say
nothing of any infraction of the many laws of the Order
—was punished according to the crime, usually by fines,
but in extreme cases by expulsion.

Social intercourse among the brethren was encouraged, not only to strengthen organization bonds but to
enable the poorly educated to learn from the better educated. Even personal manners were improved in this
way, as those who had known only crude and vulgar
ways of entertaining and expressing themselves came
into contact with men of culture and refinement. Those
who once would have taken their shameful quarrels
with fellow Jews to the public law courts now brought
them to the privacy of the lodge, where both sides were
heard and decisions were made and accepted with dignity.

The initiation fee was five dollars, and the dues were
up to six dollars a year, depending on ability to pay.
This constituted the lodge's only income. In the beginning, the Widows' and Orphans' Fund was a voluntary
one, with noncontributors enjoying no benefits, but early
in the 1850's, by constitutional amendment, it became
mandatory.

New York Lodge was innocent of what is now known
as membership promotion, but it began to attract some
outstanding men, like Baruch Rothschild, who was later

called its mastermind, Dr. James Mitchell, and Dr. Leo Merzbacher. The success and growth of the lodge during its first three months made it apparent that the time was ripe for a second group. So five members took withdrawal cards and petitioned the CGL for a charter. They interested a number of their friends, and on February 11, 1844, Zion Lodge No. 2 was installed by Isaac Rosenbourg.

It made rapid progress. A later historian described its members as "the best elements of the German Israelites," and wrote that "the meetings were not only devoted to instruction in the tenets and principles of the Order, but the foundation was laid for bringing its aims and teachings to the notice of the general public."

Evidently Zion Lodge did not believe in hiding B'nai B'rith's menorah under a bushel, with the result that "the general public" began to be more aware of the new force in its midst. The news spread even beyond the city limits, and later in 1844 Jeshurun Lodge No. 3 was chartered in Baltimore.

Then, for reasons which have not come down to us, expansion ended for a long time. Lodge No. 4 was not founded for five years, and when it was, the scene was far-off Cincinnati.

3
■
1844–1851: The quiet years

The period between 1844 and 1849 was a quiet one. No
documents of those five years have survived, except the
original book of minutes—which is almost entirely a
record of the meetings of New York Lodge—and its
later entries are about as uninspiring as those of the first
meeting. Only occasionally is it enlivened by a departure
from the routine, such as an account of the case of one
of the founders, Valentine Koon, against Solomon Buckmann, a fellow member of New York Lodge.

Koon accused Buckmann "of a violation of our laws
and customs as a Ben B'rith, in that he told uninitiated

persons the recognition sign and other secrets of the Order." The lodge officers forwarded this complaint, in writing, to Brother Buckmann, who appeared at the next meeting and denied it. He was then asked to leave the room, and each member was given two slips of paper, one marked "guilty" and the other "not guilty." He was cleared by a vote of 17 to 10, but was sternly warned by the president "to guard against similar complaints in the future."

Philipp Feital did not get off so lightly. A month after *l'affaire* Buckmann, the charge was made that Brother Feital was older than he had affirmed. This was a serious accusation, since age was very important in relation to sick and death benefits. An investigating committee of three came up with a report, immortalized as follows in the minutes:

> The Committee on Philipp Feital reports that he is not 38 but 43 years old. Feital had to leave the meeting room and after extended debate it was decided only to fine Br. Feital $25, of which $20 was to go to the Widows' and Orphans' Fund. After Br. Feital returned to the room, the President asked him whether he had any objection. Br. Feital replied that he could not express an immediate opinion. It was decided that Br. Feital must pay within a week or be expelled.

Apparently Brother Feital was guilty as charged, because he did not deny the accusation, but told the lodge he was unable to pay the $25. However, he offered $15, which was accepted, for the Widows' and Orphans' Fund.

The minutes for June 22, 1845, reveal that New York Lodge planned to participate en masse in the funeral procession for former President Andrew Jackson two days later. It was decided that "the procession should move in the same manner as at the dedication of the new lodge room. All regalia is to be draped with black crepe, to be purchased by the lodge. A committee shall be sent to the Common Council to be assigned a space."

We learn from the minutes of 1846 and 1847 something about the dues and benefits of B'nai B'rith in its early years, when it had only three lodges. The dues were governed by the member's age: between 21 and 30 he paid $10 a year; between 30 and 40, $15; and between 40 and 45, $25. These were surprisingly large amounts for those times, although it must be remembered they included a kind of primitive health and life insurance. No candidate above the age of 45 was accepted; actuarially he was too poor a risk in the 1840's.

The benefits seem meager: a member who fell ill was paid three or four dollars a week; upon his death his widow received $30 outright and $1 weekly for life, with her oldest child getting 50¢ a week and the others 25¢ until they reached the age of thirteen. For male children, "provision shall be made that they learn a trade." Upon remarriage a widow lost all benefits.

If all this appears niggardly, it should be remembered that the Order had few members then, and its resources were limited. Besides, a dollar bought a lot more then than it does now, and the lodge paid all funeral expenses by taxing each member twenty-five cents every time there was a death. Incidentally, every member of the lodge had to attend every brother's funeral, and was fined one dollar if he failed to show up without an acceptable excuse. If he neglected to wear "full regalia," the fine was fifty cents.

In 1844 some of the founders and early members organized a Cultus-Verein which soon developed into Congregation Emanu-El, which has long been the largest and most distinguished Reform congregation in the world. Dr. Leo Merzbacher, who had joined B'nai B'rith that same year, was immediately employed as the rabbi, and thus became America's leading advocate of liberal Judaism two years before the great Dr. Isaac M. Wise came to the United States.

A new development in American Jewish life began in the late 1840's which profoundly affected the community as a whole and B'nai B'rith in particular. After the liberal revolution of 1848 in Europe had been crushed, a savage reaction set in, which compelled thousands of the noblest spirits of the continent to flee to America to escape persecution. Among them were many Jewish intellectuals. Repelled by the conditions of Jewish life in New York and thirsting for creative Jewish companionship and activity, some of them joined B'nai B'rith, thus contributing to its higher standards.

One of them was Isidor Bush, a scholarly printer from Vienna, who founded *Israel's Herald,* the first Jewish newspaper in German in America. It set a high standard for the time, and therefore lasted only three months. Bush thereupon moved to St. Louis, where he prospered as a wholesale grocer and became one of the national leaders of the Order.

The steady immigration of German Jews in the 1830's and 1840's, which became a comparative influx after 1848, caused a problem. They came crowding into New York and other port cities, and few moved on to inland communities. This resulted in problems of relief, social welfare, and even some anti-Semitism. When William Renau helped found B'nai B'rith in 1843, he also was an organizer of the Jewish Colonization Society, to stimulate settlement in the interior of the country.

The chief interior community was Cincinnati, which

in the 1840's was already a huge metropolis. At the beginning of 1849 a group there applied for a lodge charter. Regular passenger trains had been running between Cincinnati and New York for several years, and a CGL delegation of three, headed by Henry Jones, promptly visited the Ohio city, met with the group, and found it worthy. They must have been armed with authority and a blank charter, because while they were there, on March 4, 1849, they installed Bethel Lodge No. 4. According to Julius Bien, who forty years later wrote a history of the Order's first sixteen years, it consisted of "the best elements" of Cincinnati Jewry, who "spread the fame of the Order throughout the western country."

Despite all this fame in the Midwest, Lodge No. 5 was organized in New York. Hebron Lodge was chartered on April 10, 1849, and soon achieved distinction by raising $106 with which to buy books for a library.

Up to that time, almost all members of the organization were Germans, or at least German-speaking, and all lodge business and documents were in that language. But as the 1850's began a group in Cincinnati, consisting of English-speaking members of Bethel Lodge, asked for a charter, and the German-language character of B'nai B'rith was at the beginning of its end, although it persisted for many years in some lodges. Jerusalem Lodge No. 6 was installed in January, 1850, by William Renau, who came to Cincinnati for that purpose.

Two months later a second lodge was established in Baltimore. Again Renau traveled from New York to do the honors. The new group was Emanuel Lodge No. 7, and the CGL had great expectations concerning it. It was composed of younger men than those organized there in 1844; they were better educated, and they got down to work with vigor and enthusiasm. But as things turned out, they caused B'nai B'rith's first organizational headache. They demanded that non-Jews be admitted to the Order!

"They did not," mourned Julius Bien in his history, "comprehend the mission of the Order as an element of education and elevation for Israelites."

Throughout the nineteenth century, Americans, conscious of their rapidly advancing industrial revolution, loved to talk about "the enlightened spirit of the age." That is what the members of Emanuel Lodge talked about. They drafted a formal application for permission to initiate "non-Israelites" and sent it, along with a strong letter, to the CGL in New York. In it they denounced B'nai B'rith for being "exclusive," declared that if non-Jews were barred it would "gravely prejudice" the standing of Jews in Baltimore, and proclaimed that such a policy was "contrary to the enlightened spirit of the age."

Thus challenged, the CGL answered with a long letter, full of references to God, the ancient Jewish credo, and virtuous rhetoric, along with a few solid arguments and some curious reasoning. For example: "We don't say non-Israelites are excluded from the Order, but we do say the Order is adapted more particularly, and if you please, solely, for Israelites." This was followed by: "'Hear, O Israel, the Lord our God is one God!' To this we draw the attention of the Brethren. Our Order will strengthen the Orthodox Jew in his belief, it will keep those who have already given up many tenets of Judaism from going still further and leave Judaism altogether." It concluded by declaring that even "if we admit that the Order excludes all non-Israelites, it is no more than some other secret societies do," and it cited the American Presbyterian Union, "the different Catholic societies, and others."

But the intransigence of Emanuel Lodge was proof against these arguments; the members continued their agitation and even clashed with the older Baltimore lodge. Unable to convince the CGL, they finally held a general meeting early in 1851 and voted to surrender the charter. It was the first time a lodge dissolved itself. But the issue of admitting non-Jews was to crop up again and again in the future to plague the Order.

The Baltimore fiasco was only a temporary setback. The B'nai B'rith idea was beginning to catch on, and in rapid succession Lodge No. 8 was chartered in Philadelphia; No. 9 in New York; No. 10 in Philadelphia; No. 11 in New York; and No. 12 in Philadelphia. By the late summer of 1851 B'nai B'rith had twelve lodges with a total of exactly 1,202 members.

"A remarkable change," wrote Julius Bien, "had taken place in the social and congregational life of the Jews, directly through the influence of the Order. New congregations had been established with a dignified service, and in the older ones decorum and order had taken the place of the former chaotic condition. Men of learning and eminence had arrived in this country to plead the cause of the Jews and of enlightened religion, and it was due chiefly, if not solely, to the activity of the Order, whose honored members they had become."

Bien's prejudice as a Reform Jew can be seen in these lines, for by "enlightened religion" he obviously meant liberal Judaism, which adjusted itself to contemporary life, as contrasted with Orthodoxy, which clung to the traditional ways its adherents had known in Europe: the entire service in Hebrew, the uninhibited weeping and wailing on certain holidays, the "chaotic condition" of men coming and going within the synagogue and chanting prayers aloud with no two worshipers in unison, the sale of honors from the pulpit for the congregation's treasury, etc.—all of which was being eliminated by Reform Jews.

But Bien's revelation that "new congregations" had been established through the Order is interesting, in light of the fact that from its founding down to the present moment B'nai B'rith, as a matter of basic policy, has been committed to neutrality between the various interpretations of Judaism. But apparently it was inevitable that the German Jews, who were virtually the organization's only members in its first few years, should, in those fiery days of the Reform movement, feel so strongly about their religious convictions that they could not restrain themselves from implementing them through B'nai B'rith.

However, with the growing influence of Temple Emanu-El and other Reform congregations, the Order's leaders became convinced that the movement was well able to progress on its own, and from 1851 on B'nai B'rith followed a hands-off policy in congregational matters, except that local lodges, in the century to come, were in countless instances to be the active forces in the founding of synagogues—Orthodox, Conservative and Reform alike—in communities where none had existed before.

4
■
The significant year 1851

In 1851, having arrived at the ripe old age of eight, and
with a dozen lodges and twelve hundred members in
four cities, B'nai B'rith felt the need for a reorganization.

The Order was not a very democratic body during its
first quarter century. The founders and other early leaders had planted a precious seed, and they wanted to be
sure it grew properly; consequently, they were more concerned with viability than democracy. They made the
laws, and they acted as judge and jury.

But the addition of nine new lodges in two years

caused a multiplication of problems, and so, at the general meeting in August, 1851, they hammered out a new constitution, of which the most radical feature was the creation of the District Grand Lodge (DGL). A new Preamble was also adopted.

The first District Grand Lodges had no set geographical borders. District Grand Lodge No. 1 consisted of the lodges in New York, Philadelphia, and Baltimore, while District Grand Lodge No. 2 was comprised of the two lodges in Cincinnati. For the time being, new lodges to be formed would belong to whichever of these centers was closest.

As for the Constitution Grand Lodge, it was to be the highest tribunal and would no longer communicate directly with the subordinate lodges but only with the District Grand Lodges. It would consist of the founders of the Order, who formed what was called a Council of Skenim (Elders), the national president, the past presidents of the Districts (as soon as they had any), former national presidents, who would be admitted to the Council of Skenim, and District Grand Lodge representatives, with each DGL entitled to one for each of its lodges.

The titles of national officers—Grand Nasi Abh, Grand Sopher, etc.—were transferred to the District officers. The president and vice president of the CGL were called Grand Saar and Deputy Grand Saar, but all the other officers were given English titles. Henry Jones was elected Grand Saar; Dr. Leo Merzbacher, Deputy Grand Saar; Isaac Rosenbourg, Grand Mentor; Isaac Dittenhoefer, Grand Treasurer; and Joseph Ochs, Grand Secretary.

The new Constitution authorized each District Grand Lodge to grant charters to new subordinate lodges it organized, install their officers, and have other routine

powers, subject to CGL review. A District Grand Lodge
was to be composed of all past presidents of its lodges.
Rules for subordinate lodges were also set forth in de-
tail, of which the most important were the requirement
to maintain a widows' and orphans' fund, to charge specified minimum fees and dues, and to elect a new president every three months. The Constitution even controlled the activities of individual members: they were
to be fined for a whole series of misdeeds, including
the use of "improper and insulting language" to the officers or other members.

The new Preamble, written by Dr. Merzbacher, differed considerably from the original one:

> The I.O.B.B. was founded to bring about a union of
> all the Israelites of America, so as to enable them to
> carry out matters of common and general interest. It
> extends to its members aid and support in the mani-
> fold changes of life where assistance is necessary, and
> thus exerts a beneficial influence. It makes it incum-
> bent on its members to assist one another in adversity
> with counsel, encouragement, and all other possible
> means. But above all, it is destined to advance the pure,
> sublime doctrines of Judaism amongst its own confes-
> sors, and to give effect to every enterprise tending to
> accomplish our objects, one of which is a dignified rep-
> resentation of the Israelites in America in a religious
> and social point of view, and the elevation of the
> masses in a moral and intellectual direction.

This was preceded by a long and flowery preface, declaring that Jews had been Sons of the Covenant for
four thousand years, pursuing "Life and Peace," and
that these were the twin aims of B'nai B'rith. "Therefore this new Covenant of Peace . . . to call into existence benevolent institutions, to found associations for
instruction, art, and knowledge, but more especially to

cultivate and guard faithfully the common inheritance of Israel, the precepts of its covenant . . ."

With this reorganization, the top national leadership retained a tight control on every aspect of the Order. To the credit of the fraternal dictators, however, it should be pointed out that they foresaw a future democratization themselves. When the CGL sent copies of the new Constitution to every lodge, it declared in the letter of transmittal: "The new Constitution is not made forever. The progressive tendencies of our age will exercize its powers over it, and those who will come after us will investigate it, use and shape it according to their own necessities; only that there should never be wanting in our Order the sacred principle of unity and brotherly love which, as the foundation of our aims, will remain for all future time."

The final phrase demonstrates how dangerous it is, in this changing world, to ordain anything forever. In the twentieth century B'nai B'rith evolved into a service organization, and lost most of its fraternal characteristics.

At the 1851 meeting it was reported that the dozen lodges had funds aggregating $19,134.23, and that during that year they had disbursed $1,100 for the benefit of sick and needy members.

But even at that early date the organization had its eyes on higher things. The New York lodges determined to create a library and erect a building to house it as well as a lecture hall and lodge rooms. In Philadelphia, Har Sinai Lodge voted to subscribe for a number of newspapers and magazines for the use of its members. And in Baltimore the lodge set a precedent, which was to become popular later, when it raised a fund not only for unfortunate brethren, but for needy nonmembers.

On September 11, 1851, District No. 1 was formally installed, and less than two weeks later it adopted a resolution to form a library association. On October 29, in Cincinnati, District No. 2 was installed by William Renau, who had settled permanently in that city. All business was conducted in English. There were only two lodges in the new District, both in Cincinnati, but on January 30, 1852, a third one was chartered in Louisville, Kentucky.

District No. 1 chartered its third Philadelphia lodge in June, 1852, and its first in Hartford, Connecticut, in August. With three lodges, Philadelphia lost no time in applying for a District charter, and District No. 3 was installed on October 17, 1852, by Grand Saar Henry Jones.

With three Districts functioning, the CGL officers met to define their jurisdiction, since it was obvious that not only would the three grow but that additional ones would ultimately be formed. It was decided that each DGL should have jurisdiction over the whole of each state in which it already had a lodge, as well as each state in which it would establish one; and that in such states no other DGL could thereafter have lodges.

With this mandate, DGL No. 1 automatically had jurisdiction in New York, Connecticut, and Maryland, DGL No. 2 in Ohio and Kentucky, and DGL No. 3 in Pennsylvania.

The year 1851 is also memorable in B'nai B'rith history because it witnessed the creation of a remarkable cultural institution and marked the first time the organization raised its voice against an injustice overseas.

The cultural institution was the Maimonides Library. Several New York lodges banded together to build a handsome structure called Covenant Hall, at 56 Orchard

37

Street. It was dedicated on the first day of 1852 and consisted of a number of spacious, well-furnished rooms for lodge meetings, a large hall for mass meetings and lectures, and a library. The first floor was leased to a member of the Order who operated a restaurant there. It was the first building erected by Jews in New York for secular purposes. The total cost, including furniture, was twelve thousand dollars.

The library, whose first books were bought with the $106 Hebron Lodge had raised the previous year, was named after the great Jewish philosopher of Spain's golden age, Moses Maimonides, and it was operated by the Maimonides Library Association, which consisted of B'nai B'rith members. A number of magazines were subscribed to, and a drive among members brought in many donated volumes.

The Maimonides Library was opened on January 25, 1852, with almost all B'nai B'rith members in the city present. Henry Jones delivered an eloquent lecture which he concluded by saying: "The Order feels that it is as sacred a duty to provide instruction for the masses as it is to provide for their physical wants." The library started out as a small institution. What made it notable was its setting. It was the first Jewish public library in the United States, and it was located in the heart of a ghetto of impoverished, uneducated Jewish immigrants.

It publicized its books, and the number of its readers grew steadily. In addition, regular weekly lectures on Jewish history, books, politics, and other subjects were delivered by notable scholars. The library became the leading Jewish cultural center in New York. It helped make self-education popular in a ghetto with low cultural standards; it demonstrated to the community what could be accomplished when Jews of diverse opinions worked together in a common cause; and it stamped B'nai B'rith as not merely a mutual-aid society but an agency dedicated to the highest ideals of Judaism.

Nor was this kind of program limited to New York. Soon the three lodges in Philadelphia, although unable to construct a building, engaged in a series of lectures and led the movement to erect the city's first Jewish hospital. And the two lodges in Cincinnati, availing themselves of an opportunity to buy a fine collection of books at a bargain price, promptly established the Mendelssohn Library Association, patterned after the one in New York.

B'nai B'rith first spoke out on a public issue in behalf of the Jewish people early in 1851, when a treaty was pending between the United States and Switzerland. It was learned that several Swiss cantons had laws forbidding Jews to live there, and that the pending treaty would exclude Americans of the Jewish faith from its benefits in those cantons. Dr. Sigismund Waterman, who a decade later was to become president of B'nai B'rith, wrote letters of protest on behalf of the Order to Secretary of State Daniel Webster and to other government leaders, including Senator Henry Clay. Webster and Clay both assured him they would take action against the outrage. Clay wrote him on February 11, 1851:

> I received your favor on the subject of the Treaty recently concluded between the United States and the Swiss Confederation. I disapprove entirely the restriction limiting certain provisions of the Treaty, under the operation of which a highly respectable portion of our fellow-citizens would be excluded from their benefits. This is not the country nor the age in which ancient and unjust prejudices should receive any countenance.

> When the Senate acts on the treaty, the matter will be fully considered and I hope disposed of.

But it was not disposed of, and the incident had a mysterious conclusion. For six years the B'nai B'rith record is silent on the subject, until the 1857 convention of DGL No. 1, which urged the Constitution Grand Lodge, meeting two weeks later, to renew action on the matter. The CGL not only passed a strong resolution condemning the treaty and calling on all other Jewish organizations to protest against it, but appropriated one hundred dollars for a public educational campaign.

Then came the mystery. Before much of the appropriation could be spent, the officers of the CGL, at their meeting in the first part of 1858, recorded the following:

> The injustice done to the Jewish citizens of this country by the Treaty of the United States with Switzerland, having been a subject of last year's convention, the matter was referred to the board of officers. We took immediate steps in accordance with the nature of our commission, and had procured very valuable documents from Europe on which to base further action, when we were arrested in our course through measures taken by other parties, which in fact neutralized our efforts completely and compelled us to abstain from further proceedings at present. We hope, however, an opportunity will appear again when this question may be agitated anew and more successfully.

Who were the "other parties"? What were the "measures" they took? What were the "valuable documents"? Deponents saith not. The matter was never brought up again in B'nai B'rith, and it remains unexplained to this day.

5
■
Growth and struggle in the 1850's

The 1850's were years of rapid growth for the young organization. By 1856, eleven new lodges had been chartered: three in New York City, and one each in Louisville, Cleveland, Albany, N.Y., Cincinnati, St. Louis, Philadelphia, New Orleans, and San Francisco. Ophir Lodge, founded in 1855 in San Francisco, was the Order's first on the West Coast.

The decade was marked by demands from the local lodges that B'nai B'rith undertake a whole series of grandiose projects, for which it was ready and willing, but not able. When the Constitution Grand Lodge held

its 1854 general meeting there were laid before it proposals for an academy to teach Judaism to youngsters,
for an institute to teach secular subjects, for the publication of an official magazine, for the establishment of
hospitals, orphanages, old-age homes, and other major
projects. None could be undertaken for lack of resources.

One of these visionary schemes was to organize a
society to interest the Jews—for two thousand years an
urban people—in farming. In 1855 a group of B'nai
B'rith members, including several founders of the Order, met at the B'nai B'rith Hall in New York and actually organized a "Hebrew Agricultural Society." They
were motivated less by the need for such a movement
than by an apologetic feeling about "the predominant
pursuit of commerce" among Jews. But the enthusiasm
lasted only a year, and when even many of the group's
directors were found to be in arrears for dues, the organization was disbanded and all the members got their
money back.

At this time, too, the question of admitting non-Jews
to the Order cropped up again. When the first lodge in
Cleveland was founded a non-Jew applied for membership. The lodge consulted the Council of Skenim, which
unanimously decided that B'nai B'rith had to be limited
to Jews.

Up to 1855 the CGL had met in New York, but in
that year, because of the growing strength of the organization in the West, it met in Cincinnati and elected
Mosely Ezekiel of that city its Grand Saar—to succeed
Henry Jones—although national headquarters remained
in New York. By that time, DGL No. 2 had its own hall,
at Sixth and Main Streets, where the sessions were held.

At that meeting the CGL considered for the first time

a motion to create a general fund, or sinking fund, as it was called, "to carry out the higher objects of the Order." B'nai B'rith was twelve years old and still had no general fund. All monies held by the Order were in the hands of the Districts and the local lodges, and the only income received by the national body—a small percentage of the dues—amounted to a few hundred dollars a year for petty administrative expenses.

But voices were being raised that it was time for B'nai B'rith, as a national agency, to begin translating into action some of its oratorically expressed intentions to raise the level of the Jewish community through specific projects. This was a study in frustration, because all the national leaders warmly favored such a course but knew it was premature because the Order was too weak financially. Then the Council of Skenim brought before the meeting a proposition it had agreed upon earlier that year, that the CGL should receive a larger percentage of income from the local lodges, so that a sinking fund could be built up. But that motion was narrowly defeated.

The opposition was partly due to a grass-roots revolt against the power of the Skenim and the CGL, but there were other reasons, too. Some members felt that "the higher objects of the Order" was too vague a definition of the purpose of the fund; others, animated by sectional jealousies, objected to the creation of any institution unless it was to be in their bailiwick; and still others opposed the method of raising funds.

The following year, 1856, when Julius Bien was elected Grand Saar for the first time, the CGL again wrestled with the problem and came up with a compromise: instead of a unified national account, each District would be urged to establish its own general fund, with a specific use for the money announced in advance, and with each District autonomous in its management. Autonomy was what the Districts wanted, but the results were disappointing. District No. 1 promptly framed a law setting up such a fund, ratified by most of its lodges, with every member assessed twenty-five cents quarterly for the purpose of building a home for the aged and widowed, or for an orphan asylum. District No. 2 proposed that its members pay one cent a week for a widows' and orphans' asylum fund, but only one lodge ratified it, and it did not come about until 1863. District No. 3 voted for a similar project, but although every lodge in the provinces ratified it, those in Philadelphia voted solidly against it, thus killing it.

In 1856 a lodge had to be expelled from the Order for the first time. Again Baltimore was the scene of the crime. For several years Jeshurun Lodge No. 3 had been a troublemaker. Investigation revealed that many "undesirable elements, unworthy of membership," had been admitted, with the result that "strife and dissension" prevailed. Julius Bien, the Grand Saar, was also president of District No. 1 at the time, and he visited Baltimore, found the situation hopeless, and the lodge's charter was revoked.

At about the same time a group in Boston applied for a charter, but before an investigation could be made a second Boston group made a similar request. Mr. Bien went up to Boston to see what was going on and found the Jews there divided into two warring camps, one affiliated with a German synagogue, the other with a Polish congregation. Bien called a joint meeting and explained the B'nai B'rith principles and the importance of Jewish unity. A few from each camp were convinced and applied for a charter, but this group was too small for a lodge. It was concluded that the antagonism between the Germans and the Poles was too strong to be overcome, and each group was granted a charter, with the hope that in time they would unite, or at least work together. And in time that happened.

The continued growth of the organization caused difficulties for the District Grand Lodges, whose members consisted of past presidents of local lodges. The term of office for lodge presidents was only three months, and there were now so many of them that District annual meetings were becoming unwieldy. Besides, the older lodges, with the most past presidents, were able to control the meetings. The Constitution Grand Lodge in 1856 therefore reorganized the District structure, granting lodge past presidents continued membership but without the vote, which was restricted to elected representatives, with each lodge entitled to at least three, depending on size.

When the CGL met in Philadelphia in the summer of 1857, it was announced that four new lodges had been instituted—in New York, Chicago, and in Easton and Danville, Pennsylvania—and that the national membership was 2,889. It was now nine years since Europe's revolution of 1848; many thousands of German Jews had poured into New York, in addition to those from other countries, and the American Jewish population was close to one hundred thousand. The character of American Jewry was consequently changing.

The immigrants who had arrived as youths in the 1820's and 1830's and their children were for the most part Americanized, and those who had arrived after 1848 were largely the better educated and more sophisticated. An increasing number of B'nai B'rith members —mainly in New York—were no longer dazzled or intrigued by the elaborate ritualism, and some felt it had already outlived its original usefulness. So the delegates to the 1857 meeting took some radical steps: they restricted the wearing of regalia to officers and discarded most of the ceremonial ritual; they replaced the candidate's initiatory oath with a simple pledge of honor; they dissolved the "degree lodges" (actually degree teams); and reduced the number of degrees from six to three.

But this brought quick opposition, chiefly in DGL No. 2—not from the District leaders but from the local lodges, whose members cherished the old customs. They resolved to reduce the power of the national body. At the CGL general meeting of 1858 their spokesmen introduced a resolution that, beginning in 1860, and every ten years thereafter, every lodge in the country should vote on whether or not to hold a convention to revise the Constitution, with each lodge entitled to at least one delegate, but the motion was lost. The following year DGL No. 2, supported by DGL No. 3, tossed a bombshell into the CGL meeting, which was held in Cincinnati.

District No. 2 demanded that the Council of Skenim and the Board of Officers of the Constitution Grand Lodge be abolished, and that all the powers, rights, and privileges of those bodies be vested in the CGL general meetings, and that between such meetings those powers be vested in the several Districts! The same motion asked for increased representation of local lodges at CGL sessions, and added that "we desire to restore and retain, in a corrected form, the customs, regalia, ritual, and usages of the Order as originally given." Significantly, too—since in 1859 women had few rights—the motion included a recommendation that wives of members be eligible for membership in B'nai B'rith! The motion was tabled, but the issues were kept alive during the year that followed.

The heavy artillery of the national leadership was fired at these revolutionary ideas, and at the 1860 general meeting the entire batch of proposals was voted down. However, their advocates managed to salvage a partial victory; although they failed to have the powerful Council of Skenim abolished, they succeeded in sharply curtailing its powers and in reducing it to "simply an honorary body of the Order," but with the right of voice and vote at the annual general meetings of the CGL.

Henry Marcus of Philadelphia succeeded Julius Bien as Grand Saar in 1860.

Another significant action was the adoption of a new Preamble to the Constitution. The new Preamble was as follows:

> The Order B'nai B'rith has for its mission the union of the Israelites of the United States of America with the purpose of developing the highest interests of Judaism most widely and most effectively.
>
> Daily experience proves that where individual endeavors, however nobly inspired and zealously prosecuted, fail of their purpose, combined efforts of men formed into societies meet with success and happy results. Past experiences of the Order have demonstrated it and justify the greatest expectations in the future. Evoking the warmest sentiments of friendship and brotherly love, it offers consolation and help to the sick, aid and sympathy in adversity and misfortune, dries the tears of the widow and orphan, and by warmhearted sympathy in all conditions and vicissitudes of life heightens its joys and lightens the burdens of adverse fate.
>
> But its further and principal aim is to advance the intellectual standards of its members, to inculcate the

knowledge of the principles of true morality, and to promote the pure and sublime teachings of Judaism, and further them to practical application.

It is true that the activity of the Order is first directed to its members, but its ultimate aim is not circumscribed by the walls of the lodge rooms. It constitutes rather a preparatory school for the highest duties of life, to work by precept and example, for the welfare of mankind to the honor and glory of Israel.

In the 1843 Preamble, the mission of the organization was set forth as "uniting Israelites in the work of promoting their highest interests and those of humanity," while this new one spoke only of "the highest interests of Judaism." This change did not mean B'nai B'rith was no longer interested in the rest of humanity—the final sentence makes that clear—but the emphasis had shifted.

It should also be noted that whereas the original Preamble mentioned the highest interests of Israelites— that is, of the Jewish people—the 1860 version said the Order was dedicated to the highest interests of Judaism —that is, the religion and culture of the Jewish people. In its pioneering days, B'nai B'rith was realistic enough to know that the survival of Judaism depended upon the survival of people, of individual Jews, whose fate as ignorant and penniless strangers in a strange land could not be clearly foreseen. But seventeen years later, after the organization had grown and prospered, as had the American Jewish community, the issue shifted to a more spiritual and idealistic plane, and the new language expressed awareness of the fact that while the people who called themselves Israelites were secure enough, the traditions they had inherited, called Judaism, still had a battle for survival ahead—in a society that was not only free but overwhelmingly Christian, with all the social pressures this implied.

The leaders of B'nai B'rith must have arrived at these conclusions, at least in part, from their own experience in trying to nurture Jewish culture in a free society— then, as now, a difficult undertaking. Not only were the majority of Jews in America ignorant of their own Jewish heritage, but even within B'nai B'rith the many efforts to raise the members' cultural level, while leading to improvements, had no revolutionary results. For example, the first fine rapture created by the Maimonides Library, with all its good books and lectures, had begun to die out by 1856, four years after its founding, and the following year its popularity had diminished to such an extent that the Association was dissolved and its affairs reverted to the Constitution Grand Lodge. In 1858 the CGL legally transferred jurisdiction over the institution to DGL No. 1, which later was able to restore it as an important force in the cultural life of New York Jewry.

In contrast, when DGL No. 1 in 1859 found it could not afford to send delegates to the 1860 CGL meeting in Cincinnati and decided to raise funds by holding a May Festival, full of fun and frolic, the District's general committee reported the result as follows: "Since the beginning of the Exile, 1,800 years ago, there have not congregated in the world so many happy, joyous Israelites, more than 7,000 participants!"

The unsuccessful attempt of DGL No. 2, in 1856, to establish a general fund for "the higher objects" of B'nai B'rith, led to an epic internal ideological struggle that lasted for years.

In 1857 Dr. Isaac M. Wise, who had been active in B'nai B'rith while he had a pulpit in Albany, New York, and who was even more active after he settled in Cincinnati in 1854, was elected president of District No. 2. The seed which was to blossom out in 1875 as Hebrew Union College was already germinating in his mind. He had so far found little support for so imposing a project, and it occurred to him that he might reach his goal through B'nai B'rith. After all, the Order, although dedicated to neutrality when it came to the religious divisions in Jewish life, was composed overwhelmingly of liberal Jews. There was nothing Machiavellian in Dr. Wise's hopes or actions. To what "higher object" could B'nai B'rith aspire than to found the first seminary to train American-born rabbis? As a young rabbi himself, who had now lived in the United States for more than a dozen years, he was firmly convinced that Reform was the wave of the future for Judaism in America. However, instead of making a direct bid for his cherished project, he proceeded cautiously.

At the annual meeting of DGL No. 2 in 1859, he moved that a committee be appointed "to devise a practical scheme for the organization of an educational institute somewhere in the West, under the control of the Order, for the general benefit of all Israelites, and in the interest of science and Judaism." As in all organizations, whoever makes a motion for the appointment of any kind of committee is at once named chairman.

Unfortunately for Dr. Wise, however, he was unable to attend the 1860 meeting of his District, and his committee declared it had no report to offer. Another committee thereupon moved that a fund be created for the construction of a Widows' and Orphans' Home, and the motion was adopted. But the following year the Civil War began, and the proposition was forgotten, or at least abandoned, until 1863, when the District met in

Cleveland. At that meeting, Benjamin F. Peixotto, as chairman of the committee to which the project had been referred, outlined a proposal for the District to establish "an Orphan Asylum Fund." The word "widows" was absent from his motion, which provided for an assessment of one dollar a year upon each member of the District. Mr. Peixotto was well aware that the influential Dr. Wise might succeed later in having the fund converted to launch a rabbinical seminary—indeed, Peixotto himself favored such a project—or that some other zealots might gain control of the money for their own favorite undertaking. He therefore shrewdly included in his motion: "No alteration of this law shall be made except the same be submitted to the lodges, and voted thereon in the same manner as this original law, and it shall require two-thirds of the lodges voting in favor thereof to make such alteration or amendment."

The proposal was unanimously adopted, because Dr. Wise and his few supporters at the meeting knew opposition was useless. Besides, he now realized it was premature to push for his own objective. Reporting as chairman of another committee at the District meeting the following year, he referred to a suggestion made by Chicago's Ramah Lodge: ". . . to change the asylum fund to a seminary fund" because "this lodge considers the education of orphans in private families preferable to asylums. There is much to be said, pro and con, in the matter; but we here have only to say that the asylum fund is not governed yet by any special laws, and may be applied hereafter, if the lodges so devise, to place orphans under the care of private families. . . . The subject of a seminary or college, however laudable and commendable it is, we do not consider ripe for action. . . . Various essays to this end have failed."

The lodges throughout the District enthusiastically raised funds for an orphan asylum, but despite his apparent surrender in 1864, Dr. Wise made another effort at the 1865 District meeting. He proposed an amendment to the District law "to erase the words 'Orphan Asylum Fund' wherever they occur and insert in their places 'Teachers' Seminary Fund of District No. 2.' " The amendment was overwhelmingly defeated, but Dr. Wise was not yet ready to give up.

This time he worked obliquely, remaining in the background. He convinced a number of B'nai B'rith leaders of the vital need to establish a rabbinical seminary, but had them advance the idea under the euphemism of an "Educational Fund." Mr. Peixotto, who by then was the Grand Saar and had always favored the seminary idea, carried the ball, although he had led the fight for an orphan asylum in 1863. In his presidential message to the CGL general meeting of 1866, he strongly urged B'nai B'rith to found a Jewish school of higher education.

The proposal was met with powerful opposition, especially from such elder statesmen as Rabbi Friedlein, Isidor Bush, Joseph and Lewis Abraham, and others. They passionately argued that it would kill the campaign for an orphan asylum, and that it would be in direct defiance of a fundamental policy of the Order: to remain neutral in all religious matters.

Mr. Peixotto's motion contained the argument that a seminary would "give to the now vacant pulpits and shepherdless flocks of Israel in America, in due time and at the moment when most required for the rising generation, Jewish ministers qualified in the language and rhetoric of the land, while learned in the laws of

Judaism . . . and develop the spiritual happiness of Israel."

Mr. Bush succeeded in having that sentence deleted, but the convention, swayed by other convincing orators, finally passed a compromise proposal by Mr. Peixotto for the establishment of an "Educational Fund." However, this turned out to be a meaningless victory for Dr. Wise, because, although Peixotto flooded the lodges with printed material and addressed many of their meetings in person, only seven of them actually established educational funds. Districts No. 1 and 2 inveighed against the project, and the latter—Dr. Wise's own bailiwick—formally adopted a resolution, lauding the idea of a Jewish college but asking "Why may not this great work be accomplished by the Israelites of the United States at large, without placing a marble slab thereon with I.O.B.B. engraven on it?" After this the project died.

The orphan fund grew so rapidly that the institution was built in Cleveland in time to be dedicated during the 1868 session there of DGL No. 2. It was described as the finest orphanage in the country, with accommodations for two hundred children and a school for them on the grounds. Dr. Wise and Grand Saar Peixotto, reconciled to the inevitable, played leading roles at the dedication.

District No. 2 framed the rules and regulations for the institution, which was the first of B'nai B'rith's "higher objects." One of the rules was that the Cleveland Jewish Orphan Home, as it was named, was to be maintained and controlled by District No. 2 and any other Districts that might be formed from its territory. Since that territory swept from the Great Lakes to the Gulf of Mexico, and from Ohio to the Rocky Mountains, Districts No. 6 and 7, which were carved out of it, later shared in the administration of the institution.

The Cleveland Jewish Orphan Home's first wards included some Civil War orphans, but for some sixty years it sheltered Jewish youngsters from many parts of the country, graduating them into the ranks of good citizens, until in 1943 it was renamed Bellefaire, converted into an institution for the care of disturbed children, and became an independent agency supported by the American Jewish community as a whole.

6

.

The Civil War and the 1860's

B'nai B'rith's relationship to the Civil War presents something of a mystery. During World Wars I and II the Order converted itself largely into a war-serving agency. But from 1861 to 1865, although hundreds of members served in the armies, and most of the lodges—which were virtually all in the North—undertook programs on behalf of the Armed Forces, the record itself is almost completely silent on the subject of the Order's participation as a national agency.

The proceedings of the Constitution Grand Lodge meeting in New York at the end of July, 1861, months after the shooting began, contain not a word about the war, and the session's only action of interest was to elect Dr. Sigismund Waterman, of New York, as Grand Saar. Strangely, the only delegates came from DGL No. 1; the other two Districts were wholly unrepresented. The following year, when the CGL met again in New York, the delegates of those two Districts complained bitterly about that, charging that they had received "official information" that there was no need for their Districts to be represented at the 1861 meeting, because no business of any importance was pending, and that the session was being held only because the Constitution required it. Later, the aggrieved delegates charged, they had received copies of the proceedings, showing that a number of matters had been acted upon in which they were interested. In short, they denounced the CGL officers, and insisted that the entire 1861 meeting had been illegal and that therefore all its actions were null and void.

To this blast the reply of the national officers was weak and evasive; they answered, in effect, that the meeting had considered only matters held over from the past and that no new business had been transacted. In fact, Grand Saar Waterman opened his annual report with the statement: "The session of the last annual convention was devoid of any transaction of interest." And DGL No. 1 had enough votes to quell the rebellion.

The only reference to the Civil War at the 1862 convention was a brief paragraph in Dr. Waterman's report: "The cloud hanging over our political horizon should induce us to draw nearer and closer together. . . . Israel's interests and Israel's hopes are closely interwoven with the results of the present gigantic struggle. Our future prospects, our religious freedom, may be secured or lost. . . . I hope and trust that we will

be ever mindful of the blessings we have enjoyed upon
our country's soil, and that the brotherhood and the
Order will in an energetic and tangible manner respond
to all its wants in this hour of trial."

The next year Dr. Waterman mentioned the war even
more briefly in his annual message. Benjamin F. Peixotto succeeded him as Grand Saar, and at the 1864 session he mentioned the conflict not at all in his report.
Finally, in 1865, after the war was over, Mr. Peixotto
concluded his message as follows: "Happily, my term
commencing in the midst of the greatest rebellion the
world has even seen . . . closes in the still bright dawn
of restored and angelic Peace. . . . How far the Sons
of the Covenant by deeds of heroic daring in the field
and patriotic support in civil life, have contributed to
this beneficent result, other pen than mine must record.
Suffice, that Israel rejoices in the new birth of the Nation, as it ever has and ever will rejoice in the triumph
of civil liberty and the disenthrallment and destruction
of tyranny, come in what form or under what guise it
may."

While these eloquent words expressed his own convictions concerning the triumph of the Union cause,
they add little to our knowledge of the part B'nai B'rith
played in the conflict. Grand Saar Peixotto declared that
some pen other than his would have to record the Order's contributions, but none ever did. Without doubt,
the Order rendered "patriotic support in civil life," as
the Grand Saar declared, but this consisted of activities
by local lodges—raising funds for needed supplies, supporting the families of members who were in the Union
army, catering to the welfare of the troops, etc.—and
not to any unified national program.

We do have evidence that when Rabbi Bernhard Gotthelf of Louisville was appointed an Army chaplain in 1863, Cincinnati's Beth El Lodge helped collect books and cash for military hospitals in his area. We also know that Chicago's Ramah Lodge in 1862 joined with the rest of the city's Jewish community in organizing and outfitting a Jewish company that became part of the 82nd Illinois Regiment. And there are a few sketchy references to local lodge social events to entertain soldiers and to raise funds for "items of comfort" that were sent to troops in the field. But the record is sparse.

One might have expected to find proud, even boastful, accounts of B'nai B'rith war contributions, perfervid resolutions of support for the Federal Government, all sorts of appeals for war drives and activities. After all, unlike the country, B'nai B'rith was not torn apart by the Civil War; during those years only a very few of its more than fifty lodges were in the Confederate States.

One can only speculate on why the Order was apparently so inconspicuous nationally during the conflict. Perhaps it was because the Jewish community, of which it was so representative a part, was largely an immigrant one, and therefore lacked a sense of real security. When the war broke out, two-thirds of all the 150,000 Jews had been in America less than ten years, and even the majority of the rest had been born overseas. This did not prevent them from enlisting in the Armed Forces in large numbers—about 10,000, it is estimated, in the Union and Confederate forces.

Perhaps the fact that the leading rabbis, almost all of whom were members of B'nai B'rith, differed violently about the war made the Order hesitant to emphasize its own role in it. One member, Rabbi Morris J. Raphall of New York, caused a national sensation when he publicly asserted that the Hebrew Bible sanctions slavery. Another member, Rabbi David Einhorn of Baltimore, was so fiery an abolitionist that he was forced to leave his pulpit, and he settled in Philadelphia. Still another, Dr. Isaac M. Wise of Cincinnati, challenged Rabbi Raphall's thesis, but hated both war and the abolitionists so much that although he was opposed to secession, he remained neutral. His Cincinnati colleague, Rabbi Max Lilienthal, another Ben B'rith, denounced the abolitionists as warmongers and radicals, although as soon as war actually broke out he supported Lincoln and the Union cause.

Maybe the anti-Semitism that erupts during every national crisis was a factor. Jews were accused of being cowards and slackers. They were charged with profiteering. They were accused in the North of being spies for the South, and vice versa.

It was on December 17, 1862, that Gen. Ulysses S. Grant issued his Order No. 11: "The Jews, as a class, violating every regulation of trade established by the Treasury Department and also departmental orders, are hereby expelled from the department within 24 hours from the receipt of this order. Post commanders will see that all of this class of people be furnished passes and required to leave, and any one returning after such notification will be arrested and held in confinement until an opportunity occurs of sending them out as prisoners, unless furnished with permit from headquartrs. . . ."

The "department" referred to in the order was the Department of the Tennessee, comprising Tennessee, Missouri, and other Midwest and Southern states. In a word, all Jews—adults and children, innocent and guilty, Unionists and Confederates—were given twenty-four hours to pack and leave their homes, their businesses, their communities. The horrified American Jewish community poured a flood of letters and telegrams of protest into Washington. Cesar J. Kaskel of Paducah, Kentucky, led a protest delegation to see Lincoln. The B'nai B'rith lodge in St. Louis sent a resolution of protest to Washington. Dr. Wise, Dr. Lilienthal, and other leading rabbis came to the nation's capital and visited their Senators and Representatives, Army officers, and even the White House. And in the end President Lincoln, who was not familiar with the facts until these groups laid them before him, promptly ordered the hateful Grant command canceled.

At this very time the chief of the War Department's Detective Bureau was Col. LaFayette Baker, notorious for his cruelty and ruthlessness. He had a young lawyer, Simon Wolf, arrested solely because he was a member of B'nai B'rith (a half century later he became president of the Order). Wolf was defending several Southern Jews arrested in Washington and charged with being Confederate spies, and it took the personal intervention of Secretary Stanton to effect his release.

In such an atmosphere most Jews were glad to shun the spotlight.

B'nai B'rith was not alone in this respect. The other Jewish organizations were similarly quiet during the war. The Board of Delegates of American Israelites, although it contained some bold and forceful members, held scarcely a meeting during the years of conflict, and limited its business to the discussion of Jewish issues. In the same way, B'nai B'rith went quietly about its work of philanthropy, education, and mutual aid. Indeed, during the Civil War the Order registered spectacular gains in membership.

In 1863 District No. 4 was installed in San Francisco;

to it were assigned California and Oregon, and the Territories of Washington, Nevada, Utah, Arizona, Colorado, and New Mexico. The Grand Secretary traveled from New York to San Francisco by boat, all the way around South America, to install it; the trip took twenty-six days. At the 1863 CGL meeting he reported that the Order had 56 lodges with a total of 4,840 members, and funds aggregating $198,736, not counting a District No. 1 fund of $13,613 for benevolent activities. There were, he said, five literary associations in the Order, each with a library, and educational funds in Boston and Louisville.

But the most important action taken at the meeting was another reorganization, with resultant changes in the Constitution. With the rapid growth had come pressure from the Districts to gain the ascendancy over the national officers. The CGL was shorn of most of its powers and became little more than a court of appeals, authorized to settle disputes. It was also empowered to grant or revoke District charters, and change the ritual. In other words, although it had formerly been both legislative and judicial, it was now reduced largely to the latter status. By the same token, the Districts increased their powers. It was at this CGL session that Benjamin F. Peixotto was elected Grand Saar.

The Preamble to the Constitution was amended again. In 1843, it had declared the Order's mission to be to unite Israelites in order to promote their highest interests and those of humanity. The 1860 version spoke only of "the highest interests of Judaism." But now, only three years later, in the middle of the Civil War, the new Preamble referred only to "the highest interest of humanity":

The Independent Order B'nai B'rith (Sons of the Covenant), having taken upon itself the mission of uniting the Sons of Israel in the sacred work of promoting the highest interests of humanity, and especially to support the poor and needy, to visit and attend the sick, to console the mourner, to bury the dead, to protect and assist widows and orphans, on the broadest principles of humanity; and, furthermore, to develop and elevate the mental and moral character of our race by a liberal support of science and art, and the inculcation of the holy and purest doctrines of philanthropy, honor, and patriotism; and chief, to promulgate the sublime and eternal doctrines of Judaism among its confessors, and to defend, preserve and spread the faith of our fathers in society at large as the very embodiment of all those dictates of humanity—hold the following first principles.

There followed five idealistic paragraphs on Brotherhood, Love, Charity, Enlightenment, and Judaism.

B'nai B'rith rejoiced with the rest of the nation when the Civil War ended, and mourned with it when President Lincoln was assassinated. Every member in New York City marched in the funeral procession there, as they had done years before for Andrew Jackson.

How quickly the wounds were healed between the many Northern and the few Southern lodges can be seen from the fact that a few months after the fighting ended the well-known Orthodox rabbi Isaac Leeser, long a member of B'nai B'rith, on a trip to Richmond, Virginia, installed two lodges there.

By the end of the war, B'nai B'rith had grown out of its adolescence and matured into the country's largest and most respected Jewish fraternal order (several others had sprung up in the 1850's, with sick and death benefits as their only reason for existence, but they did not last). It had 5,831 members in 66 lodges from coast to coast, with financial resources of $267,341. Nor were its lodges only in the large cities, as was the case with every other Jewish organization. They were also in places like Evansville and Ft. Wayne, Indiana, Harrisburg and Easton, Pennsylvania, Sacramento and Grass Valley, California, Virginia City and Carson City, Nevada, Columbus and Dayton, Ohio. B'nai B'rith had then, as it has today, a genius for attracting Jews to its banner wherever a handful or more lived, to work together for the common good. No other Jewish organization had that genius then, nor has it now.

In 1865 a terrible cholera epidemic struck Palestine, and the Board of Deputies of British Jews appealed to B'nai B'rith to aid the victims. Sir Moses Montefiore headed the worldwide relief committee. The CGL had no funds for this or any other kind of appeal, but it immediately asked the lodges to contribute, and practically every lodge in the country responded. The amazing total, for those days, of $4,522 was raised in this way. It was only the first of a series of actions taken by the Order on behalf of Palestine, and later the State of Israel; and a century later, with a flourishing program of activities in Israel, B'nai B'rith celebrated the centennial of that event by special meetings and programs all over the world.

The CGL general meeting of 1866 heard some heartwarming reports of more personal work. One concerned a lodge in Boston, which had learned that two orphan sisters were to be married on the same day. Their father, a member of the lodge, had died recently, and their mother had been dead for a long time. The lodge at once appointed a committee with full power to buy complete household outfits for the two girls, and to arrange "a grand nuptial feast with ball"—with the lodge members assessed for all expenses. The Grand Secretary of DGL No. 1 performed the ceremony.

Four years before, the CGL session had abolished regalia for all except the officers, but in 1866 the advocates of more ritual won their fight. A motion was passed requiring holders of the ritual degrees to wear different-colored aprons, with even more distinctive ones for past presidents. Every apron had to have "I.O.B.B." printed on it. In a thunderous minority report, Rabbi E. M. Friedlein denounced regalia as "against the letter and spirit of Judaism." He called them *chukot hagoyim* (foolish practices of the Gentiles) and quoted from Deuteronomy that "no man shall put on a woman's garment: for all that do so are abomination unto the Lord thy God." But the majority wanted aprons.

It was in 1866, too, that more precise territories (which were changed in time) were assigned to the Districts. DGL No. 1 was given New York, New Jersey, all of New England, and Canada; DGL No. 2: Ohio, Kentucky, Tennessee, Alabama, "and all the States and Territories West thereof, until to the Rocky Mountains"; DGL No. 3: Pennsylvania, Delaware, Maryland, District of Columbia, East and West Virginia, North and South Carolina, Georgia, and Florida; DGL No. 4: "all the States and Territories of the Union West of the Rocky Mountains, and British Columbia."

The 1867 CGL meeting was important for a number of reasons. It thwarted an attempt to introduce "religious elements of a dogmatical nature into our Order," although the meager proceedings do not indicate the nature of the attempt. P. W. Frank, of New York, succeeded Mr. Peixotto as Grand Saar. At the request of the lodges in Baltimore and Washington, a charter was granted for District No. 5, to comprise the State of

Maryland and the District of Columbia. An application
for a District charter was received at the same time
from the lodges in Chicago, Detroit, and Milwaukee, but
had to be denied because of a technicality.

But the most important action was the passage of a
motion recommending to the lodges that a general convention be called the following year. Since the 1863
meeting, which had reduced the power of the CGL, dissatisfaction had been growing, as reflected in an 1867
resolution: "The present position of the Constitution
Grand Lodge is not calculated to promote the best interests of our Order, its sphere of action being badly defined in our Organic Law, so that it is necessary that
the CGL should either be vested with larger, well-de-
fined powers, or altogether dispensed with."

B'nai B'rith had never held a general convention. The
CGL met quarterly, with the August meeting attended
by the national officers, the Council of Skenim, and representatives of each DGL. But in a general convention
every subordinate lodge would be entitled to representation. Naturally, they voted overwhelmingly (by mail) for
such a meeting, for they had long been chafing at being
ruled from above by a small group of men they had not
elected. They wanted to change a lot of things—and
they did.

They gathered in New York City on July 19, 1868,
and stayed there for nine days—a record never equaled
before or since. Most of the time was devoted to fashion-
ing a new Constitution. There were then 111 lodges,
and most of them were represented.

The delegates eliminated most of the old methods of
operation and erected a new structure. They abolished
the Council of Skenim and the entire system of a small
ruling oligarchy, substituting for it a representative leg-

islature with a decentralized machinery. The Constitution Grand Lodge was retained, but it was made up of one delegate chosen by each lodge from among its past presidents, and its annual meetings were replaced by quinquennial sessions. A National Executive Committee was established, consisting of one representative from each District plus one from the Order at large, to act between CGL meetings, but its powers were very few and largely consisted of carrying out the policies set by the CGL. A Court of Appeals was also created, with one representative from each District.

All this left the Districts pretty much free to run their own affairs between the quinquennial conventions of the CGL, although they were required to submit annual reports of their activities, finances, etc. to the Executive Committee, and while each DGL could enact whatever laws it wished, they could not be "in conflict with or inconsistent with the Organic Law of the Order," *i.e.*, the Constitution. It required each DGL to meet annually.

Since the reorganized CGL was now a democratically formed body, the delegates were happy to approve a section of the new Constitution which declared the CGL to be "supreme in the Order," with "full legislative, judicial, and executive powers."

As part of the trend toward acculturation and away from the fancy terminology and trappings of secret orders, the titles of all the national and local lodge officers were changed from the Hebrew to the standard English terms of president, vice president, secretary, etc. However, the officers of the Districts retained their old nomenclature: Grand Nasi Abh, Grand Aleph, etc. The demeaning term, "subordinate lodge," was abolished, and thereafter local groups were referred to simply as lodges, or local lodges.

A charter was granted, forming District No. 6 with the states of Illinois, Iowa, Wisconsin, and Minnesota, all taken from District No. 2.

During the convention a delegate moved that Article 1 of the Constitution be: "Any male Israelite of good moral character is eligible for membership in the I.O.B.B., if found worthy by the lodge to which the petition is presented." This caused a "lively debate," but it was either voted down or not voted on, because it was not referred to again in the proceedings. At any rate, it did not appear in the Constitution, and this was to cause some difficulty later, as will be seen. (Today's Constitution provides that "members of the Order must be men of the Jewish faith, of good moral character, and at least 21 years of age.")

Another section that was soon to result in quarrels was the following: "Every lodge is sovereign in her own internal affairs, subject only to such restrictions as are imposed by the Organic Law of the Order." A number of lodges assumed this made them immune to District laws they did not like, and their actions kept the Court of Appeals busy for years.

Evidence that B'nai B'rith was beginning to be more conscious of its international Jewish obligations is seen in the fact that the convention passed a resolution calling for the Order to "cultivate friendly relations and cordially cooperate" with the Alliance Israelite Universelle, headed by the well-known French statesman Adolph Crémieux. The Alliance not only worked for the rights of Jews in many countries where they were oppressed, but operated schools for culturally deprived Jews in the Near East. When B'nai B'rith had protested against Swiss discrimination in the 1850's, and aided cholera victims in Palestine in 1865, these had been *ad hoc* causes, but its relationship with the Alliance was intended to be of a continuing nature, and was the first of its kind in B'nai B'rith. The resolution passed by the convention concluded: "It is to our discredit as Americans that we are becoming selfish and absorbed in our own interests. Let us indicate our sympathy with our brethren everywhere."

Finally, although the Committee on Constitution recommended a new Preamble very similar to the original one of 1843, the delegates rejected it, for reasons not given, and voted instead to retain, with only the change of a word here and there, the one adopted in 1863.

Julius Bien was elected president, and was destined to serve in that office from 1868 to 1900—much longer than any man before or after him. This remarkable man was probably the outstanding cartographer in the country. Born in Germany in 1826, he studied at first for the Reform rabbinate, as his father had done before him, but his artistic bent soon took him to several fine art schools. In September, 1849, already an accomplished young artist, he emigrated to New York. Lithography was in its infancy, and in 1850 he entered that profession, which he had studied in Germany, and achieved such success that in the 1880's his plant had more than two hundred employees. He specialized in scientific and artistic works. He illustrated and published beautiful editions of books on locomotives, marine engines, city maps, etc., and during the Civil War his maps were widely used by Union forces.

Before the war he had gone to Washington and called on President Franklin Pierce, since he had a letter of introduction. Naïvely he asked the President to let him do some Government work. The amused President referred him to Secretary of War Jefferson Davis, who helped him obtain some of the Government's scientific work.

Leading scientists of the day described his productions as "the finest in the country," and some of them won international medals. Among other classics he published Audubon's *Birds of America* (1860) with hand-colored plates. In 1888 he was elected president of the National Lithographers Association. Despite so busy a life he found time and energy to serve not only as a B'nai B'rith leader for more than fifty years, but as a New York Jewish community leader as well.

B'nai B'rith ended its first quarter century with 8,802 members in 111 lodges in five Districts, with a sixth District just getting started. Its financial resources amounted to $383,423; it had just dedicated the finest Jewish orphan asylum in the nation; its libraries, lecture programs, and philanthropies were known in many communities; it was the oldest and largest of all Jewish organizations in America and was each year becoming better known as the most powerful of the forces working for the welfare of American Jewry.

But if its first twenty-five years were a time of planting, its second quarter century was to be a time of reaping. Between its twenty-fifth and fiftieth birthdays the Order not only reached new peaks of growth but achieved a whole chain of "higher objects," including expansion overseas.

During that flourishing period, however, it was

nearly torn apart by internecine warfare over its insurance program, and by the end of the period social conditions in America were so changed that the Order faced a new and entirely different kind of crisis, which was resolved only by profound changes to meet twentieth-century conditions.

7

The 1870's: Preparation for bigger things

The 1870's for B'nai B'rith was a decade of startling growth and a period of direct preparation for a profusion of institutions that were to determine the Order's character for more than half a century.

One of them was the Endowment Fund, or the Widows' and Orphans' Fund, as it was sometimes called. During the organization's first quarter century, each lodge had determined its own system of aiding members and their dependents. Dues and benefits therefore differed from lodge to lodge. But social conditions were greatly changed after the Civil War. The population was increasing rapidly, and new inventions were making life more sophisticated, as well as more expensive. One or two dollars a week had made a big difference to a widow in 1848, but the sum was less impressive in 1868. To give a widow $30 and a dollar a week was now ridiculous, and a radical change was obviously required.

In 1869, therefore, District No. 1 took the bold step of passing a law that changed the old system. Whenever a member died, every member in the District was assessed a specified sum, and one thousand dollars was paid to the widow or legal heirs, with any surplus going into a District reserve fund. Immediately Ararat Lodge, of Hartford, declared the law unconstitutional, on the grounds that the 1868 Constitution had made the local lodge "sovereign in her own internal affairs," that no lodge should be taxed to support the family of a member of some other lodge, that the new law gave the District too much taxing power, etc. But the Order's Court of Appeals upheld the constitutionality of the law, and soon the other Districts began to set up Endowment Funds.

In another kind of contest between a lodge and its District the outcome was different. District No. 2 required all its lodges to meet every week, but Zion Lodge, in Columbus, Ohio, passed a by-law providing for biweekly meetings. The case went to the Order's Court, where the lodge invoked the "sovereignty" clause of the Constitution. The District claimed the power to legislate for all its lodges uniformly. The Court ruled in favor of Zion Lodge, on the grounds that in all matters affecting the District, as such the District was supreme, but in purely local matters, such as the case before it, the lodge was sovereign, since it was not contrary to the Order's 1868 Constitution, which required lodges to meet "at least" twice a month.

Cases involving religious issues also continued to arise. Emek Beracha Lodge, in Ft. Wayne, Indiana, for instance, suddenly refused admission to any candidate married to a non-Jewess, and decreed the expulsion of any member who so married or whose sons were not circumcised. When District No. 2 objected, the lodge claimed local sovereignty, but the District's answer was that the only way to reject a candidate was by blackball. It added that to expel members with uncircumcised sons would lead to an espionage system, and that circumcision in itself was not a *sine qua non* requirement of Judaism. The Court upheld the District.

In another case, the lodge in Lincoln, Illinois, received an application from a young man whose father was a member but whose mother was not Jewish, and the applicant himself was neither circumcised nor professed a religion of any kind. Nonplussed, the lodge asked the advice of District No. 6, which passed a resolution stating that in cases where the Jewishness of an applicant is in doubt, he should be required to declare in writing that he "confesses his belief in Judaism" and does not belong to any "non-Jewish church or non-Jewish religious organization."

Two members of Detroit's Pisgah Lodge appealed against this resolution, and the case leaked out and was widely discussed in the Jewish press, pulpits, and meetings. Inevitably, it led to the question, What is a Jew? to which, of course, there was no definitive answer. District No. 6 appealed for judgments from such noteworthy B'nai B'rith rabbis as Isaac M. Wise, Samuel Hirsch, Max Lilienthal, Bernard Felsenthal, and others—but while they all agreed that according to Jewish law a Jew is one born of a Jewish mother or else formally converted, they disagreed on how strictly that principle could be applied in the latter half of the nineteenth century. The Court of Appeals finally decided that only a lodge can constitutionally determine whether an applicant is qualified for membership, and that District No. 6 had acted illegally in passing its resolution.

At the 1868 convention, a national membership of 8,802 had been reported, but a year and a half later, on January 1, 1870, it had grown by more than 1,500 and for the first time exceeded 10,000.

B'nai B'rith made a unique contribution to Jewish welfare that year. Rumania had long been one of the most anti-Jewish countries in the world, but now the reports of pogroms and other violence there were so alarming that something had to be done at once. The United States had no representation in Rumania at the time, and through the influence of Simon Wolf and other B'nai B'rith leaders the Government was induced not only to create the post of United States Consul to Rumania but to offer it to the Order's distinguished former president, Benjamin F. Peixotto. The Government provided no salary, and Mr. Peixotto was a man of modest means. However, he was willing to leave his home and country to use what influence he could muster to end or mitigate the horrible attacks on his people in benighted Rumania. Several wealthy Jews had promised to subsidize the venture, but before he could leave for his post abroad their enthusiasm wore off, and Mr. Peixotto, who had counted on them, was almost destitute.

Simon Wolf induced Gideon Lodge, of Albany, New

York, and Washington's Elijah Lodge to help, and an appeal was made to all members of the Order. A total of $5,271 was contributed, enabling the new Consul to set forth on his mission. Stopping in Washington for official instructions, he conferred with Carl Schurz, Secretary of State Hamilton Fish, a number of senators whose confidence he won, and finally with President Grant, who turned out to be a very different person from the General Grant who had issued Order No. 11 eight years before. When Peixotto had outlined the situation in Rumania, the President said to him:

> The story of the sufferings of the Hebrews of Rumania profoundly touches every sensibility of our nature. It is one long series of outrage and wrong; and even if there be exaggeration in the accounts which have reached us, enough is evident to prove the imperative duty of all civilized nations extending their moral aid in behalf of a people so unhappy. . . . I have no doubt your presence and influence . . . will result in mitigating the evils complained of, and end in terminating them. The United States, knowing no distinction between her citizens on account of religion or nativity, naturally believes in a civilization the world over which will secure the same universal views.

As the result of Peixotto's work in Rumania, "the evils complained of" were indeed mitigated, but far from terminated. However, the worst of the excesses ended, and after three years, when Peixotto's money was used up, B'nai B'rith issued another appeal which brought in an additional $3,100, enabling him to remain and continue his labors. While there, he established close relations with the Jewish community and organized a network of Zion Societies that later became a B'nai B'rith District Grand Lodge.

After the great Chicago fire of 1871, B'nai B'rith extended direct aid. An appeal to the lodges brought in the fantastic sum of $25,000, in addition to food, clothing, and medical supplies, all of which was sent to the B'nai B'rith Relief Committee in Chicago, headed by Dr. Felsenthal. Some members criticized the Order for using these funds and materials for B'nai B'rith victims, declaring they should have been contributed to the general relief agency. Dr. Friedlein answered the critics thus: "This is the obligation we are under to our brethren, that our first and most imperative duty is owed to them; when that is discharged we should labor as zealously and effectively for the common good." Many of the lodges and individual members contributed to both the B'nai B'rith and the general relief funds. Besides, those aided by the Order eased the drain on the community fund.

More than three hundred B'nai B'rith families in Chicago lost everything, and about two hundred, according to a District No. 6 report weeks later, "found themselves without shelter, bedding and clothing, out of work, and penniless. Four out of five lodges in Chicago lost their all, from the smallest book of account to their richest regalia. . . . The distress among our brethren was beyond description. But not long should they suffer and tremble. Never in the history of any society was there such a united effort made. . . . So excellent has been the management . . . that already today every one of our brethren in Chicago is now in a position to gain his livelihood."

Toward the end of 1872 the past presidents of lodges in Tennessee, Arkansas, Mississippi, and Alabama—all in District No. 2—petitioned the CGL for a District charter, and early in 1873 District No. 7 was formally

installed. Moritz Ellinger, the national secretary, who
went to Memphis for the installation because President
Bien was ill, was greatly impressed with the Southern
lodges.

"In no section of our vast country, probably, where
our Order has gained a foothold," he wrote, "has its
effects proved as beneficial as in the Southern States.
. . . Wherever a lodge is established, there also a nucleus is given for cooperation in matters of education, in
institutions of benevolence, stretching far beyond the
confines of sect or creed. Lodges have invariably been
the means of mitigating the severity of prejudice. . . .
In no few instances the establishment of a lodge has
preceded the organization of a congregation, and wherever this is the case a desire prevails to place the public
worship in concord with the principles inculcated in the
lodge room, and to it must be ascribed the establishment of many Reform congregations throughout the
South."

There were several reasons for the formation of District No. 7. Its lodges were too far from Cincinnati, the
seat of District No. 2, to attend conventions. More important, during the Reconstruction period the increase
in population brought many Jews to some of the Southern states and especially to the great Southwest, so that
opportunities for B'nai B'rith expansion in the future
seemed excellent. But the immediate reason was the
District No. 2 Endowment Fund.

Unlike that of all the other Districts it was voluntary,
with nonparticipants, of course, receiving no benefits.
But it specifically excluded all members in Tennessee,
Louisiana, Mississippi, and Alabama, because those
states were often the scene of epidemics of yellow fever
and other deadly diseases, and their inhabitants were

not considered good "risks" for an endowment plan. This attitude of the Northern lodges was not calculated to endear them to the Southern groups, who set up their own Endowment Fund as soon as they received their District charter.

Sure enough, in September of that same year, the South suffered one of its worst yellow-fever epidemics, with the greatest tragedy centering in Memphis, seat of the new District and home of its first president, A. E. Frankland. Thousands fled the city, and 1,800 died there in seven weeks, including 93 Jews, many of them members of the Order. One of the victims was Lew Wexler, District secretary. The new District was too young to have any resources, and aid poured in from lodges throughout the country. About 180 children were orphaned by the catastrophe. Some of the Jewish youngsters were sent to the Cleveland Jewish Orphan Home, while others were taken into private homes or provided with jobs.

But the District recovered quickly, and six years later, in a report to the Executive Committee of the Order, Mr. Frankland wrote:

> We have frequently been met with the query: "What good are your little country lodges? They cannot sustain themselves, they must live a miserable existence and die almost as soon as born. Why don't you condense?" To these queries I answer: The little country lodge of the I.O.B.B. is inaugurated by the sturdy pioneer who has gone West and South in quest of fortune, who builds up the waste places, and when a few are gathered together they build an altar, and dedicate it to the B'nai B'rith. This is their first commencement— afterwards come the *Minyan*, Congregation, Benevolent Society, *et al.,* and with few, very few exceptions, these little country B'nai B'rith lodges have been the

means of uniting Israel, when congregations failed; and this, as I understand it, has been the great mission of our founders.

Throughout the 1870's the size and wealth of the Order continued to grow steadily. When the first quinquennial convention was held, in Chicago in 1874, President Bien reported a membership of some 16,000 in 205 lodges. And when he declared that the financial affairs of the organization had been "conducted with economy," he outdid the British in understatement. The secretary refused to accept any salary, and although the 1868 convention had authorized the president to spend $500 a year for clerical expenses, he revealed that during the five-year period the entire administrative expense had amounted to $145.26!

From 1870 on, Mr. Bien, closely advised by Isidor Bush of St. Louis, a member of the Executive Committee, had been giving serious thought to the Endowment Fund. District after District had adopted its own version, each differing from the others, and it seemed to both men that there ought to be one national Endowment plan. Mr. Bush pointed out that the more subscribers there were in any kind of insurance operation, the more accurate were the actuarial statistics, and the less the risk of loss. In addition, some of the Districts had become exhilarated at the size of their growing reserve funds and were thinking of increasing the death benefit from $1,000 to $1,500, and even to $2,000. Since each District was autonomous in this matter, Mr. Bush issued warning after warning, reminding them that the present members would not remain young forever, and that in time death benefits would have to be paid out to hundreds and thousands of widows—to say nothing of the grim possibility of epidemics, floods, accidents, etc.

Mr. Bien recommended a national Endowment Fund to the 1874 convention, but it was narrowly defeated. Instead, the delegates passed a motion "that the establishment of Widows' and Orphans' Endowment Funds, by District Grand Lodges, is within the legitimate scope of the aims and objects of the Order." This merely legalized an existing practice.

The bigger an organization grows, the more critics and even cranks it absorbs, per thousand, and B'nai B'rith was no exception. In most of the Districts there were a few bitter-end lodges opposed to the District Endowment Funds on the grounds that they violated local lodge sovereignty. By 1874 the District No. 2 Fund had become mandatory, and in Cincinnati a lodge brought the issue to the Order's Court of Appeals. When it lost the case there, it took it to the Superior Court in Cincinnati, and lost again.

There was also widespread dissatisfaction because the long-promised B'nai B'rith magazine and a history of the Order had not materialized. The national officials kept explaining that both projects were too formidable for the organization's resources, but would be undertaken soon.

And still B'nai B'rith grew—to 17,800 in 1875; to 19,-200 in 1876; to 20,113 in 1877; to 21,480 in 1878. (In 1875 the first lodge outside the U.S. was chartered, in Toronto, and another was founded in Montreal in 1881, but both died out after a few years.) And all this growth took place in spite of the fact that those were years of severe economic depression. During the 1874 CGL convention it was even decided that B'nai B'rith should do something elaborate and dramatic—and expensive—to help the nation celebrate its centennial of independence in 1876. All the states, cities, corporations, and organizations were planning special events. So the B'nai B'rith committee, which had been given the power to act by the convention, engaged a talented and already well-known young sculptor, Moses Ezekiel, a member of the Order, and ordered "a group of statuary emblematic of Religious Liberty." The sculptor was frankly told the money for it would have to be raised through the lodges, and that nobody could predict how much would be collected. Mr. Ezekiel's imagination was so challenged by the project that he agreed to the terms, returned to his studio in Rome, and got to work. But the lodges responded so sluggishly to the appeal for funds that the sculptor could not buy the materials promptly, and the work was delayed. Instead of being delivered in time to be unveiled during the national centennial celebration in Philadelphia, the statue had to be dedicated later in the year, on Thanksgiving Day, 1876. The site was Philadelphia's Fairmount Park, where it still stands. Resting on a massive pedestal, it depicts the spirit of Liberty as a stately woman, somewhat reminiscent of the Statue of Liberty. Her left hand clasps the scroll of the United States Constitution; her right is extended in a protective attitude over the Genius of Devotion, a young boy. To one side is the emblematic eagle of Freedom, killing with its rugged claws the spirit of Intolerance, a writhing snake. An audience of some fifteen hundred people of all faiths attended the event.

District No. 3 paid all expenses of the dedication, including a dinner that followed. But after the sculptor's fee of $4,500 was paid, there were so many outstanding bills that although about $8,000 more was raised by the lodges, an additional $15,000 was needed. It took B'nai B'rith four years, but all bills were finally paid.

The Districts had plenty of money, but it was all held

in trust to pay beneficiaries of the Endowment Funds. But there were members who were not impressed by the Order's size and prosperity. In an 1876 District No. 6 report to the Executive Committee, E. C. Hamburgher, the District's secretary, wrote: "With so large an increase of membership and with so good a financial showing, we are not happy. . . . The majority seemingly join for the material benefits derived solely. I have spoken to several of the officers of our District, and they inform me that in Chicago there are many lodges who, for months, have no, or hardly, a quorum, and yet their members are all good-standing members . . . beyond which they contribute nothing to the benefit or honor of the institution." He urgently proposed that the approaching 1879 convention pass a law fixing "some *standard* of membership."

But neither the 1879 convention nor any other did anything remotely like that, although in 1877 District No. 1 created "a department of enlightenment and culture," and District No. 2 acted similarly. These departments consisted of talented young men who spoke and led discussion groups at lodge meetings in their vicinity. In 1879 District No. 4 dedicated in San Francisco a handsome $90,000 B'nai B'rith Hall, which served as a cultural center as well as District headquarters and meeting place for the local lodges.

The unromantic fact was that the great majority of members did not join the Order, or any other organization, for cultural programs. They joined then, as they do now, for a variety of reasons, including altruism, fellowship, Jewish welfare, service to others—and also self-interest, material benefits, honors, and personal publicity.

By the mid-1870's, with adequate Endowment Funds operating in every District, with most of the members not only "Americanized" but getting along more or less well in their occupations, with lengthy and elaborate secret rituals no longer capable of captivating the imagination, the lodges had no further reason to meet weekly and were meeting twice a month, while the District Grand Lodges, which had met quarterly, were assembling only once a year. And the Third General Convention in 1879 voted to have the CGL meet every seven years instead of quinquennially. Moreover, the three degrees of the ritual were consolidated into one simple and dignified expression.

Otherwise the convention changed the Constitution very little, with one surprising and unexplained exception. It rejected the Preamble and readopted the original 1843 version, except that it referred to "the people of our race" instead of "our faith," and unaccountably omitted the phrase "coming to the rescue of victims of persecution."

There had been so many disputes between lodges and their Districts over local "sovereignty" claims that the convention amended the Constitution to require lodges to obey District laws and Districts to obey CGL laws, on pain of losing their charters.

The only other action of interest taken by the convention was a motion authorizing and directing the president to write a history of the Order and appropriating $2,000 for him to use toward that end. The delegates wanted a magazine more than ever, but it still seemed beyond their means. As things turned out, Mr. Bien used little or none of the $2,000; his history never appeared in book form, and it covered only the sixteen years between 1843 and 1859, although he lived until 1909. His history was serialized in the first two years' issues of the Order's magazine in the late 1880's.

B'nai B'rith membership grew from 15,997 in 1874 to 22,814 in 1879.

8

■

The 1880's: Crisis and triumph

The 1880's witnessed the apogee of B'nai B'rith in the nineteenth century. Its membership climbed to the highest it was to reach in that century, far outstripping that of any other Jewish group; it created additional philanthropic agencies; its charitable works, including its own Endowment Funds, ran into millions of dollars; it finally acquired a magazine; and for the first time it took root overseas, spreading into Europe, Egypt, and Palestine.

But first it had to survive its Endowment Fund crisis, which brought it close to the edge of ruin.

The last frontier was being consolidated in the West,

and the old wide-open economic opportunities were beginning to shrink, although few were fully aware of it at the time. Most of the good lands were taken, and in the cities the growth of population had resulted in keener and keener competition. The worker, the shopkeeper, the average professional man worried more than ever about what would happen to his family if he died. Life insurance was costly, and social security nonexistent.

Under these circumstances, numerous endowment societies and mutual-aid associations sprang up after the Civil War, many of them little better than rackets. Engaging in fierce competition with one another, they offered cut-rate insurance and sick benefits. A large number of men had joined B'nai B'rith not for its "higher objects" but for its material benefits. A dollar meant more then than it does now, and it made a big difference if a thousand dollars' worth of life insurance cost perhaps $28 a year (at a given age) in a commercial insurance company, or only $15 (regardless of age) in B'nai B'rith. And when newly formed Jewish organizations offered the same benefits for even less, the attraction was often irresistible.

A lot of B'nai B'rith members either resigned, to affiliate with the wildcat insurance groups, or joined them and remained in the Order. In the latter case, a large number soon found that paying two or three premiums was more than they could afford, and they dropped out of B'nai B'rith. A third reaction was to stay in the Order but demand that it lower its Endowment fees.

Isidor Bush patiently explained over and over that most of the new insurance organizations were either knavish or foolish, and that far from lowering its fees, B'nai B'rith should increase them if it were to avoid financial catastrophe. He had the Order's mortality sta-

tistics over the years, and demonstrated mathematically
that an annual premium of at least $18 a year per mem-
ber was required, instead of the $15 then almost stand-
ard in the Districts. He pointed out that if a man joined
B'nai B'rith at age 30 and paid $15 a year for 40 years,
he would have paid in only $600, but B'nai B'rith would
have to pay out $1,000 to his heir, and that few men
lived to 70, and fewer remained members for 40 years.
What was essential, he pleaded, was a substantial reserve fund.

But the advocates of cheap insurance refused to lis-
ten. At their District conventions they voted down moves
to increase the assessments, and in District No. 7 the
death benefit was even raised to $1,500 without increas-
ing the premium. District No. 3 had no reserve fund
whatever. District No. 4, rejecting all advice by experts,
increased the benefit to $2,000.

Perhaps equally harmful to the organization was the
fact that the argument over Endowments began to over-
shadow everything else. It led to feuds and bitterness,
and even the Jewish press and pulpit began to scoff at
the Order, calling it an organization that hypocritically
professed to be interested in Jewish welfare and "higher
objects," but that it was actually nothing but an insurance outfit.

President Bien inveighed many times against the
whole obsession. In one of his reports he declared that
the Endowment had "attracted an element to the Order
whose *sole* purpose is to obtain *cheap* life insurance.
. . . Unless the evil is speedily checked, I fear that
disturbances and disruptions may follow which it will be
too late to heal."

The situation became so dangerous that the Executive
Committee recommended that the Constitution Grand

Lodge convention, scheduled for 1886, be advanced a year, and a majority of the lodges consented. In 1885, therefore, the Endowment problem was solved, for the time being. A law was passed which did not impose a national uniform endowment system, which Bien had asked for, but which did control the vital question of premiums in all Districts which chose to have Endowment Funds. The new law required that the annual assessment per member be fixed at not less than $15 per $1,000 benefit, and "a proportionate additional rate for any amount exceeding that sum."

All Districts complied except No. 4, which claimed it had autonomy, and that its own Endowment Fund—which provided a $2,000 benefit for less than $15 per thousand—was working well, and that compliance with the new law would ruin and even end B'nai B'rith on the Pacific Coast. The president of the Order sternly warned the District to comply with the law or have its charter lifted, but the District fought the case for two years. Finally, when it was about to lose its charter, it complied, and in the years that followed, like most of the other Districts, it built up a healthy reserve, and the immediate crisis was over. Even before the 1885 convention, District No. 2 had increased its assessment from $15 to $18, and its Endowment plan was considered the best one in all B'nai B'rith.

Between 1869, when the first Endowment Funds were established in Districts No. 1, 3, and 6, and 1885, a total of $3,118,000 was paid in benefits to the widows and other heirs of members—a fortune compared to what they could have afforded in commercial insurance.

Meanwhile the most important phenomenon in American Jewish history was under way: the beginning of the great immigration of Jews from eastern Europe, which during the next generation was to swell to millions and completely alter the character of American Jewry. President Bien gave notice of what was happening as early as 1880, a full year before the assassination of Czar Alexander II, which triggered the start of the flood tide. Even before then, the Jews in Russia were so persecuted that many were fleeing to western Europe and America.

Mr. Bien did not know, in 1880, that a whole new American Jewish world was being born when he reported: "The immigration from the East and South of Europe is heavily on the increase, and the continued persecution of the Jews in these countries will no doubt bring a large number of them to our shores. Something must be done, not only for the immediate relief of these unfortunate victims of fanaticism, but strenuous efforts should be made to place them in a position to gain an independence by honest labor, and to become good and useful citizens."

He saw what was happening merely as another temporary emergency that called for B'nai B'rith action, and did not dream of its ultimate extent. So he issued an appeal for funds to extend direct relief to the immigrants as they arrived, to find them lodgings, and, above all, jobs. The response was generous. But as time went on, it became apparent that sporadic fund-raising was not meeting the problem, and in the major cities B'nai B'rith joined with other groups and with congregations in forming local societies to aid the newcomers. This was done especially well in New York, New Orleans, and Chicago, and in all those cities B'nai B'rith officials became leaders in the concerted efforts on behalf of the immigrants.

As for taking them into B'nai B'rith, that was another matter. Apparently the lodges differed on the subject.

When a group of Litvaks in Chicago applied to District No. 6 for a charter in the late 1880's, their application was rejected, on the grounds that the Order did not admit men according to class, but only as individuals. On the other hand, District No. 3 granted a charter to a group of Russian immigrants in Philadelphia, and the Order's magazine welcomed them, declaring there was "no better means for assimilating, educating, and training our foreign coreligionists in the habits, customs, and laws of the country than in bringing them into the fold of the Order."

The fact is that very few of the immigrants could yet afford to belong to B'nai B'rith, very few felt at home in it, and very few applied for admission. The Order definitely bore the stamp of *Deutsche Yehudim,* which meant not only "German Jews" but Reform Jews, and anything outside of the strict Orthodox synagogue was anathema to most of the first-generation immigrants from eastern Europe. But on the whole, B'nai B'rith worked so effectively to improve their condition that it earned tributes from many sources. The New York *Sun,* for example, editorially declared the Order "has already been useful in transforming the immigrants of past periods . . . and the great increase of such immigration from Russia, Poland, and Rumania during recent years makes this work more necessary and more arduous."

For several years the Order had been raising money for the Alliance Israelite Universelle, because it warmly approved of that agency's program of providing schools for Jews in the benighted Near East. During Purim of 1880, it raised $2,000 from the lodges, and the following Purim, $1,000. Thereafter the collections fell off, but every year several hundred dollars were contributed, and these Purim collections became a tradition. After

1888, however, when B'nai B'rith became established in Palestine and other Near East lands, the Purim collections were donated directly to a B'nai B'rith orphanage in Jerusalem and to schools in the Orient, and when a District Grand Lodge was created in Rumania, its schools were included among the beneficiaries. The Order's contacts with the Board of Deputies of British Jews went back to 1865.

In line with this growing policy of internationalism, when a group of men in Berlin applied for a lodge charter, the Executive Committee dispatched its former secretary, Moritz Ellinger, to Germany, where on March 21, 1882, he installed B'nai B'rith's first overseas lodge. But first he had to overcome a problem. German anti-Semitism was not invented by Hitler, and in the 1880's it was particularly virulent. In fact, the group that applied for a charter was actuated by two motives: admiration for what B'nai B'rith stood for, and the hope that through a lodge in Berlin it could be more effective in fighting bigotry. Mr. Ellinger discovered that permission of the German Government would be required before any branch of a foreign secret society could be established. He was assured he could obtain such permission, but he realized that to do so would be to play into the hands of the anti-Semites. So, using the full power to act granted him by the Executive Committee, he removed all secrecy from the proceedings, thus making it unnecessary to get official permission to found the lodge. He nevertheless furnished the authorities with a copy of the Order's Constitution and by-laws, and a list of the Berlin members and officers.

The thirty charter members of Deutsche Reichsloge No. 332 were men of the highest caliber and of healthy enthusiasm, and it was not long before they spread B'nai

B'rith to other German cities and began founding institutions.

This expansion was dramatic, but the work of the Order went on as usual at home. The Maimonides Library
in New York, with twenty thousand volumes, established
a branch library, and District No. 1 taxed its members
thirty-two cents a year "to be employed exclusively for
intellectual purposes." There were also B'nai B'rith libraries in Cincinnati, New Haven, San Fancisco, and elsewhere, and scores of lodges provided stimulating local
programs in addition to their business meetings. Employment bureaus were set up by Districts No. 1 and 6 to
help their unemployed members find jobs. In 1883
alone, B'nai B'rith spent $350,000 "for benevolent pur-
poses."

On June 28, 1882, District No. 1 dedicated its $125,-
000 Home for the Aged, with accommodations for 150,
in Yonkers, overlooking the Hudson River. Members
throughout the country took so much pride in it that
some Districts suggested it be made a national project of
the Order, but it remained a District No. 1 institution.

By 1885 B'nai B'rith membership reached 25,000, including 654 in Germany. This growth, combined with a
long list of impressive educational, philanthropic, and
community achievements, aroused bitter jealousy in
other groups which had not fared nearly so well, including a number of congregations. Carping critics sprang
up on all sides. The Jewish press, eager for sensational
stories, was happy to publish their charges. An example
was the criticism of the well-known caustic Chicago
rabbi, Dr. Emil G. Hirsch, that "to elevate and develop
Judaism is none of the Order's business—that is claimed
as the exclusive prerogative of the congregation." He declared that "much safer and cheaper insurance" could

be bought from a trustworthy life insurance company than through B'nai B'rith, and that the whole lodge system was "an anachronism in our days and especially in Judaism." He also ridiculed the small attendance at lodge meetings.

Isidor Bush answered him: "Granted our shortcomings in these and other points, the reproach comes with bad grace from those who must avow that our beautiful temples . . . are just as poorly attended." He charged the Jewish press with failing "to attract better attendance in our temples or induce a better observance of the Sabbath, or a more liberal philosophy, a more active support of science and art, who have never been very successful in uniting Israelites in the work of promoting Judaism—these very editors dare to attack and belittle our Order."

At the same time there was plenty of self-criticism within B'nai B'rith. It dealt largely with the beginning of a sense of apathy which was to grow alarmingly in the 1890's. A. E. Frankland, past president of District No. 7, wrote: "Notwithstanding the lively interest manifested in everything appertaining to the welfare of the Order . . . the average attendance at the Lodge meetings is not so large as in the good old halcyon days when we were younger and not so strong." In his message to the 1885 convention, President Bien spoke of "a deplorable degree of apathy which has set in of late years," and of "a deeply felt want, a want of genuine unity and true fraternal concord among our Districts." Many others expressed similar nostalgic sentiments, not only then but later. The past always seemed better than the present.

None of these misgivings prevented B'nai B'rith in the 1880's from continuing to forge ahead. Unable to sustain a project to encourage Jews to engage in agriculture, back in the 1850's, the Order now tried again. At its 1881 meeting, the Executive Committee felt that as many as possible of the new immigrants should be encouraged to settle on farms, but realized this was too big a project for it to undertake, and decided the job should be done by several organizations, jointly.

President Bien asked Moritz Ellinger, who was also a leader in the Union of American Hebrew Congregations, to submit to the UAHC convention that year a report on the subject. The UAHC adopted the report, and named a committee to implement it. B'nai B'rith soon received a letter from the committee, inviting it to join in the project it had proposed. Mr. Bien promptly appointed a committee for that purpose, and notified the UAHC. "And here," he reported sadly to the 1885 CGL convention, four years later, "the matter dropped, and we never heard anything further on the subject." But, he added, the UAHC did launch a campaign to obtain funds "by which agricultural pursuits and Hebrew Union College were yoked together and which proved, deservedly, an ignominious failure."

This led to hostilities, for several years, between the two bodies. Dr. Isaac M. Wise had founded the UAHC in 1873 and Hebrew Union College in Cincinnati in 1875. Although he was a former leader in the Order, he grew impatient with it after it consistently refused to support his institutions. He attended no meetings of B'nai B'rith for more than a decade, but by 1883 the Hebrew Union College, of which he was president—as he was of the UAHC—was in such dire financial straits that the UAHC sent a letter to every B'nai B'rith lodge in the country, appealing for funds. In another letter, to the Executive Committee of the Order, the UAHC coolly asked that it use its authority to have every member taxed to support Hebrew Union College.

Furious at this approach to the lodges over the head of the CGL, Moritz Thalmessinger, secretary of the Executive Committee, fired back a letter to the UAHC, wryly declaring that "disregarding the questionable propriety of the method chosen to reach our Lodges, we beg to state that the object sought is entirely outside of the Province of our Order, and our Lodges have not the constitutional right to tax their members for that purpose." And he added, flatly: "To support the Hebrew Union College, directly or indirectly, *is strictly the affair of the Congregations, who are fully able to do so.*" A copy of this letter was sent to every lodge and District.

But embarrassingly, District No. 6 took exception to this ruling. Its general committee passed a resolution stating that it could see "no reason why lodges should not be permitted to act" in support of Hebrew Union College if they wished, and that Brother Thalmessinger had no right, in his official capacity, to forbid them to do so. The outraged secretary thereupon sent a form letter to all the lodges, quoting the resolution passed by the 1874 CGL convention, declaring it to be "not within the sphere of the Order to interfere with congregational or doctrinal matters *in any shape or form,*" and he reminded all concerned that any lodge or District which refused to obey any CGL ordinance was subject to having its charter suspended or forfeited.

It did not improve relations between B'nai B'rith and the UAHC when, in 1883, a leader of Rumanian Jewry appealed to President Bien on behalf of his oppressed people. There was a recrudescence of vicious anti-Semitism in Rumania, and many of the Jews there wanted to emigrate to Palestine. But that unhappy land was part of the Turkish Empire, which absolutely forbade foreign Jews to settle in it. B'nai B'rith was asked to petition the United States Government to intercede with Turkey. Mr. Bien was willing to try, but was enjoined by a B'nai B'rith constitutional limitation on his powers. He therefore referred the Rumanian request to the UAHC, "which, however, deemed it inexpedient to take any action."

"We are forced to the conclusion," Mr. Bien reported acidly to the 1885 CGL convention, "that the present Union of American Hebrew Congregations does not represent American Israel; neither its influence nor authority, if there be such, extends beyond the congregations composing it."

After Benjamin Peixotto founded *The Menorah* as the official organ of B'nai B'rith in 1886, it engaged in a running editorial battle with *The American Israelite*, founded and edited by Dr. Wise in Cincinnati. By that time, Dr. Wise had become openly hostile to the Order, but even his close friends were shocked when he published in his paper the almost psychopathic charge that "Bros. Bien and Thalmessinger hire *The American Hebrew* to abuse the Hebrew Union College and its President and pay for the same out of the funds of the District Grand Lodge." District No. 1 indignantly denied the accusation, and the battle waxed hotter.

But this nasty feud did not endure, for B'nai B'rith and the UAHC later enjoyed the friendliest relations and close cooperation. In 1875, when Dr. Wise founded Hebrew Union College, the Order had wished it well, just as it did to the Jewish Theological Seminary when Conservative Jews founded that institution in 1886.

Another controversy of the 1880's arose over an effort within B'nai B'rith to "consolidate the Orders." In his

1881 report to the Executive Committee President Bien had pointed out that "since the foundation of B'nai B'rith, a number of other Jewish Orders have sprung into existence, professedly pursuing the same objects, following similar aims, and carrying out like principles." It pained him "to see Israelites of this country divided into so many camps, when more than ever they should present a united front," and he urged that "earnest steps should therefore be taken to bring about a union of the various Jewish Orders."

This struck a responsive chord in many B'nai B'rith leaders, but nothing ever came of the proposal, even though the 1885 convention formally endorsed the idea. The four leading Jewish organizations then were B'nai B'rith, with 25,000 members; Independent Order Free Sons of Israel, with 11,000; Kesher Shel Barzel, with 9,000; and the Improved Order Free Sons of Israel, with 3,300. Their leaders might have become interested in Mr. Bien's idea except for one thing: his proposal involved the incorporation of the three other Orders into B'nai B'rith.

It was at the 1885 convention that the whole basis of representation was changed. Ever since 1868, each lodge in the country had been entitled to one delegate, but now there were more than 300 lodges, and the conventions had become unwieldy. Besides, many lodges in the Far West and the Southwest went unrepresented altogether, for lack of means to send delegates. The Constitution was therefore amended, requiring that in the future all delegates be elected by their respective District Grand Lodges, with one delegate for each 300 members. Two members of the Committee on Constitution were so bitterly opposed to ending direct lodge representation that they entered a minority report in which they actually called the new system "un-American," but it was adopted and has been the basis for such national gatherings ever since.

Another convention action that has held up to the present time was the change from taxing lodges for CGL income to levying a per-capita tax on every individual member.

Still another action that is still in effect concerned the Court of Appeals. Up to that time, all disputes had to come before a District convention before they could be referred to the Order's court. But the 1885 meeting created District courts, from which cases could be taken direct to the national court.

As usual, demands were made for the abolition of secrecy, but although the president and others explained that B'nai B'rith was not really a secret organization, the delegates were not yet ready to abandon the facade of secrecy formally. Instead they compromised by passing a resolution that it was the sense of the convention "that Lodges be permitted to hold public initiations of its officers if they desire to do so."

A motion "that ladies be admitted to full membership in the Lodges" did not fare so well. It was ruled out of order.

The indefatigable forces favoring B'nai B'rith's "moral and hearty support" of Hebrew Union College once more proposed a resolution to that effect, but it was tabled. The delegates restored the law that CGL conventions be held every five years.

And after efforts to frame a new Preamble to the Constitution were beaten down, the one adopted in 1879 was readopted, except that the important phrase "coming to the rescue of victims of persecution" was restored.

One of the most dramatic actions of the convention

was the granting of a District charter to the lodges in Germany, and soon afterward President Bien went to Berlin and personally installed District No. 8. In three years the German lodges had grown to ten in number, with an eleventh in formation, and their activities put most of their American counterparts to shame. The German groups had a special fund to supply one thousand mark dowries to poor members' daughters upon their marriage; they contributed regularly to the Jewish Deaf Mutes Institution in Berlin; they paid a pension to Jewish teachers, whose salaries were very low; they extended direct relief to Jews who were not members of B'nai B'rith but who were in desperate need; they forwarded "large sums of money" to Palestine to aid the first struggling Zionist pioneers of the 1880's; and this lively program expanded every year.

Finally the convention again authorized the publication of the long-demanded magazine for B'nai B'rith, and this time something happened. Benjamin F. Peixotto reached an agreement with the Executive Committee; he would privately publish and edit a magazine, to be called *The Menorah*, which would be the official organ of B'nai B'rith. The Executive Committee would have supervisory control over everything it contained about the Order, but no responsibility for its other contents, and no financial responsibility beyond paying for all B'nai B'rith notices and other material, at rates to be agreed upon. The organization promised to give the magazine its moral support and promote subscriptions among the members.

Vol. I, No. 1 appeared in July, 1886. It contained, aside from the expected introductory editorial, the first installment of Julius Bien's short history of B'nai B'rith; a tribute to the Order and what it stood for; the first of a long series of articles by Mr. Peixotto on his Rumanian mission; an article defining the Constitution Grand Lodge; another on the Order's Endowment Funds; several pages of brief news items about the Districts and lodges; and a section in the German language, including an account of B'nai B'rith in Germany. But succeeding issues contained more material of general Jewish cultural interest, until a balance was reached bteween B'nai B'rith and non-B'nai B'rith contents. That has remained the publication's policy down to the present time, although it has changed its name and format several times and long ago ceased to be a private venture and became wholly the property of the Order.

During 1885, as a direct result of increasing the Endowment dues, B'nai B'rith suffered a net loss of 532 American members, and although this was more than compensated by the gain in Germany, it was the first year since its founding that B'nai B'rith had a net membership loss. Nevertheless, the following year, when a disastrous earthquake wrecked Charleston, South Carolina, the lodges raised a total of $4,015 for the B'nai B'rith victims; District No. 6 appropriated $300 toward a school to teach English to the Russian immigrants; and in January, 1887, the first lodge in the Near East was installed—Maimonides Lodge, at Cairo, Egypt. The Sephardim and Ashkenazim of that city were split by so deep a gulf that it was thought it could never be bridged. The lodge members were all Ashkenazim, but in a surprisingly short time a number of Sephardim began to cooperate with the group and later even joined it.

The lodge in Cairo was installed by a Mr. Simmel, a Berlin member who represented the CGL. Afterward he visited Jerusalem, where he was appalled by what he saw. Destitution was combined with ignorance and bigotry among the Jews to such an extent that they were indifferent to the sufferings of their own kin. Children were abandoned on the streets, and many were picked up by swarming Christian missionaries who fed, housed, and converted them. Mr. Simmel realized that the charity contributions flowing to Palestine from Jews the world over were only spreading pauperism and that something constructive was needed. He found two institutions that deserved help: a German Jewish orphan asylum and a technical school that taught trades to boys.

These two agencies were given financial support first by the German District, and then by American B'nai B'rith. But the CGL felt that lodges should be founded in Palestine, and throughout the Near East, as a permanent force for better conditions, and on June 10, 1888, Jerusalem Lodge was organized with twenty charter members. That was nine years before the First Zionist Congress called by Theodor Herzl.

Jerusalem Lodge made a contribution of the first magnitude toward ultimate Jewish independence in Palestine. From the beginning it insisted on Hebrew as the language of the lodge, and for the first time the Order's Constitution and ritual were translated into that tongue. Eliezer Ben-Yehuda, the "father of modern Hebrew," was a charter member and the first secretary of the lodge. He suffered martyrdom for his unshakable resolve to speak nothing but Hebrew and teach it to others, knowing that without a national language—and it had to be Hebrew, in modernized form—Palestine would remain a Tower of Babel and Jewish national aspirations would never be realized. In this ideal the lodge concurred, without, however, espousing political Zionism as such.

Jerusalem Lodge almost immediately opened an evening school for adults, the first of its kind there, and on opening night 130 people attended. More important was the fact that they included Ashkenazim, Sephardim, Chassidim, Yemenites, and others who previously had never met together. The teachers were all qualified members of the lodge who served without pay, and they taught the Talmud, Jewish history, German, French, and arithmetic. Attendance soon exceeded two hundred.

In March, 1889, District No. 9 was installed in Rumania. The political climate had improved—temporarily—so that it was possible to convert Peixotto's old Zion Society into B'nai B'rith, with 544 members in 13 communities. The Zion Society had created a network of schools, which B'nai B'rith took over, and in which every lodge had its meeting room. The schools taught hundreds of Jewish children the Rumanian language, as well as German and Spanish, in addition to Hebrew, and of course general secular subjects. Poor youngsters were given books and clothing. Later the same year, by means of a lottery, one of the lodges built the first Jewish School for Girls in Bucharest. But of at least equal importance was that B'nai B'rith had brought together in the same lodges German and Polish Jews, who traditionally had kept aloof from one another. Later the Sephardim, who had kept apart from both groups, formed a Spanish-speaking lodge.

In September, 1889, a group in Bielitz, Austria, received a charter, and after lodges had been organized all over the country, Austria became a District Grand Lodge.

At that period, it seemed that nothing was beyond the capacity of B'nai B'rith. Atlanta's Gate City Lodge founded the Young Men's Hebrew Association in its city.

District No. 4 established a School for Technical Instruction in San Francisco. In 1888, on its twentieth anniversary, the Cleveland Jewish Orphan Home moved to a new and much bigger building, accommodating well over three hundred children. In the same year a precursor to the twentieth-century B'nai B'rith Youth Organization appeared in the form of a "Junior B'nai B'rith Lodge" in Vicksburg, Mississippi. It consisted of boys between thirteen and twenty, with a program of social, philanthropic, cultural, and communal activities. Later scores of similar groups were organized across the country, but lacking adult supervision, they ultimately died out.

The lodges contributed a large sum of money to sufferers of the Johnstown flood. Even the desperate plight of a tiny colony of Jewish farmers in the Dakotas elicited their aid. The seventy families found themselves without food or fuel after a crop failure in 1888. They asked no one for help, but their plight came to the attention of Minneapolis Lodge, which appealed to the president of the Order, who in turn asked the lodges for aid. Some thirty-six lodges, from Dallas to Washington, D. C., contributed a total of $1,435, which saw the farmers through their crisis.

And on March 28, 1889, District No. 5 dedicated an orphan home in Atlanta. For years, while it was raising a fund for this purpose, the District sent orphans to an asylum in Baltimore, paying $150 a year for each child. The District wanted representation on the board of the Baltimore Jewish Orphan Society, and decided to have its own institution only after this was refused. When it opened its own building in Atlanta, which cost $52,000 furnished, the entire agency was paid for.

9

■

The 1890's and the doldrums

In the 1880's B'nai B'rith reached the height of its numerical growth in the United States up to that time and achieved new levels of service and prestige. But it had an anomalous development in the 1890's. That decade witnessed a continuation of its achievements at the same time that its membership suffered a steep decline.

The period opened with the first Constitution Grand Lodge convention ever held in the South. It took place in Richmond, Virginia, in June, 1890. The big issue was again the Endowment Fund. The bright hopes aroused by the previous convention had soon faded. Competing organizations continued to proliferate, with lower insurance premiums, and many members left the Order to join them. Thus, in 1887, the American membership fell to just under 23,000, then to 21,846 in 1889.

Accordingly, the cry went up for optional Endowment Funds. By that was meant that unmarried men under the age of 30, as well as men over 45, who wished to join B'nai B'rith without participating in its insurance, should be accepted. Nobody demanded optional endowments for all members; the general sentiment was that widows and orphans had to be protected. Optional endowment had first been proposed by Adolph Freund, of Detroit, when he was president of District No. 6 in 1884. Now its advocates claimed it would attract many young bachelors to the Order, as well as older men who had no dependents. Its opponents scoffed at this idea, proclaiming that the young men were so materialistic that they would not join an organization solely to serve others, without reward.

Actually, the problem was a moral as well as a financial one. Under the endowment plan, not only did each District have to have an annual premium of at least $15, but it had to be uniform for all members, regardless of age. This made no sense actuarially, as many pointed out, because it penalized the young. But others insisted that the main desideratum was brotherly love—was it brotherly to have low rates for young men, who had contributed nothing to the Order and might resign at any time, and high rates for old men who had faithfully worked for B'nai B'rith and paid into its insurance fund for decades?

As a matter of fact, Districts No. 3 and 4, in 1887, amended their endowment laws to provide for graduated rates, from $16.20 a year for those in their twenties up to $30 a year for those above fifty. This was obviously a violation of the Order's Constitution, but they got away with it.

The issue was joined at the Richmond convention, which not only abrogated the 1885 ruling and left the Districts free to operate their own Endowment Funds as they saw fit, but also approved and legalized the actions taken by Districts No. 3 and 4. This was to prove (although it was not realized at the time) the salvation of B'nai B'rith, even though it took nearly a decade for the effects to become apparent. With endowments no longer mandatory within any District, and with each District free to change its insurance laws as it wished or eliminate them altogether, a long and painful struggle ensued, during which conditions got a lot worse before they got better.

Periodically, ever since the question was first raised in 1859, proposals had been made that women be admitted to B'nai B'rith, but had always been defeated. But the forces in favor of their admission were stronger in Richmond than they had ever been before. A motion to amend the Constitution soberly lectured the delegates: "If you want *Justice*, practical justice, remove your prejudice against women . . . and proclaim that they are as capable as we are to carry out the teachings of your Order." The motion went so far as to suggest that the name of the Order be changed from the masculine Independent Order B'nai B'rith (Sons of the Covenant) to the neuter Independent Order B'rith, that is, Independent Order of the Covenant.

The delegates were not prepared to go that far, but they did pass a compromise resolution: that the matter of admitting women be submitted to a referendum of all the lodges, and if two-thirds concurred, the Executive Committee was to declare it constitutional. But when the poll was taken, several months later, the proposal was defeated, with more than two-thirds of the lodges voting against it.

Despite the warm critical acclaim *The Menorah* enjoyed, not enough members had subscribed to make it pay its way, and its editor, Mr. Peixotto, had to make up its losses every year from his own pocket. By 1890 he was no longer able to do so, and the magazine continued to appear only because a number of wealthier members met the deficit. President Bien therefore was authorized to appropriate enough money for one subscription for every lodge in the country.

The continuing Jewish immigration from eastern Europe caused the convention to vote to cooperate with the Baron de Hirsch Fund and other agencies to aid the newcomers.

After the convention Mr. Bien issued a long report to the lodges, in which he recommended that the immigrants be absorbed into as many lodges as possible, to help them adjust to America. He did not hide a less altruistic reason. "We also perform thereby," he observed, "an act of self-preservation. The world knows no distinction between Jew and Jew. . . . The increasing mass of foreigners coming to these shores, who outwardly and inwardly remain foreigners, fill the public with apprehension and mistrust, and Jews as a whole are made to feel the effects of it."

In the same report, he explained the Order's decrease in membership by averring that "the higher an organization places the ideal it strives for, the slower will be its growth, because the object is so much more difficult to grasp by the masses." He also disclosed that the Executive Committee had received applications for lodges from South America, Australia, and even Russia!

A few months after the convention the Order suffered a severe loss in the death of Benjamin F. Peixotto. As his name indicates, he was of Sephardic origin and was not only one of the few non-German leaders of B'nai B'rith of his time, but the first native American to head the Order, having been born in New York (as had his father) in 1834. For several years he was associate editor of the Cleveland *Plain-Dealer*. After his return from Rumania, in 1876, President Rutherford B. Hayes appointed him United States Consul in Lyons, France. Coming home in 1885, he remained active in New York politics until his death.

He was succeeded as editor of *The Menorah* by Moritz Ellinger, former secretary of the Order, who also now became its recording secretary. He maintained the high literary standard of the magazine, but gradually reduced its B'nai B'rith content.

The 1890 convention had scarcely adjourned before most of the Districts made their Endowment Funds optional, and for a while the downward trend in membership was reversed. A goodly number of bachelors in their twenties joined, as did a lesser number of men over forty-five. In addition, several lodges of recent immigrants were chartered. B'nai B'rith made no substantial inroads among the newcomers, however, for the reasons already given, and also because, from the 1890's on, most of them who joined anything joined the most popular institution of immigrant Jewish life in the United States, the *Landsmannschaften*. These were mutual-aid and fraternal organizations of Jews who came from the same European country, or, more often, from the same town or province. In such societies they spoke not only Yiddish but their own kind of Yiddish, they enjoyed reminiscing about a common background, they were able to help new immigrants from their home towns, and they had sick benefits and insurance.

Nevertheless, B'nai B'rith's growth was such that by 1893, when it observed its Golden Anniversary, it had climbed back to a membership in the United States of 24,500, and to a total roster, including the overseas lodges, of 30,000. In 1891 it chartered the first lodge in Syria, at Beirut.

And B'nai B'rith continued to succeed in its chief mission, that of uniting Israelites. This was especially true overseas. In Beirut, for example, where the Jews had long been divided into Ashkenazic and Sephardic groups, the new lodge took the initiative and actually succeeded in uniting them in a single congregation—something no other agency had ever done. This example was soon followed in Jaffa, Palestine, through the efforts of the lodge there.

In Rumania things went from bad to worse for the Jews, who had no citizenship rights, even though native-born. Almost none were wealthy, and how the lodges were able to maintain a network of schools would be a mystery if one were not aware of how desperately important education was to them. At one point a fanatical anti-Semite, who became Minister of Education, proposed that all Jewish children be barred from public schools. A B'nai B'rith delegation immediately obtained an audience with the President of the Ministry to protest the proposal, and it was postponed until the Cabinet fell. The new officials were more moderate, and the danger seemed over. But at the same time another anti-Semite tried to have the Government create a committee to "in-

vestigate" Rumanian Jewry to "protect" the nation
against their "plots." The idea, of course, was to black-
mail the Jews and extort large sums from them. Again
the general committee of the District protested to the
Government, this time to the Minister of Interior, who
assured them the measure was aimed only at "foreigners." But the responsible press helped defeat the infa-
mous plan.

Meanwhile, in America, the cooperation of B'nai
B'rith and other groups with the Baron de Hirsch Fund
resulted in the creation of an American Committee for
Ameliorating the Condition of Russian Refugees. A plan
was worked out to establish, throughout the country, job-
placement bureaus and night schools for adults, and to
provide tools for mechanics and others who could not
find work without them. In addition, efforts were to be
made to induce as many immigrants as possible to leave
the overcrowded New York ghetto for communities in
other states.

B'nai B'rith was active in all these measures and particularly the last, because it was the only Jewish organization that had units in practically every state in the Union. They engaged enthusiastically in this program. Few
immigrants moved to the Deep South, but a great many
settled in Cincinnati, Chicago, St. Louis, Philadelphia,
Baltimore, San Francisco, and elsewhere. Cincinnati's
experience was typical. The lodges there were in the
forefront of the united Jewish community program.
More than $16,000 was raised locally, an office was
opened with a staff, and jobs were found for the new
arrivals, tools were supplied, training courses offered,
and direct relief and housing provided. "As a result of all
this," Isidor Bush reported to the Executive Committee

in 1892, "it is impossible to find any of these immigrants on the streets asking alms."

It was thus in an optimistic mood that B'nai B'rith observed its fiftieth anniversary. Every District and most of the local lodges held their own celebrations, but the national observance took place in New York on October 12, 13, and 15, 1893. The program opened at the city's finest hall, the Grand Central Palace of Industry, where more than ten thousand were seated and several thousand others had to be turned away for lack of space. President Bien, who headed a long list of speakers, reviewed the Order's history; the others paid tribute to various phases of its work. There was also a banquet for four hundred community leaders, addressed by the Governor of New York. A letter from President Grover Cleveland was read:

> I regret that I am not able to accept this invitation on account of pressing official duties. A Society formed for the furtherance of such noble purposes as that of the B'nai B'rith should not only excite the enthusiasm of its members, but should also inspire the good wishes of all who desire to see humanity bettered and the higher instincts of our nature cultivated. Accept for your Order my sincere wish that the gratifying results which have followed its effort for good in the half century that has passed, may be multiplied many fold in the years to come.

It was the first testimonial expression from a President of the United States to B'nai B'rith, but almost all of Cleveland's successors followed his example.

The leaders of the Order confidently expected that the enthusiasm and publicity generated by the occasion would make an impact on the organization's growth. In this they were to be bitterly disappointed. Between the celebrations, in 1893, and the sixth General Convention in 1895, B'nai B'rith in America suffered the stunning loss of nearly 5,000 members—from 24,500 to 19,-658! And the worst was yet to come.

There is no evidence to explain why such a massive loss occurred in so short a time, but B'nai B'rith had actually, late in the 1880's, begun to enter a period of the doldrums which, despite a few ups and downs and the continued progress of its programs, continued for many years.

As early as 1887, *The Menorah* published a letter from a District No. 3 leader which referred to "this quiet, uneventful, go-as-you-please District. . . . There is no excitement at lodge meetings, no eager contest to be representatives, no electioneering for Grand Lodge officers." In an editorial the same year, the magazine observed: "It is a sad commentary upon the 'spirit of the age' that so many of our young men, young merchants, brokers, clerks, etc., indulge in the demoralizing habit of 'playing at cards,' a frivolous pursuit at best . . . and worse still, a degeneration of manhood."

In 1888, a report to the Executive Committee from District No. 2, long considered the best one in the Order, stated flatly that "a lethargic sleep appears to have prevailed from one end of the District to another." And in 1894, a District No. 6 report complained: "The difficulty in our District, and very likely in all other Districts is, How shall we interest our young men in the mission of the Order in the larger and small cities? Their leisure time is occupied in congregational work, in social life, and charity matters, not within the reach of the Order. The most we can get out of them is an occasional visit to the lodge room and their dues."

These were not a few isolated expressions; similar ones were heard in every part of the country. Looking back now, we can see that the *fin de siècle* era marked the beginning of profound social changes in America, which were reflected within the Order. "In small places," another 1894 report from District No. 6 explained, "the B'nai B'rith is the representative of everything pertaining to Jewish life in the community. The same can be said of those parts, in larger cities, where the poorer class of our brethren live. There the B.B. lodge is the congregation, the club, the center of charitable activity, and the literary and debating society."

But the great majority of Jews did not live in "small places." They congregated in the largest cities, which were beginning to sprawl far beyond their original limits. In former years, the Jews had huddled together in downtown areas, within walking distance of everything, and there was a close-knit community spirit. But now many lived too far from the lodge rooms to walk to meetings, and few owned carriages. They made new friends in their new neighborhoods. The growth of newspapers, the spread of transportation, and the increase of inventions began to lessen the need for fraternal gatherings. The electric light, the telephone, the typewriter, the mechanical home appliances, and many other innovations made the middle classes feel they were living in a new age, in which such things as lodge meetings were anachronisms. Soon the infant movie and automobile industries would greatly intensify that impression. The masses of poverty-stricken immigrants, who remained in the downtown ghettos, worked from dawn to dusk in the sweatshops and had neither the time, the money, nor the inclination to join any fraternal orders, except their *Landsmannschaften*.

However, although B'nai B'rith suffered numerically during this period of social transition, its growth in activity continued. In 1893, District No. 3 opened a manual training school in Philadelphia for children of the immigrants and others. The Maimonides Library, having grown so large and popular that it could no longer be managed solely by B'nai B'rith, was soon to be made a free library open to the public, and eventually it was incorporated into the New York Public Library system. The number of children in the Cleveland Jewish Orphan Home increased to nearly five hundred, its capacity. The joint work of the American Committee to aid the immigrants was taken over by the United Hebrew Charities in New York with such success that the cooperating organizations were able to withdraw from active sponsorship. In Denver, the small Jewish community was plagued by thousands of Jewish tuberculosis sufferers, most of them poor, who flocked there for the climate and became social problems beyond the capacity of local Jews to handle. The Colorado lodges therefore raised enough money —$50,000—to build a modest TB hospital in Denver, although not enough to open it (the annual operating cost was estimated at $12,000).

In 1892 the lodge in Jerusalem founded the Abarbanel Library, which became the nucleus of the National Library many years later. At the end of 1894 District No. 10 was chartered in Austria-Hungary. The following year the first lodge in Algeria was installed, at Algiers. At the same time, Turkey's first lodge was chartered, in Smyrna. Almost immediately it opened a much needed public library, and through its efforts twenty-six Jewish boys, who had been lured by Christian missionaries, were brought back to the fold. The European lodges continued to grow.

Consequently, in spite of the loss in American membership, Julius Bien was able to open the CGL convention of 1895 in Cincinnati in a confident mood. Nothing dramatic took place there, however, except that, at long last, permission was given to establish B'nai B'rith women's units. The motion declared that "District Grand Lodges be empowered to establish Auxiliary Lodges for women under such regulations and conditions as may be approved by the Executive Committee." This meant not that women were to be accepted as actual members of the Order, but that groups could be organized as "auxiliaries" to lodges. Nevertheless, it was the first step in a development that today sees the B'nai B'rith Women as a national organization of some 130,000 members, with its own national and District staffs and programs, and its own representatives on all the Order's ruling bodies.

The women did not wait long to take advantage of the new dispensation. The first auxiliary was formed in San Francisco on August 8, 1897, with Mrs. Herman Gutstadt as president. She was the wife of the incumbent president of District No. 4, and the mother of Richard E. Gutstadt who, forty years later, was to be the driving force in building the B'nai B'rith Anti-Defamation League into American Jewry's leading defense and human-rights agency. Several other auxiliaries were founded in succeeding years, but the growth was very slow and spasmodic.

In 1959 the B'nai B'rith Women held an elaborate celebration of its fiftieth anniversary. A short history published at the time stated that the first few auxiliaries had all died out, and that the women's organization's real birthday was March 16, 1909, when San Francisco Auxiliary No. 1, as it was called, was installed. However, research for this volume revealed that at no time between 1897 and 1909 did all the auxiliaries disappear.

It is true that the original one did, as well as most of the others. In fact, all the women's groups in District No. 4 had melted away by 1907, when the District No. 4 convention revised its Constitution to erase all mention of them. But they continued to function in other Districts. Before the ones in District No. 4 died out, others were started in Districts No. 1, 3, 5, and 6. Early in the twentieth century, Isaiah Ladies Auxiliary in New York City was an active group, and by 1910 the president of District No. 1 recommended, at the annual convention, that a "Ladies League" be formed—presumably because there were enough groups in the District to form an association—although no such league was ever organized.

During the first decade of the century, the record spoke of "several" auxiliaries in District No. 3, although the only one specifically named was the one in Braddock, Pennsylvania. It was chartered in 1905 and functioned continuously until 1931, when it was suspended. Actually, an auxiliary was organized in Madison, Wisconsin, early in 1909, and although the exact date is not recorded, it may well have been before March 16, when San Francisco Auxiliary No. 1 was born. Incidentally, in 1901 there were ten women's auxiliaries in Germany, which continued to exist until B'nai B'rith there was destroyed by the Nazis in 1937.

In other words, there have been B'nai B'rith women's groups functioning uninterruptedly since 1897. Consequently, in 1959 the B'nai B'rith Women should have been celebrating its sixty-second anniversary instead of its fiftieth, and it will be seventy years old in 1967.

The 1895 convention also tried again to combat the prevailing materialistic atmosphere of the times, by authorizing each District to create a Standing Committee on Intellectual Advancement, to "provide lectures, musical and literary entertainments and celebrations." The delegates wanted to take over and open the tuberculosis hospital in Denver as a national B'nai B'rith institution, but had to admit the means were lacking. They therefore appropriated one thousand dollars to the institution (whenever it should open its doors) and gave it their warm moral support. They also empowered the Executive Committee to extend financial aid to "meet the unfortunate position of our Brethren in Rumania."

A motion was made that B'nai B'rith found a university—not a Jewish religious institution, but a full-fledged nonsectarian school of higher learning—"dedicated to the people of the United States as an imperishable evidence of the gratitude of the Jews of America for the blessings we enjoy under a free and enlightened government." But this was so chimerical an idea that the motion was quickly defeated.

During the final years of the century, the American membership continued to shrink—from 24,500 in 1893 to 19,658 in 1895, to 18,330 in 1897, to 17,341 in 1899. But the Order's institutions remained strong and effective, and before the turn of the century a new one, full of prestige, was added, in Denver. In 1896 the Chicago lodges created a home for themselves, called the Covenant Culture Club. The following year District No. 2 founded its Educational League, a fund to enable talented alumni of the Cleveland orphanage to continue their studies.

By the end of the 1890's, District No. 5 became so enfeebled that its Orphan Asylum in Atlanta was dissociated from it in order to avoid the risk of a possible financial catastrophe. The Home was separately incorporated, and supported for the most part by non-B'nai B'rith people.

District No. 2 decided to take responsibility for the hospital in Denver, and it was dedicated and opened in 1899 as the National Jewish Hospital, later becoming a national B'nai B'rith institution for a number of years. It accepted patients of all races and creeds, and its slogan became famous: "None may enter who can pay; none can pay who enter."

Overseas the lodges continued to flourish. Jerusalem Lodge, during the 1890's, founded a model colony called Motzah, where Jewish families worked the land and planned to found additional colonies. A member representing the lodges in Palestine visited Bulgaria and found the Jews there in "a wretched condition" despite relatively favorable political conditions. Those who were not filled with lethargy were proud and autocratic, and the Jewish community was in a turmoil. B'nai B'rith therefore chartered a lodge in Philippopolis, which in turn proceeded to form a lodge in the capital, Sofia. The work of these two groups was phenomenal; on their initiative a commission was created to revamp the country's Jewish community structure. A constitution regulating the relationships between Jewish communities was approved by the Government, and a Chief Rabbi was appointed—an action that had been blocked for years by internecine strife. Plans were made to build an impressive synagogue in Sofia, and the lodge there began to publish a Jewish weekly newspaper in Ladino, the language spoken by Sephardim. In time there were enough lodges in Bulgaria for a District Grand Lodge.

In 1897 Theodor Herzl called the First Zionist Congress in Basel, Switzerland—an event which divided world Jewry. Officially, B'nai B'rith remained neutral, in line with its traditional policy. But the great majority of its leaders and members—like most American Jews—were either opposed to the movement, or skeptical about its objective: the creation of an independent Jewish state. But Moritz Ellinger, editor of *The Menorah*, wrote and published two articles in which he spoke of "the utter irrationality" of the idea and predicted that its proponents would "only cover themselves with ridicule."

In Europe, however, the District Grand Lodges were divided. The German District was openly opposed to Zionism, partly from conviction and partly because of the virulent anti-Semitism whose advocates were quick to charge Zionists with "double loyalty." German Jews as a whole were not attracted to Zionism. The German District passed a resolution declaring: "The endeavors of Zionism, in so far as aiming at the establishment of a national Jewish state, are in conflict with the principles of the Lodge and of national sentiment. Discussions of this subject in the Lodge are deemed inadvisable because the fields of religion and politics are apt to be touched thereby."

On the other hand, in Rumania, where Jew-hatred was infinitely more vicious than in Germany, the District in 1897 passed a resolution stating: "In expressing its sympathy with the Zionist movement, the Grand Lodge warmly recommends to the lodges of the country to give their moral support to it and to suggest means whereby they could, if possible, afford to it likewise pecuniary assistance." At the same time, the general committee appointed two members to represent it as delegates at the Basel Congress, but neither was able to attend. In 1898 the general committee did not meet, so no delegates to the Second Zionist Congress could be appointed, but the District secretary and the president of one of the lodges attended as delegates representing local Zionist societies.

The records reveal no attitude, one way or the other, on the part of B'nai B'rith in Austria-Hungary or, strangely enough, on the part of B'nai B'rith in Palestine itself.

The Order entered the twentieth century severely reduced in numbers but more widespread than ever in territory, in institutions, and in determination to cleave to its already historic Covenant.

10
.
New century, new issues

The first few years of the new century were filled with events more momentous for Jewish life than any B'nai B'rith had had to cope with before. A recrudescence of pogroms in Galicia was swiftly followed by anti-Jewish violence in Rumania on a large scale. Then came the Kishinev pogrom, and further persecutions in Russia, all of which increased the tempo of Jewish immigration into New York, raising problems of the gravest kind.

At the beginning of 1900 the Order was so weakened by loss of members and widespread apathy that many wondered whether it could actually survive. Its American membership had dropped from 17,341 in 1899 to little more than 16,000, and District No. 1, the mother District, which had been booming with 8,000 members only a few years before, was down to 4,000. District No. 6 had long been at a standstill, and District No. 5 was almost ready to give up the ghost altogether. Although the Endowment Fund had been made voluntary in 1895, the problem still plagued the Order, as the older members died off, with their death benefits eating up capital and reserves. Some of the Districts, in desperation, reduced the benefits to $800 or $600—and even less—and increased the fees, which served not only to bring about even more resignations but even some law suits.

The Seventh General Convention in 1900 was therefore a grim gathering. It had been scheduled for San Francisco, but had to be held in Chicago, to save money. Very little of importance was accomplished. The delegates imposed an annual tax of twenty-five cents a member for the support of the National Jewish Hospital at Denver; they defeated another effort to abolish official secrecy in the Order; they wrangled again over the hoary question of the ritual and decided to retain it in amended form. President Bien reported that a lodge had just been chartered in Lemberg, the first in Galicia; that the German District was booming with 40 lodges and 4,000 members; and that since the founding of B'nai B'rith at least $35,000,000 had been paid out to widows, orphans, and sick brethren.

But the committee on propaganda frankly admitted that in this country there had been "a lamentable decline both in numbers and in interest," and that something would have to be done to revive enthusiasm. The Jewish Chautauqua Society, a national educational organization, had offered to collaborate with B'nai B'rith, and the convention voted to enter an arrangement whereby that Society would provide competent lecturers on Jewish subjects for lodges throughout the country, with B'nai B'rith paying all expenses (but after a five-year trial the program proved to be a complete failure and was abandoned).

The big change that did take place was in the top leadership. Julius Bien, nearly seventy-five and in ill health, refused reelection and was succeeded by Leo N. Levi, a relatively young attorney from Galveston, Texas, who had been practicing law in New York City for several years. He was a highly literate but tough-minded executive who, in his acceptance speech, declared that during his administration, if any member of the Executive Committee "by reason of his business engagements, sickness, or other cause, fails to perform the duties of his office, I shall expect his resignation, and if it is not forthcoming, I shall ask for it." And he added that if ever he himself should be unable to devote to his office the time and energy it required, "I shall demand the resignation of your President." He told the delegates "we are entering a new era in the history of the Jew," and that "the salvation of Judaism is in the American-born Jew."

The reports of the overseas Districts made it clear how dangerous was the condition of the Jews in eastern Europe, and a special committee on the Galician situation revealed that in recent months the Grand Lodges of Germany and Austria, realizing the problem was too enormous for any one organization to tackle, had called a conference, in Vienna, of the leading Jewish groups, which had worked out a relief and rehabilitation program.

Partly to pay tribute to Julius Bien and partly because

of the Order's growing interest in the field of foreign
affairs, the convention created a new office, that of
chancellor, and conferred it upon Mr. Bien. It was to
deal with everything concerning the foreign lodges.

The convention delegates had scarcely returned to
their homes when the first crisis erupted. A crop failure
in Rumania, added to a stepped-up campaign of political, religious, and social persecution, caused a quarter
million Jews in that country to flee, or try to flee. Made
desperate by pogroms, starvation, discrimination, and
utter hopelessness, they left their native land without
even knowing in many cases where they were going, except for vague notions of trying to reach Palestine or the
United States.

The first group to reach America was a band of 175
young men, who had been helped by B'nai B'rith in Germany on their way, and who confidently expected the
president of B'nai B'rith to get them into the United
States. But they were ordered deported. President Leo N.
Levi at once arranged a meeting of the Order with the
Baron de Hirsch Fund, the United Hebrew Charities,
and the Rumanian Aid Society. Jacob H. Schiff and former Ambassador to Turkey Oscar Straus, both members
of B'nai B'rith, attended as representatives of the Hirsch
Fund. A delegation was sent to Washington, where it
was joined by Simon Wolf for B'nai B'rith, and the 175
refugees were admitted to the country when the united
group gave a bond that they would not become public
charges.

But this incident only emphasized the critical nature
of the problem. A famine was raging in eastern Europe,
affecting 150,000 Jews in Bessarabia, 700,000 in Galicia, and 300,000 in Rumania—all of whom were also

suffering from increasingly severe and violent anti-Semitism.

The first big objective was to limit immigration to those best qualified for admission. It would have been not only futile, but cruel, to have encouraged immigration of people who would only have been deported. The second goal was to prevent as many immigrants as possible from crowding into the already jammed Lower East Side of New York, and finding them homes and jobs in the interior of the country. The other organizations agreed and urged that such redistribution would have to be done by B'nai B'rith, as the only agency that had lodges everywhere. The third big problem, as Leo N. Levi saw it, was to avoid "pauperizing" the newcomers by raising large sums of money and supporting them in idleness.

He contacted every lodge in the country, and demanded to know how many immigrants each could provide with jobs and what kinds of labor were most needed locally.

A few wealthy Jews, traditionally insecure, were frightened by all this, and fearful that it might stimulate anti-Semitism. They demanded that the whole project be undertaken quietly, if at all. But Mr. Levi insisted on the utmost publicity for the most effective results.

He called a meeting of the Executive Committee in August, 1900, which was also attended by invited representatives of other leading organizations. From this meeting developed the gigantic Removal Project, in which B'nai B'rith played the leading and almost the only role in settling thousands of immigrants—who otherwise would have huddled in the New York ghetto—in towns all over the country, where local B'nai B'rith lodges met them and helped them become self-sustaining.

A less tough-minded leader than Leo N. Levi would have despaired, not only because of the magnitude of the work but also because, after a few months, the early enthusiasm of the local lodges wore off. By December he wrote them again, threatening that "unless the different communities will assume willingly their proportionate share of the burden it may become necessary to relieve the situation by shipping without requisitions." This moved the lodges into action, and soon the project was proceeding so well that it was enlarged by inducing not only newcomers but some of the immigrants long settled in overcrowded New York to move west.

The Rumanian Aid Society was reorganized to bring it closer to B'nai B'rith in Europe and America, and Leo N. Levi was elected its chairman. During the first three years of the Removal Project work, nearly ten thousand immigrants were sent to more than five hundred communities. B'nai B'rith lodges were ordered to work together with other local agencies in helping them. "We are not seeking glory, but results," President Levi wrote the lodges. "If need be, let others have the place of honor, while we take the post of duty." As a result, immigrants found new lives not only in the big cities, but in scores of places like Cripple Creek, Colorado, Bloomington, Illinois, and Silver City, New Mexico.

And all this was done at a time when, at the end of 1901, B'nai B'rith had only 16,718 members in the United States. It was comparatively much stronger in Europe, where it had 7,580 members. In Germany alone, in 1901, the ten women's auxiliaries collected and spent $25,000 for charity, almost as much as the $28,000 distributed by the men's lodges there.

It was this kind of latent strength that enabled the organization to strike a blow against one of the most horrible rackets of the time: the white-slave traffic. During the 1890's, taking advantage of the poverty and despair of the Jews in eastern Europe, an international syndicate began recruiting girls there for the brothels of North and South America. Depraved Jewish young men were hired to appear in the ghettos, well-dressed and apparently well off, to propose either marriage or job opportunities in New York. Thus deceived, the girls were given boat tickets to New York or Latin American ports, where they were met by syndicate agents, and impressed into brothels. And to make matters even worse, if possible, it was charged that "the Jews" were responsible. But an investigation by B'nai B'rith in Germany proved that the majority of the criminals were non-Jews.

In June, 1902, the German District committee on this subject held a conference in Hamburg, with representatives of other organizations, and an intensive program was undertaken. An exposé of the racket was sent to a long list of rabbis and community leaders in the countries affected, many Jewish women from Germany went to eastern Europe to meet with heads of Jewish women's groups there, and the names and addresses of cooperating Jewish leaders in cities throughout the Western world were distributed, so they could be contacted in case of need. This put a serious crimp in the white-slave business but did not end it, by any means, and it remained a problem on which B'nai B'rith worked even up to the 1930's.

But the cause célèbre of Jewish life in the early years of the century was the Kishinev Massacre, on April 19, 1903. Looking back now, past the Nazi murder of six million Jews, to 1903, when forty-five were killed and several hundred injured in a pogrom in the Russian territory of Bessarabia, one marvels at the worldwide passions it aroused. The Jewish East Side of New York burst into a continuing uproar of mass meetings and demonstrations; there were uncoordinated fund-raising campaigns, frenzied Yiddish press headlines, and denunciations of the entire Russian people and Government and the Orthodox Church.

In the midst of this pandemonium, the president of B'nai B'rith, backed by the Executive Committee, insisted upon reasoned action instead of wild emotion. He was denounced by the Zionist Society and the Yiddish press when he refused to align the Order with their activities. Rightly or wrongly, he insisted that so far as was known, the pogrom had been perpetrated by hoodlums and drunken peasants, that there was no actual proof the Russian Government had instigated it, and that if American Jews hoped to appeal to that Government to prevent further tragedies, the worst way to do so was to alienate it in advance by name-calling based only on emotion. As for raising relief funds for the surviving victims, he wanted to know if such funds were really needed. His investigation proved that Kishinev had a rather large Jewish middle class, poor enough, but able to take care of the needy, and that the Jews of Europe had immediately raised what additional money was required. On the other hand, he learned, the pogrom was sure to result in increased Jewish immigration into America, and that money would soon be needed, not in Kishinev, but in New York, to take care of the newcomers.

Through its Washington representative, Simon Wolf, the Order kept in close touch with the State Department and the American Embassy in St. Petersburg, and Mr. Wolf also arranged for the entire Executive Committee to meet with the President of the United States and the Secretary of State in the White House on June 15, 1903. Before that meeting took place, a conference of all the leading Jewish organizations in the world, to determine policy regarding the Kishinev situation, was held in Berlin, with Adolph Mayer, a German B'nai B'rith leader, representing the CGL. The conference arrived at the same conclusions President Levi had reached.

The Executive Committee spent an hour with President Theodore Roosevelt and Secretary of State John Hay, after which Mr. Roosevelt himself released an account of the meeting to the press. In it he announced that B'nai B'rith had drawn up a petition to the Czar of Russia, which was being signed by leading American citizens in all states, and that the United States Government would transmit it to the Czar. The petition called upon the Russian Government to find and punish the Kishinev murderers and take immediate measures to prevent any further outrages.

But Teddy Roosevelt, a man of action, wanted to transmit the petition to the Czar without delay, although the campaign to get thousands of signatures had just begun. Another appointment was therefore made with him, and on July 14 he received President Levi, Simon Wolf, and Oscar W. Straus at his Sagamore Hill home at Oyster Bay. They persuaded him to wait. At the same time he agreed to allow B'nai B'rith to keep the original petition in its archives, while a copy was to be made for transmission to Russia.

The lodges quickly obtained nearly thirteen thousand signatures of the leading business and professional men, clergymen, public officials, military officers, educators, editors, bankers, and trade-union officers in every state in the Union. Almost all of them were non-Jews.

Nobody was surprised when the Czar refused to receive the petition. But the United States Government announced that it would be kept permanently in the State Department archives, the world press published its text, and no one doubted that the Russians got the message. Leading newspapers and magazines throughout the world joined with other major Jewish organizations in many countries to praise B'nai B'rith for its action. And in a letter to President Levi, John Hay wrote:

> Although the copy of your petition did not reach the high destination for which it was intended, its words have attained a worldwide publicity, and have found a lodgement in many thousands of minds. The petition will always be memorable, not only for what it contains, but also for the number and weight of the signatures attached to it.

Meanwhile, of course, the less dramatic work of the Order continued. In 1903, District No. 7 was able to establish a long-needed manual training school at the Orphan Home in New Orleans, thanks to the generosity of one member, Isidore Newman. During the same year, the District began discussing plans to build a hospital for arthritis sufferers at Hot Springs, Arkansas. The natural hot waters there were becoming widely known for their curative powers, and many sick people flocked to the city, including a large number of Jews, most of them poor. They soon became a drain on the tiny Jewish community, in the same way tuberculosis sufferers had strained the resources of the Jews in Denver a decade earlier. It was to be eleven years, however, before the

District, with the help of B'nai B'rith nationally, could actually build a hospital.

With the decline in membership and the continuing Endowment problem, less and less interest was expressed in *The Menorah,* and in the middle of 1901, while remaining the official organ of B'nai B'rith, it also became the official organ of the Jewish Chautauqua Society. By the end of 1902 B'nai B'rith severed all official connection with it, and it ceased publication altogether in 1907. From 1903 to 1909 B'nai B'rith issued a slender little monthly publication called *B'nai B'rith Bulletin* to the lodges (not to individual members), but during that period the need for a genuine organ of the Order was keenly felt, and one was finally established in 1909.

B'nai B'rith suffered a grievous blow when Leo N. Levi died, at the age of forty-eight, on January 13, 1904—fifteen months before the end of his term of office. Jacob Furth, of St. Louis, who was vice president, assumed extra duties for a month, when the Executive Committee met and unanimously elected Simon Wolf to succeed Mr. Levi as president.

The quinquennial CGL convention that met in New Orleans in 1905 was devoted in large part to paying memorial tribute to Leo N. Levi. The delegates also heard a report that during the previous October a conference of European District delegates had taken place in Berlin to plan aid in regulating the emigration of East and South European Jews and protect them from unscrupulous agents and give them general assistance. During the convention a telegram arrived announcing the formation of the Order's first lodge in Switzerland, at Basel. The delegates learned, too, that the District No. 1 employment bureau on New York's East Side had found jobs for at least 2,500 immigrants during the previous year, and that B'nai B'rith membership was beginning to creep upward. There was a detailed report on the Order's Kishinev and post-Kishinev activities, and despite the pall of sorrow over the loss of Leo N. Levi, a new spirit of optimism concerning B'nai B'rith began to form.

The delegates even survived one of the many ardent welcomes to New Orleans, in which the official representative of the Mayor, carried away by his own eloquence and local chauvinism, evidently forgot what kind of audience he was addressing when he declaimed:

> I welcome you to the land of the crimpled shrimp on the cracked ice; of the oyster, not in the tin can, but the juicy, salty oyster on the half shell; to the home of the crayfish bisque. . . . Oh! gentlemen of the Convention, you ought to go out to West End and sit on the verandah at Tranchina's, and there, over your soft shell crabs and amber Chateau Yquem from the sunny vineyards of La Gironde, dream of dark eyes and languorous glances!

The convention created a B'nai B'rith Washington Office (which was to be directed by Simon Wolf); increased the per-capita assessment for the National Jewish Hospital; voted to retain nominal secrecy in the Order despite passionate pleas to end it; and authorized the Executive Committee to begin publication of an official organ as soon as possible.

It was announced that the American membership had grown from 16,000 in 1900 to 18,728 at the end of 1904, while the overseas membership was 8,000. But the important factor was that the majority of members were now nonparticipants in the various District Endowment Funds. Indeed, two Districts had abolished endowments altogether for new members, and one had liquidated its insurance operation entirely by dividing the total assets equally among all policyholders. It was obviously only a matter of time until all such insurance would completely disappear. That is what happened as the old-timers died off, and from the beginning of the twentieth century it could be said that men joined B'nai B'rith solely for nonmaterialistic reasons.

The election of a new president took an unusual form. Adolf Kraus, of Chicago, nominated Simon Wolf. It is not explained why Mr. Wolf did not immediately decline but waited until the representatives of every District had seconded the nomination with long eulogies and the delegates had elected him unanimously before announcing that "circumstances over which I have no control" made it necessary for him to decline the high honor. He thereupon nominated his nominator, and Adolf Kraus was unanimously elected.

Mr. Kraus was a wealthy attorney and owner of the Chicago *Times*. He had served as president of the Chicago Board of Education, and as president of the city's Civil Service Commission, and he was a highly respected civic leader.

The convention abolished the office of honorary secretary and created instead the office of secretary. The former had been held by an official who devoted only a small amount of time to the job and received either a token fee or none at all. Now, for the first time, the secretary became the chief professional executive of the Order, devoting full time, and he was compensated accordingly. Mr. Kraus chose his fellow Chicagoan, A. B. Seelenfreund, for the post, with a starting salary of $2,000 a year. Mr. Seelenfreund was also secretary of District No. 6.

The new president and secretary lived in Chicago, but because the Constitution required it, the archives and headquarters remained in New York, where a clerk was hired to take care of them.

Soon after the convention word was received of renewed outbreaks of anti-Semitism in Russia, especially in Melitopol and Zhitomir. Early in August, through the Russian consul in Chicago, President Kraus arranged to meet with Count Witte, Russia's Prime Minister, who was in this country to attend the peace conference that ended the Russo-Japanese War. The conference took place in Portsmouth, New Hampshire. The B'nai B'rith delegation included President Kraus, Simon Wolf, Julius Bien, Oscar S. Straus, Jacob H. Schiff, and J. B. Klein of the District No. 1 executive committee. The session lasted several hours, during which both sides frankly discussed Russian anti-Semitism. It was emphasized to Count Witte that Americans of all faiths were shocked at the situation, that not only Jews but public opinion generally wanted Jews in Russia to be given equality before the law, and nothing more nor less.

Count Witte created headlines in the world press at that meeting by announcing, for the first time, that his Government had decided to permit the calling of a National Assembly (the Duma), to which Jews would have the right to be elected.

It seemed that a new day was dawning in bloody Russia. But no more than three months later, in October, pogroms broke out in far-separated Russian communities, apparently the result of planned action. Men, women, and children were brutally massacred, and Adolf Kraus concluded that further diplomatic approaches would be useless. The only thing Jews could do was raise money, since thousands were reported starving. After obtaining Jacob H. Schiff's promise to serve as treasurer, he invited the presidents of the leading national Jewish organizations to join with B'nai B'rith in a great campaign. The Order's Executive Committee launched it with a gift of $1,000, and the seven American Districts quickly raised more than $50,000. In addition, members gave money to local joint committees formed in their own communities.

As though in reply, the anti-Jewish press in Russia threatened a new and worse pogrom at Easter. Mr. Kraus therefore wrote to Count Witte in February, 1906, calling the threat to his attention, reminding him that none of the pogromists had been caught and punished, and that if the Government could not prevent further violence, "a movement is being seriously considered . . . for the removal of the Jews from Russia. . . . If the plans for such a movement are put into effect, the Society over which I preside will take an active part."

In his reply, the Russian Prime Minister gave strong assurance that the Government would protect the Jews; he also forced the Minister of Interior to take measures to prosecute all offenders. There was no pogrom or other disturbance that Easter. The Chicago *Daily News* published a cable from its St. Petersburg correspondent that "the publication of a letter written by Adolf Kraus of Chicago and Premier Witte's reply thereto has caused a sensation in Russia. The entire press recognizes the Chicagoan's letter as statesmanlike and humane." A Jewish member of the Duma credited the letter with saving the lives and property of many Jews.

But few American Jews trusted the Czar's Government, and a movement began in the United States to raise money with which the Jews of Russia could buy arms to defend themselves against future attacks. The Order's Executive Committee opposed this, declaring it favored "only the employment of moral forces and legal instrumentalities" to aid Jews. Nevertheless, some money was apparently sent to Russia for the purchase of weapons, because Jewish homes were searched by police, and when arms were found, it served as a further excuse against granting full rights to the Jews.

As a result of the critical situation in Russia, the American Jewish press had been agitating for the creation of a permanent central organization to speak and act for American Jewry. B'nai B'rith opposed the plan. It held that, while B'nai B'rith did not presume to speak for all American Jews, it was so representative, consisting as it did, by that time, of Germans and Russians, Reform and Orthodox, rich and poor, and all other elements of the Jewish community, that "it seeks to attain the high ideals to which every intelligent Jew aspires," and that it was already doing all the work that any new central body could do. Moreover, it added, it had proved, during the Russian emergency, that it was willing at all times to join with other bodies to meet emergency situations.

Consequently, B'nai B'rith sponsored a conference in Chicago, on December 17, 1905, at which all the organizations which had participated in the Russian relief campaign were represented, as well as a number of others. Mr. Kraus was elected chairman. The conference declared that American Jewish organizations were ready, willing, and able to cooperate in all crises and that any new organization for that purpose was unnecessary. It also dealt with a number of other pressing subjects: it favored preliminary physical examinations of prospective immigrants at points of departure to avoid the tragedy of deportation after arrival in New York; urged all Americans to use the influence of Church and State to bring about concerted international action to end atrocities as being contrary to the law of God and man; set up a committee to study conditions in North and South America to provide prospective immigrants in Europe with better guidance when they emigrated; voted to aid children who had lost both parents during the Russian pogroms; and agreed to try to stop the agitation for sending arms to Russian Jews.

Nevertheless, a committee created by the conference called another meeting of organization representatives in New York the following May to discuss the need and feasibility for a new central Jewish body "to promote the welfare of Judaism" and speak for American Jewry. The Order's Executive Committee issued a long letter to the chairman of that meeting, declaring that the B'nai B'rith would not attend, that the sponsoring committee had no authority to call such a meeting but was supposed to be merely a coordinating group, that a new organization could only lead to duplication and waste, that it was bound to fail anyway, that it would probably "fall into the hands of radical theorists" whose views would be generally considered to be those of American Jews as a whole, and that the whole scheme was "not only inexcusable but dangerous."

The new organization remained unborn, although the American Jewish Committee was founded soon after.

In June the Executive Committee passed the following resolution:

> Be it resolved, that the Independent Order of B'nai B'rith, while rigidly maintaining its separate identity in the fulfillment of the tasks it has undertaken, nevertheless stands ready to cooperate temporarily in all critical emergencies with other recognized Jewish organizations for the achievement of immediate results in matters affecting the Jewish cause. At the same

time, this Executive Committee deems it antagonistic to the principles of the Order and subversive of its mission to enter into any permanent alliance or federation with other institutions limited in their scope and lacking the universality which has ever characterized the B'nai B'rith.

But everything else was crowded off the agenda on April 18, 1906, when San Francisco was largely destroyed by the great earthquake and fire. This was an even more stunning disaster than the Chicago fire of 1871, and so much relief money poured in from everywhere that there was no need for B'nai B'rith to raise a direct relief fund for its members. It did, however, issue an appeal to the lodges for the creation of a loan fund from which those who needed credit might draw. This appeal drew $22,000, which helped many members reestablish themselves. The fire that raged after the earthquake completely destroyed the beautiful B'nai B'rith Hall, the B'nai B'rith Library, all the records of the ten San Francisco lodges, and most of the records of District No. 4.

The ceaseless influx of immigrants stimulated efforts in Congress to pass restrictive legislation. B'nai B'rith took the position that all immigrants who were healthy and who would make good citizens should be admitted. When one restrictive bill seemed near passage, President Kraus asked all the lodges to stimulate prominent citizens of all faiths to oppose it in letters to their congressmen, and the bill was defeated.

At the end of 1906, District No. 7 amicably withdrew its support from the Cleveland Jewish Orphan Home, which was thereafter maintained by Districts No. 2 and 6 and later, for a number of years, by B'nai B'rith generally. District No. 7 was forced to take this action because of its large subventions to the Jewish Widows' and Orphans' Home in New Orleans and the Touro Infirmary there, and because it was deeply involved in raising money for the new hospital to be built in Hot Springs, named after Leo N. Levi.

In 1908 Los Angeles Lodge took the lead in founding a Hebrew Orphan Home, which was widely supported by the Jews of southern California.

In 1906 the American Jewish Committee was founded. Early the next year there was a proposal that representatives of that organization, the Union of American Hebrew Congregations, and B'nai B'rith should hold a conference "relative to the manner in which the most effective work can be done in questions affecting the Jewish interests." Such a meeting was held, in New York, but a report to the Order's Executive Committee told succinctly with what result:

> An effort was made to come to an understanding as to what joint or particular work each organization desired to undertake for the Jewish cause. As, however, the representatives of the American Jewish Committee stated that all the questions of the hour which affected Jewish interests throughout the world were to be embraced within its sphere of effort, thereby including nearly all work which the other two organizations were created to do, and have in a large measure heretofore done, it soon became clear that no plan for joint action, acceptable to all, could be agreed upon.

The seemingly endless Jewish immigration from eastern Europe was the innocent cause of an increase in expressions of anti-Semitism. Dressed in their unfamiliar clothes from the Old Country, speaking a language no Americans understood, engaging in religious practices that seemed weird, keeping to themselves, and in general acting in ways that seemed strange, they soon furnished the anti-Semites—and even otherwise friendly but careless people—with an impression of the Jew which became a stereotype. Many people readily believed that all Jews were rich, contrary to the evidence of their own eyes; others, that all Jews were poor, and therefore "anarchists"; and some, that all Jews were usurers, tricky, and dishonest. Many otherwise kindhearted people laughed cruelly when any of these Jewish stereotypes was portrayed on the stage (usually, alas, by "Jewish comedians") or in cartoons or books. When they met a Jew whose family had been in America for several generations, they called him an exception.

It was therefore not surprising that, at the 1908 meeting of the Order's Executive Committee, Rabbi Joseph Silverman of New York proposed that B'nai B'rith should establish an agency "for the defense of the Jewish name," to do something about the "stage Jew," and even about such things as the study of Shakespeare's *Merchant of Venice* in the public schools. It was not until five years later that B'nai B'rith did just that by founding its Anti-Defamation League, but long before it set up that agency it was engaged in such work. In 1908, for instance, Adolf Kraus wrote a letter to Melville E. Stone, head of the Associated Press, which became famous in view of Mr. Stone's reply:

> If A. B., a non-Jew, commits a crime, the Associated Press dispatches furnish the public with the news without any reference as to whether he is a Methodist, a Catholic, or whatever Christian denomination. If, however, A. B. happens to be a Jew, then almost invariably the news item informs us that A. B., a Jew, committed an offense. Is there any good reason for making such a distinction?

The letter continued with an appeal to Mr. Stone's sense of fair play, and the latter promptly replied:

> I think your suggestion is a perfectly proper one and I see no reason on earth why we should say A. B. was a Jew any more than we should say he was a Methodist. Based on your suggestions I will issue precisely the instructions you indicate.

Meanwhile, as the incubus of the Endowment Fund lightened rapidly, as B'nai B'rith maintained leadership in all matters of philanthropy and international relations affecting Jews, and as its prestige rose to new heights, its strength increased. At the end of 1905 its American membership stood at 18,729; at the end of 1907, at 21,016; and at the end of 1909, at 22,847, plus 10,276 overseas.

With this kind of growth, in size and activity, the absence of an official organ became intolerable, and in January, 1909, the Executive Committee began publication of a large tabloid newspaper, the *B'nai B'rith News*, with Secretary Seelenfreund as editor. Like its predecessor, *The Menorah*, it published feature articles on all phases of Jewish life, and a great deal of specifically B'nai B'rith material, covering the activities of the Order internationally, nationally, and locally. At first it was sent only to members who subscribed, but soon the percapita tax was increased so it could be sent to all American members.

When the venerable Julius Bien died at the end of 1909, at the age of eighty-three, it was almost symbolic of the end of an era. The position of Chancellor of Foreign Affairs was abolished.

By 1910, when the Order's quinquennial convention was held, B'nai B'rith was well over the thirty thousand mark internationally, and at new levels of purpose and prestige.

During the first decade of the twentieth century, B'nai B'rith reached half its present age.

It knew it had outgrown many of its former activities, and that it had to develop new ones to meet new challenges. Its leaders were unable to predict such twentieth-century phenomena as world wars, five-year depressions, Communist revolutions, Nazism and the slaughter of six million Jews, the establishment of an independent Jewish state, unprecedented American prosperity, and other remarkable events. But they did know that lodge meetings, sick and death benefits, pious ideals, and even large-scale philanthropy were not enough to justify the organization's existence.

President Adolf Kraus got to the root of the matter in a statement he made to the Executive Committee in 1905:

> For many years our orators have pointed with pride to the institutions which the Order has established or maintained . . . the orphan asylums, homes for the aged, libraries, the Statue of Religious Liberty, and all the other institutions. . . . But useful and necessary as such institutions are—and in fact owing to the very necessity that existed—it might well be presumed that sooner or later the Jews of this country would have established the same or similar institutions in the course of time, even though this Order had never existed. . . .
>
> But such things may well be left to other organizations. This Order must stand for greater things; its aims must be higher. It is the only international Jewish organization of its character in existence. As such, it must take up the cause and bear the burden of the Jewish race wherever existent, and with every peaceable means at its command strike with the strength of

a mighty and united host at the strongholds of wrong and oppression, until the shackles of prejudice shall fall and rust, and the Jew shall stand in every clime a free and respected man. . . . It must be alive to all the grave questions which arise from time to time affecting our people, and it must be ready to meet them courageously and unselfishly.

To be entitled to exist as a Jewish organization, we must never forget that we are Jews; that whatever affects any of our race affects us all; that we are Jews not by birth alone but also by virtue of our religion. . . . Let us then take up our work, and do it.

This demand—perhaps yearning would be a better word—for B'nai B'rith to do "greater things" and to be always more consciously Jewish, can be traced back to the beginnings of the Order, and forward to the present moment. It is the prime ingredient of the organization's personality and philosophy, even though large numbers of its members have failed to match the ideal. No matter who were the leaders, no matter what were the times or circumstances, the ideal persisted: to be greater, to do more, to fill all possible needs, and above all to preserve and strengthen the Jewish heritage.

This is a remarkable phenomenon, because in no similar period of history have changes been so swift and so basic. And all the leaders were different—in education, personality, experience, background. Yet all, in their different ways, were pointed in the same general direction, vague though it sometimes was. Nothing could stop them, neither the economic "panics" of the nineteenth century, the vast apathy of the members during the 1890's, the "thirty years' war" of the Endowment Fund fiasco, the great depression of the 1930's, the Nazi nightmare, or the double-barreled test of modern times —the most fateful of all—in which it remains to be seen whether Jews, who have survived two thousand years of poverty and persecution, can also survive unprecedented freedom and prosperity.

Perhaps it was this devotion to basic ideals, this feeling that B'nai B'rith, with all its faults, was the one agency in Jewish life flexible enough to meet the changing challenges, that caused the organization, under totally differing leadership, to refuse to participate in the many attempts to set up a permanent central body to speak for American Jews, just as it was the same spirit that caused all the different leaders to insist on Jewish unity of all groups in great emergencies. Perhaps it is because B'nai B'rith is the oldest of all Jewish organizations in America that it has always been so closely in tune with the American spirit of voluntarism, turning away from anything that even seemed authoritarian, to say nothing of extremism either of the left or right.

In the early years of this century, after living half its life so far, B'nai B'rith slowly began to change into something quite different from what it had been, just as the world did in which it functioned.

11

■

1910–1915: Historic events

Nothing very substantive took place at the Ninth General Convention in Washington, D. C., in 1910. However, it marked the only time in all B'nai B'rith history, even down to the present, that a President of the United States personally addressed a national convention of the Order. William Howard Taft was guest of honor at a glittering banquet, and the previous day he had entertained all the convention delegates at the White House.

At the banquet he delivered the kind of speech that might have been expected at such an occasion ("I have the profoundest admiration for the Jewish race"), but in his case it had the virtue of being completely sincere. In the same spirit he declared: "I have known the B'nai B'rith for many years, for its good work, for the social opportunities that it gives, and as a model Jewish society." President Taft had had many friendly contacts with the Order, and especially with Simon Wolf, and one of his law-school classmates had been Alfred M. Cohen, a fellow Cincinnatian, who was to succeed Adolf Kraus as president of the Order. Only a year before the convention Mr. Taft had addressed a meeting of Argo Lodge in Washington.

At the business sessions the delegates backed the plan to build the Leo N. Levi Memorial Hospital at Hot Springs, Arkansas, by assessing every member ten cents a year; expanded the Educational League of District No. 2 into a nationally endorsed activity by asking every lodge to set up local committees to arouse interest in and raise funds for the League; demanded again that a book telling the history of the Order be written and published, and accepted the offer of Rabbi Edward N. Calisch of Richmond, Virginia, to write it; finally moved the headquarters of B'nai B'rith from New York to Chicago and amended the Constitution to provide that the seat of the Constitution Grand Lodge should be wherever the president of the Order lives; and rejected a proposal that B'nai B'rith engage in the Jewish education of children because that belonged to the home and synagogue.

The old question of abolishing secrecy inevitably cropped up again and again was beaten down by a large majority. President Kraus won the day for its formal retention by pointing out that six of the seven American Districts still had endowment laws applicable to a dwindling few thousand members, and that if B'nai B'rith did away with its ritual it would lose its character as a fraternal body, thus making it impossible to carry out its obligations to endowment members in states which had laws governing the subject.

The next ten years were a period of remarkable growth and achievement, although saddened and embittered by many Jewish tragedies. Only a few days after the convention, the Executive Committee held a meeting at which Dr. Schmarya Levin, of the Jewish Technical Institute at Haifa, appealed to B'nai B'rith to make available a number of scholarships for that institution. Palestine was being colonized by enthusiastic but not very qualified farmers from the ghettos of Russia and Poland. They needed technicians. B'nai B'rith provided many scholarships for them during the following years, just as today the Order is providing high-school scholarships for Israeli teen-agers and seeking out technicians of all kinds in North America to take jobs in the new Jewish State.

In May, 1911, the Orient District was chartered, with eighteen lodges in Bulgaria, Serbia, Turkey, Egypt, and Palestine.

A few weeks before the 1910 convention, the first B'nai B'rith lodge in London had been established, and a few weeks after the convention it took a leading role in helping the stream of Jewish refugees from Czarist Russia who settled in England or stopped there on their way to the United States. On one occasion that year, when a shipload of such migrants was not allowed to land in England or have access to legal counsel, the British lodge appealed to Winston Churchill, then Home Secretary, who cut through the red tape and allowed B'nai B'rith lawyers to board the ship. Hundreds of the immigrants were then enabled to enter England.

Two years later, when the German Hilfsverein

founded a school in Palestine, B'nai B'rith supported fif-teen of its students for five years, at $250 a year per student. During the same year, 1912, the first lodge in Scandinavia was founded, in Copenhagen.

The Order's American membership grew from less than 22,000 in 1910 to more than 24,000 in 1911, and finally, in 1912, to 25,000—a size it had not enjoyed since the 1880's.

The five years between 1912 and the entry of America into the First World War were crowded with stirring and fateful events for B'nai B'rith. The first was its role in bringing about the abrogation of the commercial treaty between the United States and Russia. It dated back to 1832, and almost from the beginning it was violated by Russia, which refused to recognize the American pass-ports of Jews, Catholics, and missionaries. During the nineteenth century there were sporadic protests against this open insult to the American people, but no President and no Administration saw fit to take any action in the matter.

However, with the dawn of the twentieth century and the increasing public awareness of the cruelty and op-pression of the Czarist regime, the time became ripe for effective countermeasures. Because Jews were the chief sufferers it was natural that the lead should be taken by Jewish organizations. The Union of American Hebrew Congregations deserves the credit for taking the initi-ative; early in 1911 it passed a forthright resolution on the subject, urging the United States to abrogate the treaty. Simon Wolf was the Washington representative of both B'nai B'rith and the UAHC at the time, and largely through his influence President Taft invited the presidents of the two organizations, along with the head of the American Jewish Committee, to have lunch with him at the White House on February 15, 1911.

They spent an hour together, and although no report of their discussion was published, it is easy to guess what happened. The *B'nai B'rith News* gave a broad hint when it declared, in an editorial: "It is probably too much to ask that President Taft take the initiative. . . . The people must make the demand." And not just the Jews, the paper added, but Americans of all faiths, *i.e.*, public opinion.

The American Jewish Committee was small; the UAHC was not geared for the kind of action required; and B'nai B'rith, while always acting in concert with both of them, spearheaded the campaign. Through its membership everywhere it was able to interest the press in scores of cities and towns in editorializing on the situation, to stimulate a torrent of letters to Congress, to inspire many ministers to deliver sermons on the subject, to have organizations pass resolutions, etc. A wave of indignation against Russia arose, and demands were voiced from all sides that America abrogate the treaty. Resolutions to that effect were introduced in Congress, and before the end of 1912 President Taft abrogated it, with the unanimous consent of both houses of Congress. And the President gave B'nai B'rith the pen he had used to sign the abrogation.

The 1910 convention had authorized the creation of a B'nai B'rith Medal to be given annually to the person who had made the greatest contribution to the Jewish people, and its first presentation was to President Taft during a meeting of the Executive Committee in Washington during the first week of 1913. The entire Executive Committee were luncheon guests at the White

House for the ceremony. Two weeks later the President was the chief speaker at the celebration of the Order's seventieth anniversary at a mass meeting in a New York synagogue.

The next great event was the founding of B'nai B'rith's Anti-Defamation League. At the same Executive Committee meeting during which President Taft was given the B'nai B'rith Medal, it was decided to form a "National Caricature Committee" for the purpose of "eliminating the caricaturing and ridiculing of the Jew in literature, art, drama, and the press." By October, President Kraus was ready to announce the formal creation of the Anti-Defamation League, with a committee of a hundred prominent Jewish leaders from coast to coast to launch its work.

From the beginning B'nai B'rith made it clear that the ADL, while it was organized to defend the Jewish people, had the long-range goal of working for the rights and dignity of all peoples, in the spirit of the Order's Constitution. Mr. Kraus put it this way in his original announcement of the founding of the League in October, 1913:

> The immediate object of the League is to stop, by appeals to reason and conscience, and if necessary by appeals to law, the defamation of the Jewish people. Its ultimate purpose is to secure justice and fair treatment to all citizens alike, and to put an end forever to unjust and unfair discrimination against and ridicule of any sect or body of citizens.

The tentative original name, "National Caricature Committee," indicates the nature of anti-Semitism in 1913. The Jew was widely caricatured in the press, in cartoons, in the movies, on the stage. He was depicted as a repulsive and sinister fellow, always engaged in lying, cheating, and plotting.

So the task the ADL set for itself was a twofold one: to fight overt expressions of anti-Semitism, and to educate the public, so far as possible, to the truth about the Jews. Actually, the word "fight" is too strong a term for its early efforts. The approach to an editor, a public speaker, a theater manager, a businessman, or anyone else who had held up the Jew to ridicule was quiet, private, polite. There were no Jewish demonstrations, picket lines, threats, or boycotts, or even public exposures. The ADL representatives always gave the offender the benefit of any doubt. But they let him know how harmful his thoughtless expressions had been to millions of innocent fellow Americans. They were confident he would not repeat them. And in the great majority of cases he admitted the ADL was right; he was sorry and said it would never happen again. In fact, some of his best friends were Jews.

When an offender became a backslider, the ADL contacted him again, and that usually closed the case. When he was defiant, other methods had to be used. Sometimes the man had business associates or friends who were willing to help him see the light. When a "Jewish comedian" refused to alter an insulting act, the ADL appealed to the theater manager. There was no boycott. But Jews soon hear about such things, and they are very sensitive, and that affects box-office sales. In some cases, of course, nothing availed, and the ADL had to admit failure.

This kind of anti-Semitism was not new. Actually, B'nai B'rith had been doing ADL work long before it founded the ADL. Most of the work was handled by an alert young lawyer from Bloomington, Illinois, who had settled in Chicago and risen to the presidency of District No. 6. His name was Sigmund Livingston, and as chairman of what was called the Publicity Committee of his District he compiled an impressive record of successes in coping with anti-Jewish expressions of all kinds. He was consequently named the first chairman of the ADL, with Leon Lewis as secretary. Mr. Livingston became so identified with this program that he was credited with being its founder, and he remained its national chairman until his death in 1945. But the ADL's greatest work did not begin until the 1930's, when historic events made great work indispensable.

In the summer of 1914, the outbreak of World War I was followed by a new series of pogroms. On the Eastern Front, millions of Jews lived in ghettos in Russia and Poland, in Rumania, Galicia, Austria, and elsewhere, and the contending armies rolling forward and backward were like gigantic steamrollers, crushing Jewish life.

In London the B'nai B'rith lodge established a hostel for Jewish war refugees, but the only ones who reached its shelter were from the relatively humane Western Front, and they amounted to only a few hundred.

The European lodges informed the CGL of Jewish conditions in the war zones, and President Kraus called upon the lodges in America to raise a fund equal to at least $10 per member for the victims. Although that goal was not reached, B'nai B'rith did raise and send to Europe the then staggering sum of $101,000. But as the war progressed, this money was used up in no time. Thousands of Jews served in the Russian Army and fought in the frozen trenches while pogrom mobs at home killed and maimed their families. Jews were accused of being slackers, spies, and saboteurs—all pretexts for more and more violence against them.

Soon after the war began, B'nai B'rith's Executive Committee began to discuss what might be done to bring postwar protection and equal rights to the Jews in eastern Europe. As in most wars, people generally, indulging in wishful thinking, assumed the conflict would soon be over. Nor did any foresee the Bolshevik Revolution and its profound effects on the Jewish masses. As early as the end of 1914, therefore, B'nai B'rith leaders began to formulate demands for civil, social, and religious rights for Jews, to be presented to the peace conference, no matter who the winner.

The United States was not in the war, and public sentiment was by no means all hostile to Germany. Millions of American citizens were of German descent, the Czar was universally hated, and it was not until the U-boat attacks on American ships that sentiment changed. B'nai B'rith was able to maintain fairly normal mail contact with its European lodges.

In Germany the members, like German Jews generally, were fervently patriotic. Practically all the young members were in the Armed Forces, and the lodges made significant contributions to the war effort. The most dramatic was sponsorship of a huge railroad train which made regular trips to various parts of the front, delivering doctors, nurses, medical supplies, special foods, and other items to the German troops.

Meanwhile, in the United States, the demands made upon the Order were unending. In 1911, the Jewish section of Constantinople was destroyed by fire, and the CGL raised more than 23,000 francs for the victims. The Balkans were another source of tragedy for Jewish civilians, including a severe earthquake in Turkey; B'nai B'rith sent nearly $27,000 for direct relief. Right after the start of the war, many Jews in Turkey, Egypt, Palestine, and elsewhere in District No. 11 faced starvation, and the CGL cabled them $9,000. Five thousand dollars was sent to war sufferers in Palestine alone, and another $5,000 was contributed to a food ship going there. To aid Jewish refugees from Palestine who were in Egypt, B'nai B'rith sent 5,000 francs. In 1915, Henry Morgenthau, the United States Ambassador to Turkey and a member-at-large of the Order's Executive Committee, informed B'nai B'rith that the Jews in Constantinople were in dire poverty, and the Executive Committee sent 20,-000 francs. The following year $5,000 was sent to the Rumanian District for direct relief.

In September, 1914, District No. 3 opened its Orphan Home at Erie, Pennsylvania, consisting of twenty modern buildings that could house five hundred children; it was an even more magnificent institution than the Cleveland Jewish Orphan Home. In November the Leo N. Levi Memorial Hospital began operation in Hot Springs, Arkansas, supported and administered by the Order as a whole.

B'nai B'rith had long been active in social service programs, but now there was a demand that this work be placed on an organized and professionally directed basis. Consequently, when B'nai B'rith held its tenth General Convention in San Francisco in 1915, it appropriated the huge sum of $25,000 for the creation of a Social Service Bureau and engaged Rabbi Rudolph I. Coffee of Pittsburgh to direct it.

During the same year the Order set up an Immigration Commission, consisting of one representative from each American District. Immigration had virtually

ceased because of the war, and the Commission's purpose was to help as many immigrants as possible move
from crowded New York to other communities.

B'nai B'rith was able to afford such developments because of its continuing growth, from 25,000 American
members in 1912 to 27,600 in 1913—plus 13,000 overseas. By early 1915 the American membership leaped to
nearly 32,500, a gain of almost 5,000 in one year—the
largest net increase in that time in the organization's
history. Only in District No. 5 had B'nai B'rith foun-
dered; it was on the verge of collapse several times, and
for a number of years there was not a single lodge in
Baltimore, its largest city. But in 1915 Menorah Lodge
was founded, and even District No. 5 began to move up-
hill again. In 1913, a lodge was formed in Montreal—
the first in Canada since the death of the Order there in
the 1880's—and it was the forerunner of a great expansion in the Dominion.

The new Social Service Bureau planned to encourage
the Big Brother and Big Sister movements, provide religious and social service for Jewish prison inmates, help
prevent juvenile delinquency, and fill many other social
needs. But it proved to be a bigger bite than B'nai B'rith
could chew; after two years of professional direction, its
work was taken over by volunteer members, and in time
even their programs withered away as public agencies
became stronger in the field.

Rabbi Edward Calisch had been unable to fulfill his
promise to write a history of B'nai B'rith, and in 1915
Dr. Gotthard Deutsch of Cincinnati agreed to undertake
the project. An appropriation was made for research assistance, but the book was never written.

Overseas and at home the man-made and natural catastrophes were so numerous that it became obvious that

for B'nai B'rith to appeal for funds each time one occurred was self-defeating. Often the same lodges and individuals responded, while others gave nothing. The 1915 Convention therefore created a permanent Emergency Relief Fund, by assessing every member a given sum per year (twenty-five cents, at first) as part of his dues.

The convention also, for the first time, set the Order's age minimum at twenty-one; before, each District had set its own.

But the most significant action taken by the convention was its decision to end its system of taxing every member a given sum per year for the support of charitable institutions. Instead, the Executive Committee was empowered to appropriate annually to such institutions amounts it thought proper. This was actually the beginning of the end of philanthropy as a major program of the Order, although it still remains a minor one. The convention Committee on Propaganda put it this way:

> Union in Israel cannot be founded upon charity and philanthropy. . . . The supreme altruism of the Order is deeper and more profound; far greater is the power within the Order to create of the Order a center of vital forces which shall ultimately evolve a complete freedom for Israel. . . . Our duty in the largest interpretation of propaganda must be to make of the Jew today the Jew of history, and of the old historic ideals.

12

.

1915–1920: War and peace

B'nai B'rith was not the only agency, early in World War I, that hoped the peace conference might bring a better life for the tragedy-ridden Jews in eastern Europe. Early in 1915 there arose two major factions in American Jewish life dedicated to the same idea. One of them, which included the American Jewish Committee, the UAHC, and other important groups, wanted a representative conference to discuss how Jewish rights might best be secured; the other, which included the Zionist Organization and bodies sympathetic to it, wanted an American Jewish Congress.

The distinction was important; a conference implied a joint effort to do a specified job and then disband, while a Congress implied an ongoing organization of increasing scope. To make matters more difficult, each group was suspicious of the other: The conference backers feared the other side wanted to establish a permanent agency to speak for all Jews and thus threaten the autonomy of existing organizations and at the same time promote the cause of Zionism. The Congress people were afraid the conference groups might not be "militant" enough. Both sides wooed B'nai B'rith, which yielded to neither. The Order resolved, instead, to try to bring the two movements together, in its traditional unity role.

And in this it succeeded—for a while.

On October 3, 1915, at President Kraus's invitation, the presidents of the twenty-two largest groups from both sides met in New York to discuss their differences. All philosophies were represented in the persons of independent people like Louis D. Brandeis; Dr. Solomon Schechter and Dr. Cyrus Adler of the Conservative Jews; Dr. William Rosenau of the Reform wing; Dr. Bernard Drachman of the Orthodox congregations; and the Zionists, the fraternal orders, Jewish labor, the Rumanian and Russo-Polish groups, etc.

The president of B'nai B'rith presided, and the secretary of the Order took the minutes. The differences of opinion expressed were sharp, but the meeting was a friendly one. No votes were taken, but it was the first time the contending parties had faced and spoken directly to each other, and there was a feeling of unity in the air.

But, as is traditional in Jewish life, the convictions on both sides were so deep and passionately held that the friendly spirit did not last, and the following months witnessed one verbal battle after another. In the middle of 1916, B'nai B'rith was again invited by each side to participate in separate meetings, and again declined. It offered its cooperation to both sides "in any plan which may make for the betterment of our people," but explained that, as an international organization, it could not commit its overseas members to decisions made by Americans.

After much negotiation, a compromise was reached, and the two opposing sides united toward the end of 1916. They agreed upon a Congress, but "exclusively" to define methods of achieving "full rights" for Jews. "The securing and protection of Jewish rights in Palestine" was listed as another purpose, but without the endorsement of any "general theory or philosophy of Jewish life." The autonomy of all constituent groups was to be guaranteed. The Congress was to meet before the end of the war.

B'nai B'rith found all this compatible with its policy, and its entrance into the Congress made that body representative of the overwhelming majority of American Jews. The Order's attitude toward the Zionist controversy had changed during the previous few years, although not its policy of neutrality. In the late 1890's its magazine had published many articles critical and even contemptuous of Zionism, but from 1910 on it presented articles giving both sides of the argument. In December, 1917, editorially commenting on the Balfour Declaration of the month before, it went even further: "There is only one event in our long history to which the British announcement may be compared, and that is the edict of Cyrus. . . . What harm to anyone if these Palestinians manage their own affairs in their own way on their own soil? . . . Let us decide to help those who will go there."

The first meeting of the Congress' Executive Committee took place in New York on Christmas, 1916. Immediately there was a clash. Adolf Kraus and Louis Marshall were nominated for temporary chairman, with Mr. Kraus winning, 49 to 45. He was also chosen for permanent chairman by the nominating committee, but Cyrus L. Sulzberger nominated Mr. Marshall, his fellow leader of the American Jewish Committee. In doing so, he said Mr. Kraus was head of a "secret organization" and that that would be injurious to the Congress.

Mr. Sulzberger had been a member of a B'nai B'rith lodge in New York which had been suspended for violating the Order's rules, and he knew B'nai B'rith was not really a secret organization. Mr. Kraus replied calmly, "It is well known that B'nai B'rith is not a secret organization in the sense sought to be given it here by the minority spokesman. The Order has no secrets objectionable to any government on earth. . . . Even Russia understands why we are organized. I have furnished that government our ritual and advised it fully concerning our aims, for I intend to apply to that government for permission to start lodges in that land."

Whereupon he offered to withdraw as a candidate if Mr. Marshall would do the same. Mr. Marshall agreed, and Nathan Straus was chosen. Mr. Kraus and Mr. Marshall were elected to the administrative committee.

But the entrance of the United States into the war on April 6, 1917, made everything else secondary. B'nai B'rith did not undertake a war-service program immediately because several groups had jointly founded the Jewish Welfare Board to do just that. However, when the Executive Committee met in Chicago at the end of

July, the public had not yet been informed of any activity by the JWB, and B'nai B'rith therefore organized its
American Soldiers' and Sailors' Welfare League, and
boldly asked the lodges to raise a million dollars for its
work.

At the time, there were some thirty military canton-
ments in the country, and B'nai B'rith pledged to serve
every one of them by establishing a recreation room outside of each, and to help meet the spiritual, social, and
other needs of the men in uniform by offering regular
programs of entertainment, opportunities for religious
services, lectures, visits to the homes of nearby Jewish
families, and other activities.

The Jewish Welfare Board immediately came to life,
announcing it had finally met and elected Col. Harry
Cutler as chairman. In September, he was in Chicago,
where he conferred briefly with President Kraus. They
agreed to avoid duplication, that all money raised for
soldier welfare work would be sent to the JWB, that
B'nai B'rith would have three representatives on the
JWB administrative committee, and take complete
charge of the program in nine camps, which were specified. Mr. Kraus emphasized that while the two organizations were to cooperate, they were to remain completely
separate, and that any merger was to be of the work and
not of the organizations. All appeals for funds, it was
decided, should be issued jointly in the names of the two
organizations.

But the very first fund appeal sent out by the JWB
after that was signed by individual names, not the
names of organizations. And soon Colonel Cutler ordered all stationery in the camps to contain the name of
the JWB only, for the sake of "uniformity." But when he
notified B'nai B'rith that the JWB had reorganized, and

that the Order was now considered one of its many constituent bodies, it was too much for Mr. Kraus. He informed the JWB it had abrogated the agreement and
that the partnership was over.

B'nai B'rith then went ahead with its own original war
program. It set up recreation rooms outside many of the
camps, which were used by soldiers of all faiths, and
arranged home hospitality and religious services for
thousands of Jewish soldiers. It sold Liberty Bonds. Its
lodges presented many ambulances and other needed
pieces of equipment to the Red Cross; its women's auxiliaries did all manner of Red Cross work, and although
no centralized records were kept that have survived, it
conducted an impressive war-service program. About 10
percent of its male members were of military age and
served in the Armed Forces. It suspended their dues for
the duration, of course, and performed many services
for their families where needed. The Order's program
was warmly endorsed by the War Department.

Undoubtedly it was this success that caused the JWB
to regret its break with B'nai B'rith, because in January,
1918, Colonel Cutler came to Chicago and conferred
with President Kraus again. They negotiated a new partnership, which went into effect on April 1, as a result of
which they conducted a joint operation amicably until
the end of the war.

Even while the United States was at war with Germany and its allies, B'nai B'rith in America received reports of the work of its lodges in enemy territory. Those
lodges, in addition to war work, continued many of their
peacetime projects. Thus in Constantinople the lodge
operated a kindergarten, and it appealed to the CGL for
funds for it. But much of the lodge work in Europe dur-

ing the war consisted of helping the distressed families of men killed or wounded in action.

In September, 1918, a great mass meeting was held in Chicago to celebrate the seventy-fifth anniversary of B'nai B'rith. A service flag was dedicated in honor of 3,256 B'nai B'rith members in the Armed Forces.

As soon as the war ended, all Jewish organizations turned their attention to the coming Peace Conference, and the American Jewish Congress held its first plenary session in Philadelphia on December 15, 1918. But even before then, in November, President Kraus expressed B'nai B'rith's concern over the fate of East European Jewry in a letter to President Wilson, who said, in his reply, that the subject "will be very much in my mind" during the Peace Conference. On November 28, Mr. Kraus, Henry Morgenthau, Simon Wolf, and A. B. Seelenfreund were received by the President at the White House, where Mr. Kraus presented him with the B'nai B'rith Medal.

The American Jewish Congress formulated an impressive list of demands to be presented to the Peace Conference. The delegates agreed to work with representatives of Jewish bodies from other nations. In addition, they voted to demand that Jews of all other countries join with them in establishing a permanent international Jewish Congress, and to demand that Palestine be made a Jewish commonwealth.

These last two votes were plainly illegal, for the Congress' official agreement barred ideological causes and limited its scope to efforts at the Peace Conference on behalf of Jewish rights in Europe. But nothing in the record indicates that B'nai B'rith or any other representatives objected.

President Kraus was unable to attend the Peace Conference in Paris; the Order was represented by Herbert Bentwich of London. This is not the place to relate what the Congress accomplished or failed to accomplish; that is a long story, full of frustration, and internecine Jewish strife. After the Peace Treaty was adopted, the Congress delegates failed to convert the organization into a permanent international one. Dr. Stephen S. Wise and others invited all leading American Jewish organizations to form a permanent American Jewish Congress, but B'nai B'rith, the American Jewish Committee, and other major groups, declined. However, Dr. Wise succeeded in founding an organization he called the American Jewish Congress in 1922, and it is still functioning.

But the ineffectiveness of the minority clauses in the Versailles Peace Treaty was immediately demonstrated when pogroms broke out in all the lands of eastern Europe, and continued periodically for years. B'nai B'rith in Europe could do little to cope with such frightful happenings. In Bucharest the lodge opened a soup kitchen and fed 2,500 starving Jews one meal a day. Secretary Seelenfreund visited Europe in 1919 for a firsthand report, and he returned with data showing unimaginable poverty, persecution, torture, sickness, and death among the Jewish masses. He also learned that many once prosperous members of the Order were impoverished, and to help them the Executive Committee appropriated $20,000 from the Emergency Relief Fund. An appeal to the lodges brought in another $50,000, but not all of it was needed.

In most parts of Europe, lodges and Districts ceased to function temporarily, although a few managed to continue their work. The war altered many national borders, and some German lodges were now in French territory. The Austrian District became the Czech District, taking over No. 10. In 1922 Austria again became a District, No. 12. In Vienna the lodges joined with other groups in trying to care for two thousand Jewish war orphans.

The appeals for aid that came to the CGL from Europe were like a broken record endlessly repeating itself. The Executive Committee relayed the stream of reports about pogroms and discrimination to the Government, but the financial appeals totaled tens of millions of dollars, and B'nai B'rith could do nothing but turn them over to the American Jewish Joint Distribution Committee.

During every war there is so much sloganizing about liberty, justice, democracy, and freedom that after the carnage there is bound to be a reaction. By 1920 this reaction was at its height, with a Red scare comparable to the one in the 1950's led by the late Senator Joseph McCarthy. The press was filled with stylized editorials and cartoons warning against "Bolsheviks." Such caricatures came more and more to be identified as Jews, and since the majority of Jews in America had been born in Russia, the resulting syllogism was widely used by anti-Semites.

In such an atmosphere the Anti-Defamation League rapidly emerged as B'nai B'rith's most effective and glamorous program. Considering its limited staff and financial resources, it did remarkably good work. It nailed every spoken or published lie about the Jew. It scotched ugly rumors, published mountains of leaflets giving the truth about unfair charges, induced many business firms to end discriminatory practices, convinced movie producers to delete scenes that were not only false but potentially dangerous to Jews, and exposed the machinations of organized anti-Semites.

The ADL was thus the hero of the Eleventh General Convention in Cleveland in 1920, which authorized a special appeal to the lodges which by the end of 1924 was to bring in an ADL Fund of more than $192,000.

The reactionary postwar climate had a great deal to do with influencing the convention delegates, finally, to abolish the last vestiges of secrecy in B'nai B'rith.

One of the most appealing projects in the Order's history was begun when the convention authorized the "adoption" of one thousand Jewish war orphans in Europe—although enough money was raised to provide for only six hundred. These homeless waifs were not only in need of food and shelter, but they needed to feel they belonged to somebody who cared about them. The Executive Committee allocated a fund large enough to care for one hundred of them in approved orphanages or private homes in Europe, and called upon the lodges to support the rest. Each lodge that contributed a specified sum was assigned an orphan. But more than merely money was sent. Each contributing lodge had a committee that wrote personal letters to the children, sent them gifts on their birthdays, and helped with paternal advice on many matters. The orphans were cared for until the age of fourteen. B'nai B'rith spent a total of a quarter million dollars on them.

B'nai B'rith's Americanization Department also originated at the 1920 convention. Sig Livingston was head of the convention committee that made the recommendation, which was accompanied by a suggested actual program, the goal of which was the acculturation and application for citizenship of as many aliens as possible —plus, of course, the cultivation of patriotic projects. Sidney G. Kusworm, of Dayton, Ohio, was appointed chairman of the project, which he organized and headed for forty years, after which he was named its honorary chairman.

A motion to admit women to membership in B'nai B'rith was defeated, but for the first time they were recognized in the Constitution. A section was included authorizing the District Grand Lodges to establish "auxiliary lodges, composed of women, with such rights and powers and under such rules and regulations as the Executive Committee may prescribe." The women's auxiliaries up to that time were few in number, with little independence and less program. It was to be twenty more years before they became an important force in the life of B'nai B'rith.

The growth of the Order in the 1910–20 decade was so great—nearly 100 percent—that the convention created a Central Administrative Board, of Executive Committee members, to meet several times a year, between Executive Committee sessions, to handle the growing volume of business.

It is nowhere indicated when or how a relaxation of the Order's membership admission policies took place. Probably no overt action was ever taken; the change developed gradually, and undoubtedly more rapidly in some communities than in others. But after 1910 growth was so rapid that the old methods—thorough investigation of every applicant, blackballs, etc.—must have been increasingly abandoned (although District No. 1 did not officially abolish the blackball until 1948!). There were no national membership campaigns, such as have been annual events for the past generation, but greater efforts by lodges to acquire members must have been combined with more casual admission standards after 1910.

In that year the American membership was 23,000, in round numbers. By the beginning of 1920 it had risen to 42,000. The overseas membership was 17,500 (13,000 of it in Germany), so that the organization's total membership was just under 60,000.

13

■

1920–1925: Birth of the youth agencies

B'nai B'rith entered the 1920's with considerable strength, and during the decade undertook the most significant program of its entire history—its youth agencies. But the decade ended in such disaster, because of the depression, that for a time early in the 1930's it seemed that its very survival was threatened.

The 1920's are looked back on now as a glamorous and prosperous period, but for the great masses of Americans it was neither, especially at the beginning. The immediate postwar years were ugly ones, filled with economic unrest, Red scares, xenophobia, and the rise of a new kind of anti-Semitism much more serious than America had ever known before. Henry Ford began to publish a viciously anti-Jewish tabloid, the *Dearborn Independent,* which, thanks to his boundless wealth, was circulated everywhere. The Ku Klux Klan, trumpeting hatred for Jews, Catholics, Negroes, and foreigners, enjoyed a resurgence not only in the South but in many northern states. The generation-old "Protocols of the Elders of Zion," long discredited as a forgery in Europe by leading scholars, was introduced to America and spread all over the country like a poisonous fog. It charged that the Jews were plotting to overthrow all governments and take over the world, and although its charges were so ridiculous and its lies so self-evident, millions of Americans had been conditioned to believe anything about Jews.

Anti-Semitism reached such a pitch of intensity that in September, 1920, B'nai B'rith called an all-day meeting in Chicago of its Executive Committee, the ADL board, the Central Conference of American Rabbis, and the National Council of Jewish Women. This group decided to help the ADL intensify its work, and it enlisted Dr. Gotthard Deutsch to head a nonsectarian committee of American leaders to write and publish pamphlets containing the truth about the Jews and distribute them widely. A few months later the group issued a manifesto denouncing anti-Semitism as false, un-American, and unchristian. It was signed by 116 of the nation's leading citizens, all Christians, headed by President Woodrow Wilson, former President William Howard Taft, and William Cardinal O'Connell.

In 1921 B'nai B'rith initiated another major project which, like the adoption of the war orphans, no other agency could, or would, attempt to fill. In May the Executive Committee met in Washington, where all the members were received at the White House by President Warren G. Harding. The business meeting itself was uneventful, except for a subject brought up by Archibald A. Marx, of District No. 7, who lived in New Orleans. It concerned a resolution passed by his District dealing with Jews in Mexico.

As the result of increasingly restrictive immigration laws, hundreds of Jews from eastern Europe had gone to Mexico, hoping to be able from there to enter the promised land. Many of them were victimized by racketeers, who sold them faked Mexican passports, and they were arrested and faced with deportation when caught crossing the border. Others, strangers in a strange land, were in serious difficulties, since they did not know Spanish, had little money, and the relatively few Jews living in Mexico were not affluent and could not help them.

One of the few Jewish leaders who felt strongly about all this was Rabbi Martin Zielonka of El Paso, Texas. Early in 1921 several Jews came to his office after they had been smuggled across the border from Mexico. From them he learned about the smuggling racket, and also that a large number of Jews in Europe were in ports waiting for ships to Mexico, so that they, too, might illegally enter the United States. Rabbi Zielonka went to New York and tried to interest the Industrial Removal Office, the HIAS, and the American Jewish Committee in the problem, but all declined to tackle it. In April, he took his case to the annual convention of District No. 7, which passed a resolution outlining the facts and urging national action by the Order. Mr. Marx presented this resolution to the Executive Committee, which promptly sent him and Rabbi Zielonka to Mexico to investigate conditions.

On the basis of their reports, B'nai B'rith created its Mexican Bureau, for whose work it eventually spent a quarter million dollars. For years the Jews who had been living in Mexico had been divided, but B'nai B'rith brought them together to cooperate in the work. The Order made it clear to the immigrants that they could not enter the United States legally, that Mexico was a good land, with freedom and opportunities, and that B'nai B'rith stood ready to help them help themselves.

The Mexican Bureau established classes in Spanish, provided loans for small business ventures, arranged for health care, sponsored social and cultural events, as well as religious services, and in 1924 rented a large house in Mexico City as a kind of Jewish community center. There was not a single Jewish organization in all Mexico at the time. Through B'nai B'rith intervention with the Mexican Government the passport racketeers were curbed, and the dangerous smuggling of immigrants into the United States was virtually ended.

The Order was aware of the notorious instability of Mexican governments up to that time and tried to discourage Jewish immigration from Europe. Nevertheless Jews kept arriving, and in a decade B'nai B'rith served some ten thousand of them. In 1927 the Emergency Refugee Committee in New York appropriated $50,000 to the program and became part of its management, but under the name of the B'nai B'rith Mexican Bureau. But the Order withdrew from this work gradually, year by year, as the newcomers became capable of managing their own affairs. By the beginning of the 1930's they had made such a good adjustment that a firm foundation had been laid for the development of a healthy and permanent Mexican Jewish community, loyal to its new homeland. Today it numbers more than forty thousand, and it has made enduring contributions to Mexico.

Two years after B'nai B'rith began its work in Mexico it undertook still another mission in human engineering, but this one was largely a failure. Jerusalem was crowded with postwar Jewish immigrants from Europe, and the need for housing was so great that Jerusalem Lodge proposed to build a B'nai B'rith Garden Community outside the city. It planned to build one hundred modest homes and sell them to the immigrants on easy long-term loans. It hoped that another one hundred homes would be built by people who could do so independently. All it needed was $250,000, and it asked the CGL for the money. The Executive Committee sent $25,-000 and tried to raise the rest from the lodges, but after more than a year, less than $7,000 was thus raised. About two dozen homes were actually built, but the project had to be abandoned, although the repaid loans formed a building loan fund which Jerusalem Lodge administers to this day.

In 1923 the Executive Committee met in Memphis, where Secretary A. B. Seelenfreund died suddenly. Leon L. Lewis, while remaining secretary of the ADL, also became secretary of the Order. During the same year the venerable Simon Wolf died and was replaced as the Order's Washington representative by Maurice D. Rosenberg.

Another event that occurred in 1923 was the chartering of the lodges in Poland as District No. 13. Still another was the replacement of the tabloid newspaper *B'nai B'rith News* by a monthly magazine called *B'nai*

B'rith Magazine. Another effort was made to have some-
one write the history of the Order, but Dr. Gotthard
Deutsch had died, and again the effort failed.

During the first half of the 1920's the Executive Committee and the lodges sent a total of $25,000 to the vic-
tims of a flood in Pueblo, Colorado. Postwar inflation
was so terrible in Germany that in 1923 the Order sent
$5,000 from its Emergency Relief Fund to distressed
members there, but the impoverished German members
were themselves managing to operate Toynbee Hall in
Berlin, where a soup kitchen fed even poorer people, and
the Executive Committee voted another $2,000 for that.
After a tornado hit Lorain, Ohio, $10,000 was contrib-
uted to aid the victims. This list could be extended at
great length.

But B'nai B'rith's work was not all philanthropic. The
meeting of the Executive Committee held in Chicago in
April, 1924, gives an idea of the catholicity of the Order's activity.

The Executive Committee dealt, of course, with much
organizational routine, but it also had, as its guest, Dr.
Chaim Weizmann, president of the World Zionist Organization. The Hebrew University had opened its doors
that very month, and Dr. Weizmann pleaded for the Order's support. It responded by appropriating one thousand dollars a year for five years to establish a B'nai
B'rith Research Fellowship. It also voted to establish a
Mexico City office, with a director and assistant, for the
Mexican Bureau. And it discussed, again fruitlessly, the
old problem of how to have a history of B'nai B'rith written.

In addition, the meeting heard Dr. Israel Auerbach
plead for aid to the Academy for Jewish Science in Germany, which was largely maintained by the German,

Austrian, and Czech District Grand Lodges, and was
housed in the German District's building. The Executive
Committee granted it two thousand dollars. It heard reports on the spreading program of the Americanization
Department, which had already influenced thousands of
aliens to become American citizens, and reports on the
work of the Anti-Defamation League.

But the most important item on the agenda was the
appearance of Rabbi Benjamin Frankel. The year before
he had founded an agency on the University of Illinois
campus which he called the Hillel Foundation, and he
begged B'nai B'rith to adopt it and found similar agencies on other American campuses.

The reason he was invited to appear at the meeting
was because B'nai B'rith was already concerned with the
problem of Jewish college students and was pondering
whether or not it should establish some kind of Jewish
centers at American universities. Its officers had consulted with other Jewish leaders, who all emphasized
that B'nai B'rith—which represented a cross section of
American Jewish life—was the ideal organization to
sponsor such a program, which was becoming increasingly necessary.

By the early 1920's the great majority of American
Jews was still foreign-born, and although they were
Americanized spiritually, their mother tongue was Yiddish, and the conditioning they had received overseas
would remain with them throughout their lives. But
their children who were born here grew up in the free
atmosphere of American life on the streets, in the public
schools, among playmates of various religions. To many
of these youngsters the broken English of their parents
was embarrassing socially, and so were their ways, their
names, their total way of life—and their religion. They

cringed when schoolmates called them "dirty Jew," and they soon became convinced that the way to get ahead in the world was to play down their Jewish identity.

When they went to college or sought a job, that is what they did. At college, with the first taste of a course in freshman science or philosophy, they considered themselves sophisticated, and since their only knowledge of Judaism consisted of what they had learned in Jewish religious schools up to the age of thirteen, plus the unacceptable practices of their old-fashioned parents, they wondered how any mature person could believe in such a farrago of supernatural nonsense.

Benjamin Frankel was ordained a rabbi at Hebrew Union College in this kind of atmosphere. During his senior year he served the Reform congregation in Champaign, Illinois, on a biweekly student basis. He loved young people, and met with a great many Jewish students at the University of Illinois. To his sorrow, he found a lot of them totally ignorant of their own Jewish heritage, and militantly uninterested in it. He discussed this situation with Isaac Kuhn, a prominent local merchant and a long-time member of the B'nai B'rith. He also became friendly with a Christian professor of literature, Dr. Edward Chauncey Baldwin. Dr. Baldwin, a philo-Semite of long standing, was upset because American Jews, who were so generous philanthropically, were doing nothing to bring the richness of their Jewish heritage to their own college students, who seemed headed toward the exits of Judaism, instead of toward its future leadership. The Catholics and Protestants, he pointed out, had Newman and Wesley Foundations for their collegians, but the Jews had nothing.

Even before he was ordained, Ben Frankel decided on what he would do. First, he would accept the pulpit offered him in Champaign, and then he would somehow find the money with which to start an institution that would get through to the Jewish students and influence them—in a way no adult synagogue could do. He would "talk their language."

He got $1,000 from the Union of American Hebrew Congregations, and $11,000 from wealthy Jews in Champaign and especially in Chicago, where Dr. Louis L. Mann, a well-known rabbi, paved the way. Then he rented two rooms above a store near the campus and announced that this was the "Hillel Foundation." He named it after a gentle rabbi of the first pre-Christian century who is famous in Jewish history for first formulating the Golden Rule and emphasizing the humane, rather than the coldly legalistic, approach to life and religion.

The Foundation opened in the autumn of 1923. It took a while, but the word got around that here was something different, and worthwhile. There were Reform services on Friday evenings and Orthodox services on Saturday mornings, and students were encouraged not only to attend but participate in them. For the more studious there were classes in Hebrew, Bible, Jewish history and thought; for others there were lively discussion groups, with no holds barred. There were plays, dances, and other social events, held in the local synagogue, and observances of Jewish holidays. There was a primitive library and magazine rack, and quiet corners in which to study. The rabbi's office was open at all times for anyone who wanted to talk over with a sympathetic adult any of the vexing problems with which students are traditionally beset. The rabbi was not shocked if a youngster declared himself an atheist, but welcomed the opportunity to discuss the matter, man to man, and if the student remained unconvinced, he was still welcome to return at any time.

Perhaps most important of all, the students governed themselves. They had a Hillel student council, democratically elected, and committees for all activities. It was not like an adult congregation, where the rabbi and the board of directors ran everything.

All of this Ben Frankel explained to the Order's Executive Committee. He also told them he hoped, the following year, to engage a scholar to give courses on Jewish subjects at the college level, for which the University would grant full college credits.

The rabbi's report was received enthusiastically, but was cautiously referred to the finance committee, which recommended that the Hillel Foundation at Illinois be taken over by the Order, and that its name be changed to B'nai B'rith Hillel Foundation, that a second Foundation be opened as soon as possible at the University of Wisconsin, that a survey be made to determine the schools where additional Foundations should be established, and that a one-year appropriation of $25,000 should be made for the two Foundations and the survey. The committee further recommended that all this should be done only on condition that no other organization was doing anything similar—in other words, that B'nai B'rith should enter this new field "exclusively, or not at all." Finally, it was recommended that the entire project be supervised by a national commission, which would deal with the budget and set policy.

The Executive Committee adopted the report unanimously, and after the meeting President Kraus appointed the first National B'nai B'rith Hillel Foundation Commission, with himself as chairman by virtue of his office. The members included, among others, Rabbi

Mann as vice chairman, Rabbi Frankel, Sigmund Livingston, Isaac Kuhn, and Secretary Leon Lewis.

Less than nine months later, at its meeting in January, 1925, the Executive Committee heard another young man plead the cause of Jewish youth. He was Sam Beber, twenty-two, fresh out of law school, who had begun to practice law in Omaha. He was concerned about the same problem that had worried Ben Frankel, but his target was the teen-ager. He saw all around him Jewish adolescents going to religious schools until they were thirteen—and then drifting away from Jewish interests. Many of them joined neighborhood groups out of a deep need for social contacts. But such groups, even when all the members were Jews, had no interest in anything Jewish.

Sam Beber felt that if the gap between Bar Mitzvah and voting age could be bridged in a way that would keep these youths close to their Jewish community, they could be counted on to remain close in their adult years. But how could that be done?

He was pondering this question when a committee from one of Omaha's many youth clubs asked him to become its adviser. The club was called AZA, letters without any meaning except that the boys were trying to imitate the Greek-letter high-school fraternities from which they were barred as Jews. Sam agreed to become its adviser provided it took on Jewish content and programs. He and the boys worked out a name that retained the club's initials, but made them stand for three Hebrew words: *Ahavo, Zedakah, Achdut* (love, charity, unity). He induced B'nai B'rith's Omaha Lodge to sponsor the group, and on May 3, 1924, it became AZA Chapter No. 1.

But like the founders of B'nai B'rith itself, Sam Beber

had a larger vision. "I wanted to start a national organization of clubs," he wrote later, "with everything that made Greek-letter fraternities glamorous—ornately titled officers, symbolic rituals, initiation ceremonies, secret handshakes, jeweled pins, national tournaments in basketball, debating, and oratory," but based on a love for, and interest in, everything Jewish.

He knew that such a development could take place only if the new group was sponsored and financially helped by a great national Jewish organization, and he decided to try to interest B'nai B'rith. But first he wanted to have something more substantial to offer than one chapter. He therefore enrolled a group of adult advisers, grandiloquently called the Supreme Advisory Council, won the sponsorship of District No. 6—together with an allocation of three hundred dollars, "which seemed like a million"—and then quickly formed three more chapters, in Lincoln, Nebraska, Kansas City, and Des Moines. He called AZA's first "national" convention for July 4, in Omaha, where the four delegates elected Charles Shane of Des Moines as the first Grand Aleph Godol, or president.

Word of the new Jewish teen-age organization spread rapidly, and before the end of 1924 District No. 2 and District No. 4 authorized the formation of AZA chapters. Thus armed with achievements, Sam Beber obtained permission to appear before the Executive Committee in January, 1925. He urged the Order to recognize AZA as its official junior auxiliary, and he made such a favorable impression that the Executive Committee created a subcommittee to investigate and make a detailed report at the forthcoming CGL convention in April.

Yet two more important seeds were planted at that meeting of the Executive Committee. Juliet Eisendrath,

the Jewish social worker at the Mayo Clinic in Rochester, Minnesota, appeared before it and described a growing need there. She said that thousands of Jews from all
over the United States and many other countries were
patients at the Clinic every year, that most of them were
accompanied by relatives, that they presented a multitude of social problems, and that neither the Clinic authorities nor the tiny Jewish community in Rochester
could cope with them. Great numbers of these Jewish
patients could speak only Yiddish; almost all were poor;
sometimes they created anti-Semitic reactions through
misunderstanding—and, in short, that there was so
much social work to be done in Rochester that a full-
time office should be established there.

The B'nai B'rith leaders were sympathetic, but,
weighed down with a dozen major commitments, they
could not take on another. They urged District No. 6 to
undertake the project, but when that body pointed out
that the problem was not a regional one, the Constitution Grand Lodge in 1927 founded in Rochester a B'nai
B'rith Social Service Bureau which is still functioning,
although it is now called the B'nai B'rith Center and oc-
cupies a building of its own with a rabbi-chaplain in
charge.

The financial squeeze that delayed the adoption of the
Mayo Clinic operation was also the origin of B'nai
B'rith's first effort at national fund-raising on a sus-
tained and professional basis. The new Hillel Founda-
tions, the War Orphan Fund, the Palestine House Build-
ing Fund, the Anti-Defamation League, the B'nai B'rith
Mexican Bureau and other activities were draining the
Order's resources. Henry Monsky, representing District
No. 6, therefore moved that a committee be appointed to
develop a plan for an annual fund-raising campaign in

the Jewish community to support the activities of the Order, and to report at the 1925 CGL convention. The motion was passed, and in accordance with tradition, its maker was named chairman of the committee.

This seemingly routine step signaled the end of a whole era and the beginning of a new one in B'nai B'rith history. For eighty years the Order had always raised funds internally. But now it was embarked on a wider scope of activity, which would serve not only its own members but the entire Jewish community, and it was deemed only fair that Jews in general should help support the agencies from which they or their children would benefit, whether they were members of the Order or not. Appropriately, when this new kind of fund drive was launched the following year, it was called the B'nai B'rith Wider Scope Campaign.

In a sense, the nineteenth century lasted until 1925 for B'nai B'rith, and the twentieth began the following year.

14

■

1925–1933: The slide toward catastrophe

The Constitution Grand Lodge convention of 1925, in Atlantic City, unanimously endorsed the Executive Committee's adoption of the Hillel Foundations, and went so far as to mandate that two new Foundations be established every year for the next five years. The delegates were almost equally enthusiastic about adopting AZA as the Order's junior auxiliary. It was reported that in less than a year thirteen chapters had been organized, with twenty-five more on the way, and the convention "endorsed and approved" the AZA, without, however, officially adopting it (that was done the following December by the Executive Committee).

In 1924 the Executive Committee had chartered the Palestine lodges as District No. 14, and in its report to the convention the new District explained why. The lodges in Palestine had been considered politically alien and geographically remote from the other lodges in District No. 11, with its headquarters in Constantinople, and "recent events"—meaning the British Mandate over Palestine—"made it both desirable and necessary to give our Order a special position of prestige within Palestine."

Today's controversy over religion in the public schools was anticipated by the convention, which passed a resolution branding required Bible reading in such schools "contrary to the principle of separation of church and state." The Constitution was changed so that District Grand Lodges, not the CGL, would govern women's auxiliaries.

The Jewish colonization of Palestine, which had been interrupted by the war, had been resumed early in the 1920's, and although B'nai B'rith was a non-Zionist organization, the convention passed a resolution expressing its "full sympathy with the practical work and construction" there.

Finally, the delegates endorsed and authorized campaigns among American Jews as a whole for funds to help support all "special activities" of the Order—such as the Hillel Foundations, Mexican Bureau, ADL, Americanization Department, and any future activities.

The American membership stood at 57,000 men (and fifty women's groups), with some 22,000 overseas members. This represented a quinquennial growth in America of 16,000, and an overseas growth of 9,000. District

No. 2 was the largest American District, with 12,421 members, but German District No. 8, with 15,000, was the largest in the world.

In the first contested election for president in B'nai B'rith history Alfred M. Cohen, 66, of Cincinnati, won over Henry Monsky, 35, of Omaha, and the Order's national headquarters were moved from Chicago to the new president's community. A few months later Leon L. Lewis resigned as secretary both of the Order and of the ADL. He was succeeded in both posts by Dr. Boris D. Bogen, a noted Jewish social worker. But that left the ADL virtually without professional direction, since Dr. Bogen's work as secretary of B'nai B'rith took practically all his time. Happily, the second half of the 1920's in America required less attention to anti-Semitism than the first half had.

The events of those five years in general, in B'nai B'rith, were constructive but hardly exciting. There were no crises. All the European Districts formed an *Arbeitsgemeinschaft,* or Cooperative Body of Non-American Districts, to act jointly on matters of common interest. In Germany a former house painter named Adolf Hitler had organized a gang of street toughs into what he called the National Socialist German Workers Party, and proclaimed that the Jews were Germany's misfortune, but everybody knew that Germany was the land of Goethe and Schiller and the Nazis were only a lunatic fringe, to be laughed at. Henry Ford was feared much more, but in 1927 he made a complete public apology to the Jews, after years of pressure from the ADL and other organizations. Four-fifths of the American people had very modest incomes, but the other fifth was making so much money that it proclaimed prosperity throughout the land and to all the inhabitants thereof.

And through all this B'nai B'rith lodges met every month, committees reported, and charitable and civic activities were conducted. They began to pursue prospective members more aggressively, and middle-class Jews, who were neither rich nor poor, joined because they were aware, in a vague sort of way, that the Order was doing "good work" and deserved the eight or ten dollars a year dues that were then universal. Other members, rarely attending meetings, dropped out, and the membership turnover was very high.

There was no sense of excitement in the organization, even though it continued to make important contributions in a number of fields. Will Hays, the "Czar" of the movies, invited President Cohen to New York and asked B'nai B'rith to be his counselor on films dealing with Jewish angles. Districts No. 2 and 6 raised a half million dollars and dedicated the B'nai B'rith Infirmary of the National Jewish Hospital in 1926. The same year, B'nai B'rith appropriated $6,000 to the Commission on Good Will Among Jews and Christians, and renewed it annually. The Order generously aided the 1926 hurricane victims in Florida. In 1925 the lodges of Great Britain and Ireland became District No. 15. In 1927 the Executive Committee voted $4,000 to Shaare Zion Lodge in Tel Aviv so it could start construction of its own building, and two years later contributed $5,000 to the Hebrew Teachers College in Jerusalem. The members approved all these actions, but their minds were on other things: prosperity, getting ahead, the good life.

The slow but steady growth of the Hillel Foundations, however, did arouse wide interest, because they were so new and unique—and necessary a phenomenon. After units were established at Illinois in 1923 and Wisconsin in 1924, a third Foundation was opened at Ohio State in

1925, a fourth at Michigan in 1926, a fifth at the University of California in 1927, a sixth the same year at Michigan State, a seventh at West Virginia in 1928, an eighth and ninth at Cornell and California (Berkeley) in 1929, and a tenth at Texas in 1930.

AZA was growing, too; the number of war orphans still under fourteen had shrunk to only a few scores; the Jewish immigrants in Mexico were gaining a foothold there so rapidly that the Order's Mexican Bureau began to plan an early withdrawal; the Anti-Defamation League fought what anti-Semitism there was and bolstered the "Good Will" movement; and in 1927 the CGL took over the Jewish social service program at the Mayo Clinic.

All of this activity required much more money than the organization's income, and consequently more attention was turned to fund-raising. A Wider Scope Committee was organized in the summer of 1926, with Henry Monsky as chairman and Dr. Bogen as director. Its goal was $2,500,000, based on pledges payable over a five-year period. The campaign did not get started until early 1927, because of careful planning, but it was at first so successful that by June the first million dollars had been pledged, although something less than $200,000 had been received in cash.

At the end of 1927 Rabbi Frankel died suddenly, at the age of thirty. He was succeeded as director of the Illinois Hillel Foundation by Dr. Abram L. Sachar, a young history instructor at the University; and Dr. Mann of Chicago was appointed acting national director, without salary.

B'nai B'rith life went on. In 1927 the lodges in New York City formed a Metropolitan Council in an effort to increase membership in the big city, which had fewer than two thousand members—but without visible effect.

The following year a lodge was chartered in Shanghai, China, where thousands of Jews from many countries formed a lively community (later a second lodge was organized).

Herbert Hoover was in the White House and all was well with the world. AZA's fifth annual conference met in Denver, where Dr. Bogen told the young delegates: "There are no important specifically Jewish problems facing American Jewry except those having to do with Jewish education."

Adolf Kraus died at the end of 1928, and Dr. Bogen, of a sudden heart attack, in the middle of 1929. President Cohen appointed as the latter's successor Dr. Isaac M. Rubinow, a renowned social worker, social insurance pioneer, and Jewish Federation executive, who had headed Hadassah's first medical unit in Palestine in 1919. In 1929 one of many anti-Jewish riots was stirred up in Palestine by Arab agitators, and B'nai B'rith sent $2,500 to help the victims.

But the most fateful event of the decade—the stock-market crash in October, 1929—meant no more to the Order, for a while, than it did to the rest of America . . . another bear market. But ominously, B'nai B'rith membership had been slowly declining in 1928 and 1929, although it was little noted until Dr. Rubinow, who, among his other accomplishments, was a statistician and an actuary, made his report to the Thirteenth General Convention, held in Cincinnati in 1930.

His figures showed that although the overseas membership had remained constant during the previous five years, the American membership had suffered a net loss of more than 5,000, most of it since 1927. But what shocked the delegates even more was the secretary's report that during the five-year period 40,539 members had been suspended for nonpayment of dues, while only 34,151 new members had been acquired, and that the turnover had been an almost incredible 90 percent! The American membership at the beginning of 1925 had been 56,375; at the beginning of 1930 it was down to 51,632. There were nearly 22,000 members overseas. District No. 2 was the only one to register a net gain (of some 500) and was still the largest in the United States. The German District had slipped from 15,000 to 14,300, but it still led all the others in the world and continued to do so until it was destroyed by the Nazis. There were 399 lodges in the United States and Canada, and 83 women's auxiliaries; with 203 lodges overseas.

Dr. Leo Baeck, president of the German District and a profound Jewish scholar who was destined to survive a concentration camp, attended the convention and delivered an inspiring address which did not once mention the Nazis. The only reference to them was in one sentence in the report of President Cohen, who declared: "In Germany anti-Semitism still constitutes an important plank of a strong political party which manifests itself in many crude ways and is forcing from the Jews of Germany active organization for combating this movement."

Few important actions were taken at the convention. The ADL and Hillel Commissions were reorganized to include one representative from each American District. Similar representation was provided on the Wider Scope Committee. The ADL Fund started in 1920 had long been spent, but support of its program since 1929 had come from the Wider Scope campaign. It was reported, however, that that campaign, since the great days of 1927, when a million dollars had been pledged, had almost collapsed. Only $300,000 had been subscribed in

1928, and a mere $40,000 by the middle of 1929, when Dr. Bogen's death had disrupted activity altogether, since Dr. Rubinow was not engaged until four months later. Moreover, pledges and cash were two different things. It was reported that the largest single pledge had been for $5,000, and there were only a half dozen of that size. District No. 2 was the only one to meet (and even exceed) its quota, and by 1930 Districts No. 1 and 7 had not even begun their campaigns.

It was announced there were only thirteen adopted war orphans still under the age of fourteen. The Palestine delegate reported that Chaim Nachman Bialik, the greatest Hebrew poet of modern times, had joined Shaare Zion Lodge.

The convention sessions were enlivened by a passionate debate on the extent to which B'nai B'rith ought to allocate money to philanthropic institutions. The younger men argued that the giving of large sums to hospitals and other charitable institutions was out of date, and that the Order had Wider Scope obligations of such magnitude that all its resources should be devoted to them. Other delegates, however, spoke heatedly of B'nai B'rith's philanthropic traditions. They won the debate, and $12,000 a year each was appropriated to the Denver and Hot Springs hospitals.

The convention shortened the Order's name to B'nai B'rith, deleting "Independent Order of."

The delegates went home, but the problems remained, most of them spawned by the deepening economic depression. New lodges were established in Buenos Aires and Baghdad, and in Paris, France, and Sarajevo, Yugoslavia, in 1931, but very few new ones were formed in the United States. On the contrary, the American membership of 51,632 as of January 1, 1930, plunged to

46,278 by midyear, although the decline had really begun back in 1927, as the result of prosperity, apathy, and the wretched administration of so many local lodges. The Executive Committee, alarmed, lured Richard E. Gutstadt away from his position as executive secretary of District No. 4, and made him the Order's first national membership director, in November, 1930.

But although he was a spellbinding orator and a tireless and inspired organizer whose whole life was passionately devoted to the Order, he was helpless in the face of economic conditions, and membership continued to shrink. Wider Scope income was also on a downhill course, and at Dr. Rubinow's urging, B'nai B'rith, for the first time in its history, began a policy of joint fundraising with others. The larger Jewish communities were becoming increasingly irritated by the scores of separate appeals, for local and national and international causes, and one by one they were forming federations and welfare funds which held one campaign a year and then allocated what was raised to a multitude of agencies. In 1930, B'nai B'rith began to influence as many federations as possible to include Wider Scope among their beneficiaries.

With millions unemployed, many Jews found themselves more than ever discriminated against in finding or keeping jobs. The problems became so grave that Dr. Rubinow suggested the leading Jewish organizations tackle it jointly, and in November B'nai B'rith convened a meeting with the American Jewish Committee, American Jewish Congress, National Council of Jewish Women, and the Jewish Welfare Board, which were later joined by several other groups. They formed a National Conference of Jewish Employment. But after several meetings it was obvious that a staff was needed, and although B'nai B'rith offered to contribute $1,000 toward the budget, money was so tight that none of the others could do the same and the whole effort fizzled out.

The depression grew steadily worse, and in 1932 and 1933 the Order cut all staff salaries by 10 percent across the board. American membership continued its downward course. Many lodges, unable to collect dues from large numbers of their members, were unable to meet their per-capita debts to the District and National offices, and appealed to the Executive Committee to accept fifty cents on the dollar, or even wipe out all debts.

To compound the crisis, the Wider Scope campaign had been collecting less cash each year since 1928. In the five years since its inception it had raised only $758,-000 against pledges of $1,250,000 and an original goal of $2,500,000. Hundreds of communities remitted absolutely nothing, and at the beginning of 1932 Dr. Rubinow issued a warning that "the re-opening of all Hillel Foundations in the Fall may be financially impossible."

At the same time he pointed out that the depression alone was not responsible for this dangerous state of affairs. He noted that Jewish community life had become so complex that many of the services B'nai B'rith had once rendered were being conducted locally by all kinds of organizations; that the lodge as a place of social gathering had lost the importance it once had; and that the interest of people in philanthropic institutions was in direct ratio to their geographical closeness.

Louis J. Borinstein of Indianapolis had succeeded Henry Monsky as chairman of the Wider Scope Committee in 1930, but despite his efforts, income continued to decline until, by the middle of 1932, the Wider Scope Fund was faced with a deficit of $20,000. In addition to salary cuts, budgets of all the agencies were reduced arbitrarily, and their directors had to find ways of operating on less money. What enabled the Order to pull through the year at all was the Emergency Relief Fund. The 1930 convention had wisely ruled that whenever that Fund exceeded $150,000, the surplus should go into the General Fund. During the first quarter of 1932 there were no calls on the Emergency Fund, and a surplus of $25,000 wiped out the Wider Scope deficit.

But the economic future grew darker every month. At its meeting in January, 1932, the Executive Committee eliminated the office of field director of the Wider Scope, whose salary was $6,000. Although it provided, instead, for four field agents at $4,000 each, none was ever hired, for lack of funds. Thus, in a vicious circle, the lack of field agents resulted in a still greater lack of funds. The lodges were depended upon to raise Wider Scope funds, without professional help, but with the exception of District No. 2 and a few communities, they did not do it. At that same January meeting a Department of Special Activities was created, with Dick Gutstadt as director. As such, he was responsible for the work of the ADL and AZA, in addition to being national membership director.

How B'nai B'rith managed to survive the challenge of the depression—and without closing a single Hillel Foundation or eliminating any other activity—was a miracle. True, it exercised Spartan economies, and borrowed from Peter to pay Paul from among its various funds, but such measures alone could not have done the trick. Despite the widespread apathy combined with fear in the lodges, in most of them there were small groups of devoted members who were willing to make sacrifices, and it was that tiny minority that proved to be the survival factor.

But in 1933 Dr. Rubinow told an associate, confidentially, that although there were some 33,000 members on the books, only about 28,000 were actually paid up in dues, and that he doubted that B'nai B'rith could survive beyond 1935.

It not only survived, but even in those desperate years it continued to serve in a surprisingly large number of ways. Its Hillel Foundations on ten major campuses served thousands of Jewish students; its AZA did the same for boys of high-school age in the communities; its ADL, through the leadership of Sigmund Livingston and without a professional staff, handled hundreds of cases of anti-Semitism and helped strengthen the Good Will movement. By 1931 the Order was able to liquidate its Mexican Bureau, and by 1934 the Jewish community was well enough established there to found Mexico's first B'nai B'rith Lodge. In 1933 District No. 16 was installed in Egypt and District No. 17 in Bulgaria—both carved out of the old Orient District No. 11.

In 1933 Dr. Mann, because of the press of his rabbinical duties, resigned as acting national director of the Hillel Foundations, and the post was made a full-time professional one, with Dr. Sachar filling it. Through it he became the architect of the Hillel movement, which today is functioning on more than 260 campuses around the world, but that development did not really begin until the end of the decade.

Meanwhile, in the immediate pre-Hitler years, although Jews everywhere were worried about the growth of the Nazi movement in Germany, most people refused to believe it could ever actually come to power. Nevertheless, as early as September, 1931, after Nazi assaults on Jews in the streets of Berlin, President Cohen cabled Dr. Baeck: DEEPLY CONCERNED BERLIN EVENTS. IS ANY

ACTION BY B'NAI B'RITH OR AMERICAN JEWRY DESIRA-
BLE TO AROUSE PUBLIC OPINION HERE? Dr. Baeck's
cabled reply was: HEARTY THANKS. AT PRESENT
NOTHING. In a follow-up letter, Dr. Baeck added, in
part:

> We are very grateful that American public opinion
> has reacted so quickly and energetically to the regret-
> table events. Perhaps it has done no harm that news-
> paper reports . . . have somewhat exaggerated the
> sufficiently sad events. This reaction of American pub-
> lic opinion has made a very strong impression here.
> Nevertheless, I would advise you to do nothing more
> about it, for any further action might weaken the ef-
> fect of earlier protests.

Ironically, on January 29, 1933—the day before Hitler became Chancellor of Germany—President Cohen,
in his report at a meeting of the Executive Committee,
declared: "Happily, it seems that Hitlerism is on the
wane!" And he went on to quote from a recent letter he
had received from Dr. Baeck: "The strong wave of anti-
Semitism is already beginning to ebb off; one cannot
speak of an imminent National Socialist danger in the
same terms as one had spoken half a year ago." Thus, in
those incredible days, were even brilliant leaders, who
were right on the scene, misled by fluctuating events.

At the same meeting Mr. Cohen reported that the previous April he had been invited to discuss "an important
matter" with the president of the American Jewish Congress the next time he was in New York. He accepted the
invitation, only to learn that the Congress wanted to organize a World Jewish Congress and wished B'nai B'rith
to join with it in issuing an invitation to important Jewish organizations in a number of countries to meet in
Geneva in August to discuss the matter. Nahum Soko-

low, then president of the World Zionist Organization, was at the meeting, and said he was emphatically opposed to the idea. That took the words right out of Mr. Cohen's mouth, but he explained he could do nothing without the advice and consent of the Order's Executive Committee.

He wrote to every member of it, at home and abroad, soliciting their reaction. Every member who answered opposed B'nai B'rith's joining a World Jewish Congress, and some wrote they were opposed to such a Congress altogether. The American Jewish Committee also declined to participate, and another in the long chain of battles over Jewish "unity" ensued.

B'nai B'rith was founded "to unite Jews," but it meant unity within diversity. When Jews of varying origins and clashing ideas worked together in an American B'nai B'rith lodge, they were unified, but they retained their differences. B'nai B'rith's idea of Jewish unity, then and now, meant unity of action by those who could agree on a given course of action, regardless of their other differences.

President Cohen explained this to the Rabbinical Assembly (Conservative Rabbis) in 1932, when that body invited B'nai B'rith to help it "study the type of organization needed to represent American Jewry." He made a counterproposal, which was not accepted, that representatives of all Jewish organizations and communities, democratically elected, should form a Board of Deputies, so that all could work together, avoid duplication and over-hasty action, and coordinate activity of the constituent agencies while retaining their identity and autonomy.

This struggle between the forces that wanted unity

based on voluntarism, and those which insisted upon a single assembly with everything decided by a majority vote, was to convulse American Jewish life in the critical years ahead.

15

.

1933–1938: The early Nazi years

When Hitler became Chancellor of Germany on January 30, 1933, the B'nai B'rith treasury was nearly empty. The membership had sunk to 33,000 (publicly announced), but to less than 30,000 (privately admitted), and the Wider Scope collections were down to a sporadic few thousand dollars here and there. Of the $2.50 received by the Constitution Grand Lodge from each member's dues, 50¢ went into the Emergency Relief Fund, which meant an income of, at most, $60,000 a year. Yet it was somehow found possible to send $2,500 to sufferers from the 1933 earthquake in southern California, and to add an eleventh Hillel Foundation at Northwestern the same year, a twelfth at Alabama the following year, and a thirteenth at Penn State in 1935.

The economies of the past were intensified, and money was often borrowed from the Emergency Relief Fund. Allocations to the Denver and Hot Springs hospitals were cut from $12,000 each in 1930 to less than $3,000 three years later. The youth agencies were treated the same way. At the beginning of 1932, the Hillel budget was $108,000; by June it was cut to $86,000; by autumn, to $70,000; and by the following January to $50,000. Hillel directors and other employees periodically went for weeks without salaries, until Wider Scope monies came in, or until some of the Order's meager stock of investment bonds had been sold. In 1932, the $18,000 AZA budget was slashed to $10,000. The leaders hung on grimly, hoping for better times.

Then came Hitler.

Up to the time he became Chancellor, most Americans, including the Jews, were woefully ignorant of the true situation in Germany, and considered the little man with the Charlie Chaplin mustache a clown. Even after he was Chancellor, they refused to believe he would ever actually have real power. As late as March, 1933, B'nai B'rith's official magazine declared editorially that "he is surrounded by judicious men . . . Hindenburg . . . and von Papen. And responsibility generally puts curbs on the folly and viciousness even of the most irresponsible demagogue."

In February, 1933, the president of B'nai B'rith, at the direction of the Executive Committee, won the agreement of the American Jewish Committee and the American Jewish Congress to attend a meeting in New York at which they agreed on joint action in all matters pertaining to the German situation. But this unity lasted only a short time. The Congress wanted the three organizations to stage mass protest meetings, which the other two insisted would do more harm than good to the Jews in Germany. The Congress therefore left the group.

As 1933 advanced, the Anti-Defamation League became the Order's most important activity. Its founder, Sig Livingston, convinced the Executive Committee to move the ADL office back to Chicago, with Dick Gutstadt as its full-time secretary, although the Executive Committee continued to pay his salary. Nazi-minded German-Americans were beginning to organize, and the Nazis in Germany, seizing control of German Government resources, financed American fascist groups and flooded the United States with Nazi and anti-Jewish propaganda.

Mr. Livingston and Mr. Gutstadt started to build a small professional staff in Chicago to meet the threat. Attempts were made to have the postal laws amended to ban hate-inciting propaganda; the new American fascist groups were infiltrated and exposed; a speakers' bureau was formed to tell the American public the truth about Nazi machinations; a press department was organized; the FBI and other government agencies were furnished with evidence of the direct links between Berlin and American anti-Jewish groups, as well as the sources of the latter's funds and the nature of their interlocking relationships. To pay for all this, Mr. Livingston proposed to raise a special ADL fund of $200,000, and Mr. Gutstadt addressed audiences the country over, trying to raise the money.

This caused one of those embarrassing internal collisions common to many organizations from time to time. Supporting the fight against anti-Semitism was much more popular than supporting Jewish culture and youth work. The Wider Scope fund raisers therefore found themselves competing with their own colleagues of the ADL for the B'nai B'rith dollar. Many lodges raided their own treasuries to help the ADL, and had nothing left for Wider Scope. Mr. Livingston had promised the Executive Committee he would raise ADL funds quietly from a select list of wealthy individuals, but from such people he obtained almost nothing, and soon lodges were writing to the president of the Order that they were being solicited and even pressured for ADL contributions, and could not afford to give to that cause and also to Wider Scope. Mr. Livingston appealed to federations, welfare funds, and other sources, many of which were already allocating funds to the Wider Scope campaign.

The Executive Committee blew the whistle on this situation when its Administrative Committee directed that Wider Scope and ADL funds be raised jointly, with 25 percent going to the ADL and 75 percent to the Executive Committee for all the other activities of the Order.

Soon after the Nazis came to power, the American Jewish Congress and other groups launched a boycott of German goods and asked B'nai B'rith to participate. The Executive Committee, after painful soul-searching, refused, on the grounds that B'nai B'rith alone, of all Jewish organizations, had members in Germany—some 14,000 of them—who would probably suffer directly if the Order joined in the boycott. A few members of the Executive Committee voted in favor of participation, but President Cohen declared that no Jew with any self-respect would buy German goods anyway, that a nonsectarian boycott might be worthwhile but a Jewish boycott could be harmful to Germany's Jews, that it was easy to be a hero five thousand miles from the battlefield, and that B'nai B'rith could not, in good conscience, risk the arrest—or worse—of 14,000 of its members. The boycott organizations and the Jewish press, completely ignoring these arguments, thereupon began a frenzied campaign of slander and vilification against B'nai B'rith, which hurt the organization but did not change the minds of its leaders. The boycott, as it turned out, was totally ineffective. In the midst of all this, and without publicity, B'nai B'rith sent $5,000 to the German B'nai B'rith on the appeal of Dr. Baeck. It also sent $1,000 to the *Arbeitsgemeinschaft*, which moved from Vienna to London in 1933, and changed its name to the B'nai B'rith European Committee.

By June, 1933, B'nai B'rith succeeded in bringing the American Jewish Congress and American Jewish Committee together again to form a Joint Consultative Council, to work together, when they could agree, on all matters concerning the German crisis.

The need for joint action seemed so critical that the Jewish members of the U. S. House of Representatives invited the three organizations to consult together in Washington, and the Council really grew out of that conference. Its first united action was to present a strong plea to the Government for sympathetic treatment of applications from German Jewish refugees who wanted to enter the United States. As a result, thousands received American visas. Later, B'nai B'rith determined to try to have the Council extend its scope to Jewish problems the world over. But although the Council lasted for several years, the same basic disagreements that had caused its first collapse caused its final one.

Throughout the rest of the decade B'nai B'rith did all the pitiful little that any agency could do to try to help Germany's Jews. Together with other organizations, or alone, it kept in constant touch with the U. S. State Department, and President Cohen made many trips to Washington to see Secretary of State Hull and others. He appealed to them on humanitarian grounds, and also made the point that B'nai B'rith in Germany was a branch of the American B'nai B'rith, and that therefore tens of thousands of American citizens were directly concerned about it and the people it served. He furnished facts on the dozens of old-age homes, orphan asylums, youth hostels, libraries, hospitals, and other institutions B'nai B'rith was operating in Germany.

Toward the end of 1933 President Cohen and Secretary Rubinow represented the Order in London at a Conference for the Relief of German Jewry. James G. McDonald had just been named by the League of Nations as High Commissioner for Refugees, and the Conference prepared to work closely with him, because it was still possible for Jews to escape from Germany at that time. However, despite the Conference's best efforts and intentions it accomplished very little, and the same was true of the High Commissioner's office, because most of the nations that condemned the Nazis refused to admit refugees from Germany as immigrants. The Order collected 250,000 names of Americans of all faiths on a petition asking President Roosevelt to denounce the Nazi persecution of the Jews, and Mr. Cohen personally presented it to the White House.

In Jerusalem, the lodges opened a shelter home for the refugees who were beginning to stream into the country, without money or connections. Under the guidance of Henrietta Szold, they were given food and lodgings until they could find work or a better place to stay. During 1934 and 1935 this shelter cared for more than 3,500 refugees.

But crisis or no crisis, most of the work of any organization consists of day-by-day routine functions, and B'nai B'rith agencies somehow carried on, with starvation budgets. The birth of the New Deal was a turning point in the depression, and although substantial effects were not felt for some time, they were beginning to take place. From January, 1930, to January, 1933, the Order's American membership dropped from about 52,000 to less than 30,000, but by the end of 1933 it rose to slightly more than 35,000. It was not until the following year, however, that the recovery from the depression became noticeable. The membership at the end of 1934 reached 43,000. In addition, there were 100 women's auxiliaries with a total of 10,000 members, and 5,000 AZA members. It was at this time, too, that teen-age girls began to form Junior Auxiliary chapters which developed later into a national B'nai B'rith Girls organization.

But more important was the change that rapidly took place in American Jewry after the Nazis came to power. There was a revival of Jewish consciousness such as had never been witnessed before in this country. Assimilated men and women, who for years had had nothing to do with organized Jewish religious or community life, stood up to be counted as part of the Jewish people; and those whose devotion had never flagged became even more active. The Zionist Organization of America, long regarded with indifference or hostility by most Orthodox and Reform groups, began to swell in size and the prominence of its leaders.

When the Wider Scope Appeal ended in 1932—it had been announced as a five-year project in 1927—the Executive Committee faced a dilemma. Most of the five-year pledges had not been redeemed, either in full or in part; the depression made it clear they would never be; and the Order's activities needed more funds than ever. It was therefore decided to have Wider Scope campaigns on a continuing basis, without long-term pledges—in effect, annual campaigns.

But great faith and hope were placed in the growing welfare-fund movement, and an increasing number of welfare funds included Wider Scope as a beneficiary of their campaigns. The trouble was that those campaigns did not raise nearly enough, either for local or overseas causes. Nevertheless, beginning in 1934, B'nai B'rith's income, both from membership dues and fund-raising, slowly but steadily increased, and by 1935 it was possible to finance AZA from the Order's general fund, thus releasing more money from Wider Scope to ADL's swiftly growing programs. In 1934 Sidney G. Kusworm became treasurer of the Order, and he still holds that post in 1966.

At the beginning of 1935, B'nai B'rith was part of a national committee that sponsored the first National Conference on Palestine, organized by the Zionist Organization of America. It united Zionist organizations of all ideologies with non-Zionist groups, like B'nai B'rith, which were dedicated to the upbuilding of Palestine but without political commitments. The National Conference coordinated the Palestine programs of all fifty national groups that participated. At the same time, B'nai B'rith helped form a Committee on German Jewish Immigration Policy, with a program of bringing hundreds, and if possible thousands, of German Jewish children (not orphans) to the United States, to be placed in Jewish homes until they could be safely returned to their parents. But this effort was not notably successful.

By 1935 the ADL program was so ramified that Dick

Gutstadt's title of director of Special Activities was dropped, and he became, simply, national director of the ADL, and was relieved of all other responsibilities. The ADL's work was largely fact-finding, related to Nazi propaganda, but somehow it also continued to handle the hundreds of routine cases of anti-Semitism. Although Henry Ford had shut down the *Dearborn Independent,* and had forbidden the use of his name in connection with any anti-Jewish propaganda, the "Protocols of the Elders of Zion" was widely circulated all through the 1930's under his name, and Ford agents promoted the poisonous radio propaganda of Father Charles E. Coughlin, who by 1936 was broadcasting over 475 stations. Fritz Kuhn, head of the German-American Bund, was financed by Ford money as he organized branches of the Bund throughout the country.

The Nazis in Germany poured hundreds of millions of dollars into propaganda in America, and the ADL later estimated that during the late 1930's there were more than five hundred anti-Semitic organizations in the United States, although most of them were merely small rackets. Concentrating on the big ones, the ADL developed voluminous fact files on such groups as the Bund, the Silver Shirts, the Vigilantes, Ku Klux Klan, the Paul Reveres, the Nazi Organization of America, and scores of others, all of which published periodicals and pamphlets. After the United States entered World War II, the ADL files proved a gold mine to the FBI in its surveillance of hundreds of enemy agents.

The Fourteenth General Convention in Washington in 1935 was an important one for several reasons. It was the last quinquennial session to be held, since the delegates voted, in view of the swifter pace of modern times, that conventions thenceforth be held every three years.

The name of the Constitution Grand Lodge was changed to Supreme Lodge, and it was voted to incorporate the organization, as well as the Hillel Foundations—and soon AZA as well—under the laws of the District of Columbia.

More important, the convention changed the Constitution to require that permanent headquarters of B'nai B'rith be established in the nation's capital before the next convention, in 1938. Practically all the delegates knew they were going to elect Henry Monsky of Omaha as president then, and it was evident that B'nai B'rith headquarters could no longer move every ten or fifteen years when a new chief executive was chosen. Besides, they felt the headquarters should be near the great masses of Jewish population, namely, the East Coast, and in Washington rather than New York because the Order's growing international work and interests required closer relationships with many government agencies. The Washington Bureau, a one-man operation on a part-time basis, had become wholly inadequate, and indeed it was abolished altogether as soon as Supreme Lodge headquarters were established in the capital in 1938.

The convention also streamlined the Hillel Foundation Commission and made it more representative of all the American Districts. There were, at the time, Women's Grand Lodges in five of the seven American Districts, and 136 AZA chapters. Provision was made for a Canadian ADL office. It was announced that District No. 18 had just been chartered in Yugoslavia, of lodges formerly in District No. 11, and that, for the first time, a B'nai B'rith lodge had been formed in the Sudan, at Khartoum.

Of special interest was President Cohen's report that

B'nai B'rith was still functioning in Germany, and was the only international organization still represented there. There had been no direct contacts with the German members since 1933, but in that year, after Mr. Cohen had attended the Conference on German Jewry in London, he had met with two German B'nai B'rith leaders and had made arrangements for indirect contacts. He informed the convention that although the German brethren were suffering the common fate of all Jews there, only a few of the lodges had had to dissolve, and that miraculously the network of B'nai B'rith charitable institutions, which were needed more than ever before, was still functioning. As soon as the Nazis had achieved power, they had ordered all German units of international organizations to liquidate themselves, and the Masons, Odd Fellows, and others had promptly obeyed. With supreme courage, however, Dr. Baeck had told the Nazi authorities that B'nai B'rith was resolved to serve its people, and would not end its existence voluntarily. Unaccountably, it was allowed to live.

Three issues stirred the convention delegates to hot debate and significant decisions. The first was a continuation of the 1930 dispute over how much emphasis B'nai B'rith should place on philanthropy and how much on its other activities. Some delegates demanded that all support for the Denver and Hot Springs hospitals be gradually withdrawn over the next five years, with a corresponding increase in allocations to "our own activities."

Dr. Rubinow, as secretary, did not take sides, but he produced statistics showing during the previous decade "a definite trend from philanthropy . . . towards greater efforts in the cultural field and for the protection of Jewish political, economic, social, and religious rights." Thus, of the total expenditure by B'nai B'rith of $1,331,000 between 1925 and 1930, cultural-protective activities had received 54.6 percent and philanthropic activities, 28.3 percent, while from 1930 to 1935 the amount spent on cultural-protective work rose to more than two-thirds of the total, while the amount allocated to philanthropy declined from one-fourth to one-eighth. Although the proponents of more philanthropy won, time proved the victory a hollow one, since allocations to philanthropic institutions gradually shrank to an infinitesimal percentage of the Order's budget.

The second lively dispute grew out of a recommendation that members at large, who would pay annual minimum dues of $25 but not belong to any lodges, should be admitted. But this was defeated because the delegates were opposed to more than one class of members.

The third controversial issue was whether the Order's growing financial needs should be met by fund-raising or by assessments on the members. Fund-raising won, not only because the members could not afford the large assessments that would be required, but because most of the work B'nai B'rith was now doing was benefiting Jews generally, and not merely the members.

Wider Scope campaigns were beginning to bring in more money; during the first quarter of 1935 the American membership climbed from 43,000 to 45,000; and with the depression diminishing in intensity, a new mood of confidence and optimism began to mark the period.

A few months after the convention the groundwork was laid for one of the most dramatic actions ever taken by the organization. Dr. Chaim Weizmann, World Zionist president, wrote to Mr. Cohen, suggesting a project on behalf of the Jewish National Fund. "As you probably know," he wrote, "the most pressing need in Palestine at present is for land." He proposed that the Order buy enough land for an entire colony and present it to the JNF, which would name it after B'nai B'rith and hold it in perpetuity as the property of the Jewish people. He suggested the acreage be purchased in the Beisan area, in northern Palestine, which possessed "considerable strategic as well as economic importance."

Mr. Cohen laid the matter before the Executive Committee which, at its meeting in February, 1936, enthusiastically voted the then unheard of sum of $100,000 for the purchase of one thousand acres. The money was to come from the Emergency Relief Fund and be paid out over a period of seven years. But before any public announcement could be made, severe Arab anti-Jewish rioting broke out in Palestine, and it was feared that such an announcement might exacerbate the situation. But when the riots continued all summer and into the autumn, the Order's leaders realized that an announcement would have the effect of telling the Arabs—and the rest of the world—that American Jewry, through its largest and oldest organization, had confidence in the future of a Jewish community in Palestine.

The story was featured in the nation's leading newspapers and in publications around the world, and practically every Jewish leader hailed B'nai B'rith for its action. A colony of German refugees was later established on the land, and the community today is known as Moledet B'nai B'rith.

During the same year a fascinating revelation was made when the Order's magazine published an article on the occasion of Sigmund Freud's eightieth birthday. It included the full text of a little-known letter Freud had written to the B'nai B'rith lodge in Vienna ten years before. He had joined the lodge in 1897, at a time when his new theories had earned him the obloquy and even hatred of much of the scientific community. But the lodge invited him to lecture to it on his theory of the interpretation of dreams, and this expression of confidence in him by a responsible body of men was extremely important to his morale. In 1925, after he had achieved worldwide fame, the lodge wanted to honor him at a special celebration, but illness prevented his appearance. He wrote the lodge, in part:

> I want to tell you how I became a Ben B'rith and what I sought in your companionship. . . . The announcement of my unpleasant findings had the result that I lost the largest part of my human relations. I felt like one who is ostracized. In this loneliness, there awoke within me the longing for a circle of select, high-minded men who would accept me in friendship in spite of my daring opinions. . . . The fact that you were Jews could be only desirable to me, for I myself was a Jew, and I had always deemed it not only unworthy but nonsensical to deny it.

He went on to confess that neither the Jewish religion nor its concept of nationhood was of any interest to him, although he admired its "ethics." But what made "the attraction of Judaism and Jews irresistible" to him included "many obscure forces of emotions" and "an inner identity in common with yours"—as well as the advantage, as a Jew, of being "free from many prejudices which limited others in the use of their intellect. Thus," he concluded, "I became one of you. . . . You were my first audience."

The great economic depression taught people many bitter lessons: that education was all important in getting or holding jobs, that unskilled labor was getting more expendable, and that many people were unhappy at their work because they were in the wrong jobs. And Jews needed no depression to know that discrimination often worked against them. But what was the answer to all this?

As early as 1933, AZA undertook an occupational study of Jews in a number of cities, and later determined to create a Vocational Service Bureau. But by 1935 the Hillel Commission, in order to plan for intelligent expansion, asked B'nai B'rith to set up a Research Bureau, under Hillel auspices, to find out how many Jewish students were on American campuses. The Executive Committee liked the idea, and employed Rabbi Lee J. Levinger, a former Hillel director, to head the project. To everybody's amazement he discovered there were 105,000 Jewish students—more than anyone would have guessed. This led to further research, into the vocational interests of these students. The AZA turned over its own research findings to the Hillel Bureau, and the Executive Committee realized there was an urgent need for vocational guidance among young people, and especially among Jewish youths, who suffered from anti-Semitism in so many occupations. Early in 1936 a committee was appointed to work out a plan of action, and in January, 1938, B'nai B'rith founded its Vocational Service Bureau, with Alfred A. Benesch, of Cleveland, as its first national chairman. Dr. Levinger, his work completed, was asked to write the history of B'nai B'rith, but he left B'nai B'rith service. Max F. Baer was named the first national director of Vocational Service.

The Bureau for many years confined itself, for budgetary reasons, to group guidance and vocational and educational research and publication. It replaced the Hillel Research Bureau, made a decennial census of Jewish college students, and in more recent years added individual counseling to its program, setting up professionally directed offices in more than twenty cities.

Although the worst of the depression was over by 1936 and the work of the ADL was proving more important every year, B'nai B'rith membership increased very slowly as a whole, although rapidly in some communities. New York was not one of them. With a million and a half Jews, it had only thirteen hundred members in six Manhattan lodges, and one lodge each in Brooklyn and the Bronx. There had been no National Membership Department since Dick Gutstadt had become ADL director in 1933, but in 1936 a young rabbi was engaged to organize one. He took the long-term view that Jews who knew their own heritage would flock to B'nai B'rith, and he organized adult Jewish education programs in a number of large cities. But they resulted in no increase in membership, and there were still less than fifty thousand in the United States in September, 1936, when Dr. Rubinow died.

Shortly before, in August, while a British Royal Commission was preparing to go to Palestine to investigate the latest Arab riots, word leaked out that England intended to suspend all Jewish immigration into the Holy Land, to appease the Arabs. B'nai B'rith joined with other national Jewish organizations in making strong protests to the U.S. State Department, pointing out that the refugees from the Nazi hell had no place else to go. The threat was temporarily averted.

But a threat that could no longer be averted was the complete destruction of B'nai B'rith in Germany. After tolerating its existence for four years, the Nazis struck in April, 1937. Storm troopers suddenly appeared at the central B'nai B'rith building in Berlin, and at all the lodge quarters and philanthropic institutions throughout the country, as well as at the homes of the most prominent members. The officers of many lodges were arrested, some were badly beaten. The troopers invaded the lodge rooms, hospitals, orphan homes, widows' shelters, and other buildings, and threw the old, the young, and the sick into the streets. All property and bank accounts were confiscated, and B'nai B'rith was declared dissolved.

During the four years from 1933 to 1937 the German B'nai B'rith, led by Dr. Baeck, had helped bolster the courage and morale of German Jewry, and it had sheltered many aged and infirm people, and orphans. During that time American members had contributed more than $30,000 to their brethren in Germany, to help them survive and carry on this work. Now it was over.

During 1937 B'nai B'rith renewed its efforts to forge real Jewish unity. It proposed that the ADL should work closely with the American Jewish Committee, American Jewish Congress, and other agencies, in an exchange of information, common programs in certain fields, and as a clearing house to avoid friction and duplication. Such an arrangement was actually made, but the historic old centrifugal forces were too strong, and it did not last long. It was called the Joint Consultative Council.

There were three speakers at a huge B'nai B'rith Unity Dinner in New York later that year: President Cohen; Dr. Stephen S. Wise, president of the American Jewish Congress; and Dr. Cyrus Adler, president of the American Jewish Committee. Mr. Cohen challenged the other speakers by proposing that in the field of defending Jewish rights there should be one agency to speak for all, consisting of organization representatives who, after their election, would be responsible to American Jewry and not to the groups that had elected them. He indicated that B'nai B'rith was ready to support such a plan. But although the two other speakers paid devout tribute to the theory of Jewish unity, neither accepted the B'nai B'rith president's challenge.

And the Joint Consultative Council continued to die of inanition.

On July 1, 1937, Maurice Bisgyer was appointed secretary of the Order. He had been director of the Jewish Community Center in Washington, D.C., for many years. During the same year, the Anti-Defamation League opened a branch office in New York City. A few years later that branch office became the National ADL headquarters. In 1937, too, the name of the Americanization Committee was changed to Americanism Committee.

At the end of the year the Supreme Lodge headquarters moved to rented offices in Washington, in accordance with the mandate of the 1935 convention. President Cohen, who was then seventy-eight, of course remained in Cincinnati. The Washington staff began to prepare feverishly for the 1938 triennial convention, which was to be held in the nation's capital.

16

■

1938–1941: Henry Monsky opens the throttle

The only action of any significance taken at the 1938 convention was the election of Henry Monsky as president—and that was a major one.

He was the first "Russian Jew" to head the Order; all of his predecessors had been "German Jews." Actually, Alfred M. Cohen, Leo N. Levi, and Benjamin F. Peixotto had been born in the United States, but they were "German Jews" psychologically. All the others, from 1843 on, were born in Germanic central Europe.

Henry Monsky was born in Russia of poor Orthodox

parents, but he was brought to Omaha as an infant of less than a year and lived there all his life, graduating from the Catholic Creighton University law school. He cared little about Jewish denominationalism, and as a matter of principle he belonged to a Reform, a Conservative, and an Orthodox congregation. He was a successful attorney but never became wealthy. He had the common touch, and it was symptomatic of his personality that nearly everybody called him Henry. At a time when most of the "best Jewish society" favored the upbuilding of Palestine as a philanthropic activity but shuddered at the idea of a Jewish nation, he was an ardent Zionist.

He had a razor-sharp mind and abundant courage and energy. Although far from being a radical (he was a Republican and a corporation lawyer), he was a liberal and an experimenter. All these attributes, and more, he brought to the presidency of B'nai B'rith. During his three terms, the Order shed most of the vestiges of its nineteenth-century practices.

The state of the Order had never been better, in some respects. American membership—in 457 lodges—stood at 60,000, an all-time high. There were 13 Hillel Foundations. There were 17,000 women in 178 auxiliaries. In AZA, there were 6,244 active members in 233 chapters, and 5,352 alumni. There were 13 chapters of teen-age BB Girls. And although money was still tight, the budget was balanced, with a small surplus.

But the convention undertook no new programs, no bold steps. The rapid growth of women's activities emboldened them to seek representation at Supreme Lodge conventions. But the best the delegates in Washington could do for them was—conveniently without changing the Constitution—to permit each women's District, at the next triennial convention, to designate one representative to attend, with voice but no vote, and at her own District's expense.

A constructive motion was made that a national committee be formed to organize a program of adult Jewish education for the Order. But it was laid on the table "indefinitely"—after a delegate declaimed that "if you will tell the adults to read their Bible and study the Psalms, they will be getting a good deal of adult Jewish education without spending thousands upon thousands of dollars."

Shortly before the convention the American Jewish Congress had made an extraordinary effort to become recognized as the spokesman for all American Jewry. It had invited B'nai B'rith and other major Jewish organizations to participate in a "referendum" by voting on a list of important issues facing the world Jewish community, at ten cents per voter. The hitch was that the registration blank, which all voters had to sign, carried the declaration: "I herewith endorse the purposes of the American Jewish Congress and join in its effort to mobilize American Jews in defense of Jewish rights the world over."

The Supreme Lodge convention gave short shrift to that stratagem, refusing to have B'nai B'rith participate, and telling Dr. Stephen S. Wise why, in a letter that crackled with righteous indignation. Most other organizations reacted similarly, and the Congress hastily abandoned the field.

But immediately after the convention, B'nai B'rith joined in yet another effort at forging Jewish unity. This one was made by a group of Pittsburgh Jewish leaders, at whose invitation B'nai B'rith, the Committee, the Congress, and the Jewish Labor Committee sent representatives to Pittsburgh, where they all pledged themselves to join forces in defense of Jewish rights, in a new agency called the General Jewish Council. Moreover, they agreed that additional organizations should be invited to join them, and that decisions of the body should, by a two-thirds vote, be binding upon all constituents. However, B'nai B'rith later interpreted the agreement as meaning that any constituent organization that disagreed with the majority vote on any given issue would not be committed to it.

Under Henry Monsky's leadership the work of the Order began to hum. The convention had authorized a Bogen-Rubinow Forest in Palestine as a memorial to the Order's two great secretaries. Mr. Monsky quickly saw to it that shortly thereafter the Supreme Lodge planted five hundred trees; the lodges planted thousands more. When Hadassah, at the post-convention Executive Committee meeting, appealed for help in bringing 1,000 Jewish youths from central Europe to Palestine as part of the Youth Aliyah, some members wanted to allocate $1,000 as a token gift, but after Mr. Monsky finished talking to them, they voted $10,000—and a year later, without being asked, another $2,500.

Even before Germany's ghastly "Crystal Night" in 1938, thousands of German Jews had been beaten and starved in concentration camps, and the lucky ones were those who managed to flee the country. But because of the strict United States immigration laws, they could enter this country only if responsible American citizens signed affidavits guaranteeing they would not become public charges. B'nai B'rith set up a national committee to obtain such affidavits from members, with the result that thousands of German Jews were enabled to enter the United States and start new lives. In a few scores of cases Jews were actually released from concentration camps and allowed to emigrate to the United States when B'nai B'rith produced affidavits in their behalf. At the same time, $1,000 was sent to Germany to enable the German-Jewish Children's Aid to bring additional youngsters to America.

The 1938 convention had authorized the creation of a National B'nai B'rith Committee on Social Service, and it was organized the same year. The convention had also authorized Hillel extension service. The Order could not afford to place full-time Hillel Foundations in dozens of universities that were clamoring for them, but President Monsky backed up Dr. Sachar, the national Hillel director, in his plea for expansion as soon as possible. Meanwhile, at small cost, it was found feasible to extend part-time Hillel programs, called Counselorships, to schools near those with Foundations. This marked a change from the slow, ultra-conservative policy, and was the beginning of the process of dotting the entire country—and later other countries—with a network of nearly 100 full-time Hillel Foundations and more than 160 Counselorships.

Early in 1939 another bold step was taken when the Executive Committee authorized the Hillel Commission to raise funds for buildings for the Foundations at Illinois and Penn State. Up to that time all Foundations had operated in usually modest rented quarters, but in time most of them acquired and remodeled existing structures or built new ones, through capital fund campaigns by B'nai B'rith men and women in the region.

At the beginning of 1934 the *B'nai B'rith Magazine* had changed its name to *B'nai B'rith National Jewish Monthly,* and five years later to *The National Jewish Monthly,* published by B'nai B'rith.

The question of B'nai B'rith's joining the anti-German boycott had been brought up from time to time ever since 1933. A curious resolution was passed at the 1938 convention, calling on the whole civilized world to prevent any persecution which threatened Jew or Christian, but without mentioning a boycott, even though B'nai B'rith no longer existed in Germany. But early in 1939, with the General Jewish Council in favor of the boycott, the Executive Committee passed a forthright resolution, calling for support of "generally organized boycotts." It even organized a National B'nai B'rith Boycott Committee, with a $5,000 budget.

Later in 1939 it became known that Great Britain intended to issue a white paper, allowing restricted Jewish immigration to Palestine for five years, then none at all. Seldom did any democratic nation's action more violently outrage all Jews—and many others—coming as it did when Europe's tortured Jews had no other place on earth where they could find refuge in substantial numbers, if they were lucky enough to escape from the Nazis. The Supreme Lodge joined with the National Emergency Committee for Palestine in the resulting protests. President Monsky was one of a five-man delegation that met with Secretary Hull, and he directed the activities of other B'nai B'rith key men in the matter.

But despite all protests, England issued its notorious white paper.

By this time, even the most optimistic had to admit that nothing could save Germany's Jews. The Nazis were as impervious to threats as they were to pleas. Cincinnati's Rockdale Temple congregation tried to save Dr. Baeck before it was too late, offering him a rabbinical position, and B'nai B'rith offered to help pay his salary. But the gentle scholar proved to be a tough martyr, preferring to remain with his people, who needed him. Within a couple of years he was sent to Theresienstadt Concentration Camp, where he narrowly escaped death and was rescued by the Red Army. He lived out the rest of his life in London.

Before Pearl Harbor, B'nai B'rith leaders joined with most other responsible Americans in pleas for United States neutrality. But the country was preparing psychologically for war, and after President Roosevelt declared a state of national emergency, a great civil-defense program was launched. B'nai B'rith played a role in this effort out of all proportion to its size. The men and women members raised $50,000 during 1940 for Red Cross war relief, and the Order and the Red Cross cooperated in the field of home service. The American Armed Forces were being steadily expanded, and the cooperation largely involved welfare work on behalf of servicemen's families. By January, 1941, Mr. Monsky organized a National B'nai B'rith Defense Committee, with himself as chairman, to plan a program of aid to national defense agencies, with emphasis on the preservation of morale at home and in the Armed Forces. Through hundreds of lodges, it enlisted tens of thousands of civil defense volunteer workers.

President Monsky and Secretary Bisgyer were sympathetic to the aspiration of the women to become more effective in the B'nai B'rith programs. Consequently, in the autumn of 1940 the presidents of the six women's Districts (District No. 7 had no women's District organization yet) met in Washington and formed the B'nai B'rith Women's Supreme Council. The grandeur of this title belied reality, because it had practically no power or influence. Its purpose was to coordinate the activities of the auxiliaries, but for its first six years it had no professional national director, and its Executive Committee represented the six women's Districts, all of which were jealous of their autonomy. And everything was tightly under the control of the Order's Executive Committee, anyway.

Mrs. Lenore D. Underwood, San Francisco, was elected the Council's first president. At the time the auxiliaries had some 35,000 members, and inspired by this national recognition, however hollow, they threw themselves into B'nai B'rith work with even more than their usual vigor.

During Henry Monsky's first ten months as president, B'nai B'rith's male membership in the United States and Canada zoomed from 60,000 to 80,000! This enlarged manpower, plus increasingly successful Wider Scope campaigns, enabled the Order to expand the Hillel, AZA, Vocational Service, and ADL programs—and that, combined with the popular civil-defense work, attracted still more members. It also led to renewed friction, even competition, between the Wider Scope and ADL fundraisers. It was the mid-1930's all over again. ADL received part of its income from Wider Scope, but in addition it solicited contributions from wealthy individuals. Its director, Dick Gutstadt, was so effective a speaker and fund-raiser that many lodges he addressed wanted to give money directly to the ADL instead of through the Wider Scope. This led to charges and countercharges.

But before an explosion could take place, the issue was resolved by an unexpected development. B'nai B'rith had been trying to have the General Jewish Council enlarge the scope of its work and even raise funds jointly. When this effort failed, the ADL and American Jewish Committee decided, although remaining within the Council, to raise funds jointly while retaining their complete autonomy. They created an instrumentality called the Joint Defense Appeal, with one staff of fund-raisers, in 1941, just before the Supreme Lodge convention, and it lasted for more than twenty years.

The Sixteenth General Convention, held in Chicago with Henry Monsky presiding, was as lively as the previous meeting had been dull. It electrified world Jewry again with a second $100,000 contribution to the Jewish National Fund for the purchase of land adjoining the Alfred M. Cohen Colony for the creation of a second colony, to be named for Henry Monsky (it is now called Ramat Zvi, Zvi being Hebrew for "Henry").

Mr. Monsky announced that B'nai B'rith had spent more than $250,000 during the previous three years on war relief and refugee aid, sending money, ambulances, mobile kitchens, medical supplies, clothing, and food to war victims overseas. The convention voted to place B'nai B'rith's "entire membership and resources at the disposal of the President and the people of the United States" during the "grave crisis that confronts our country." Henry Wallace, Vice President of the United States, was the speaker at the convention banquet.

During their sessions, the delegates created a national committee to direct the Vocational Service Bureau, and a national Wider Scope Committee; provided, for the first time, District and field secretaries for AZA; resolved that the Order should "render full support to all nations resisting totalitarian aggression"; and organized a National Americanism Commission, with Sidney G. Kusworm as chairman.

Another important step was the decision to create a B'nai B'rith Foundation, to receive tax-exempt contributions for the Order's philanthropic, educational, and religious activities (after Mr. Monsky's death, it was re-named in his memory).

Another long and bitter discussion on a motion that B'nai B'rith undertake a program of adult Jewish education repeated all the 1938 arguments, but this time the proponents succeeded in having the subject referred to the Executive Committee, with power to act if and when financial resources permitted. America's entry into the war in December made it necessary to abandon all ideas on the subject, but it blossomed into a major B'nai B'rith activity in the postwar years.

President Monsky was able to report that the organization's American membership had reached 95,000 men, 42,000 women, and 6,000 girls in junior auxiliaries—now called B'nai B'rith Girls. AZA reported 12,000 members in 450 chapters, and 10,000 alumni. And Dr. Sachar revealed there were 55 Hillel Foundations and Counselorships operating on campuses with a total of 30,000 Jewish students.

Mr. Monsky was enthusiastically reelected.

17
■
The 1940's: A historic decade

Henry Monsky was in Chicago, attending a meeting of the Hillel Commission, on Sunday, December 7, 1941. When news of the Japanese attack on Pearl Harbor was received, he told his colleagues that B'nai B'rith would have to retool for war work immediately. The same day he sent a pledge to President Roosevelt, declaring that B'nai B'rith stood ready "for any and all sacrifices of blood, treasure, talent, and toil in defense of our country." The following day he announced that the Supreme Lodge had given another $5,000 to the Red Cross for war relief, and asked the lodges to contribute $45,000 to the same cause—which they did.

Thus began the Order's four-year war service program, one of the greatest private organization contributions to the nation in its history. But how can the story of so massive a program be told briefly?

The only way to give even a general idea is to list the statistics that were scrupulously kept, and published after the war. But even they cannot convey the variety of functions, the millions of work-hours of literally tens of thousands of men and women in hundreds of local B'nai B'rith committees, the raising of huge sums of money, the enthusiasm and dedication of countless people who participated. To cite only one of countless examples, B'nai B'rith's San Francisco Lodge provided food, lodging, and entertainment for more than one hundred thousand servicemen at a Hospitality House it maintained during the four-year period.

The dues of all members in the Armed Forces were, of course, suspended for the duration. Their elders, not qualified for active duty, made their contribution through the B'nai B'rith War Service Program, with Robert Lurie as national director, and Col. Elliott Niles as chairman.

This, then, is the record:

31,280 members of B'nai B'rith and its youth agencies served in the Armed Forces.

553 were killed or reported missing in action.

466 were decorated.

46,000 served as volunteer workers in civil defense, plus 1,500 who were in Home Guard or militia units.

1,507 recreation facilities for servicemen were furnished by lodges and chapters, including company, squad, and battalion day rooms, hospital solaria, chapels, and recreation centers.

800 Navy ships were served, from submarines and hospital vessels to battleships. Their crews were supplied with every comfort not provided by the Navy, including birthday gifts, mechanical cows, books, games and hospital parties in port.

72,000 pints of blood were donated to the Red Cross.

67 pieces of major mobile equipment were contributed by the lodges and chapters to the Red Cross. They included canteens, ambulances, buses, passenger cars, etc.

$711,456,000 worth of War and Victory Bonds were sold.

5,000,000 surgical dressings and 380,000 sewn and knitted garments were turned out by 21,570 B'nai B'rith women and girls in 283 Red Cross sewing units.

2,500,000 servicemen and women were entertained by B'nai B'rith at social events of all kinds.

2,000,000 games, books, and magazines were distributed to the Armed Forces, and 650,000 gift kits and packages were sent to the wounded.

200 Torah scrolls were borrowed from local synagogues and made available for the religious services of Jewish military personnel all over the world.

250,000 servicemen of all faiths (estimated) read copies of the Order's *National Jewish Monthly,* which were supplied free every month to chaplains and military posts around the world.

26,000,000 pounds of scrap metal and other needed materials were collected during the critical shortage period by lodges and youth groups.

342,000 United Nations troops were entertained at traveling shows sponsored by B'nai B'rith in Canada, who also supplied them with 360,000 gift boxes and furnished 54 recreation huts.

$900,000 was contributed to the Red Cross and other war relief agencies, and for direct relief to refugees.

$560,000 was raised within B'nai B'rith for its National War Service Program, in addition to millions of dollars spent by local B'nai B'rith units for local war projects.

This record caused the Navy to confer on B'nai B'rith its first citation for outstanding war service by a civilian agency. It was presented to President Monsky by Admiral Forrest P. Sherman at a mass meeting in Boston, where B'nai B'rith had served so many ships, on December 12, 1945. On February 4, 1946, in his office in the Pentagon Building, General Dwight D. Eisenhower awarded to B'nai B'rith the Army's first citation to any civilian agency.

Two months later, in April, at a luncheon in honor of General Omar Bradley, President Monsky pledged that B'nai B'rith would continue to serve the veterans of the war so long as such service was needed—and although most other organizations allowed similar programs to die out after the war, B'nai B'rith still has a lively veterans' activity to the present time.

After V-J Day, the Order reorganized for peace. It replaced its War Service Department with a Postwar Service Department, and engaged A. B. Kapplin, a World War I veteran, to direct it as well as the work of the American Commission. B'nai B'rith in Canada, however, had grown so large that in deference to it the name was changed to Citizenship Commission, and this joint work of veterans' and community service in general is known today as the Community and Veterans' Services program.

In addition to the Order's principal war program, all

its regular departments, while continuing to pursue their basic objectives, also oriented them in the direction of war service. Thus, when the Government sent 250,-000 picked servicemen to the nation's campuses for technical training, the Hillel Foundations created special religious, cultural, and social programs for the thousands of Jews among them. AZA lost most of its member over eighteen to the Armed Forces, but the younger boys engaged in their own sales of War Bonds, scrap collections, and a dozen other community projects. The Vocational Service Bureau did special vocational research and its publications were used by the War and Navy Departments. *The National Jewish Monthly* supplemented its regular editorial program with patriotic material and news of special Jewish contributions to the war effort.

Meanwhile, unknown to the outside world, in 1942 the Nazis made the decision, at their Wannsee Conference, to kill all the Jews in Europe—and later throughout the world—as the "final solution" to the Jewish problem, and implementation began almost immediately. News of this incredible plot did not leak out until the end of the year. President Monsky was one of the first to learn about it, in December, from what was called "secret sources" at the time. Actually, he heard it from a Polish Jewish leader who managed to reach the United States.

Together with a delegation of officials of other Jewish organizations, he lost no time in presenting the evidence to White House and State Department officials. The State Department already had knowledge of the Wannsee Conference, and President Roosevelt told the Jewish delegation he was horrified to learn that two million

Jews had been killed already and that millions more were scheduled to suffer the same fate. The delegation urged him "to receive and examine all evidence of Nazi barbarities against civilian populations and to submit this evidence to the bar of public opinion and the conscience of the world."

But "the conscience of the world" had already been dulled by so much slaughter, barbarism, and unprecedented cruelty that it did not react as it had earlier in the century. Jews the world over were aghast, but also frustrated by their helplessness.

Refusing to surrender to this feeling, Mr. Monsky, although admitting there was little the Jews could do, insisted that they do at least that little. In January, 1943, he took it upon himself to call a national conference in Pittsburgh of all the major Jewish organizations to try to forge Jewish unity in the crisis. His invitation emphasized one immediate goal—to save as many lives as possible—and two long-range goals: "the post-war status of the Jews, and the upbuilding of a Jewish Palestine."

Only B'nai B'rith's president could have organized such unity, it was freely admitted by other Jewish leaders. All other Jewish organizations would have been suspected of ulterior motives if they had taken the initiative. But everybody had to admit that B'nai B'rith had no such motives, and that it was the only truly neutral and unifying force on the American Jewish scene. The result was that 32 of the 35 invited organizations sent delegates to Pittsburgh on January 23, and they agreed to form an American Jewish Conference a few months later.

In those few months American Jewry witnessed something never seen before in this country. In every community, delegates were democratically elected by secret ballots, and more than 500 of them were at the Conference's first session in New York on August 29.

The successes and failures of the American Jewish Conference are not part of this history, except insofar as B'nai B'rith was involved. As we have seen, its president called the Conference into being. He delivered its keynote address and served as temporary chairman. Of the 502 delegates, 200 were members of the Order, although only 65 registered as members of the official B'nai B'rith bloc, which was the third-largest at the meeting. B'nai B'rith leaders were active on the Executive Committee.

In its four years of existence, the Conference set up machinery that saved an indeterminate number of Jews from death, helped inspire the postwar reconstruction of European Jewish life, and acted as a spur to public opinion in connection with the 1947 United Nations decision to partition Palestine into Jewish and Arab states. It is impossible to determine the extent of the Conference's influence in these matters, but one thing is certain: it represented the most solid unity ever achieved in American Jewish history. It did not last for the same reason that all its predecessors died: because elements within it demanded that it become a monolithic superbody in American Jewry, a single voice to speak for all Jews on all matters.

B'nai B'rith's one hundredth anniversary arrived on October 13, 1943—right in the middle of the war. The 1941 Convention had authorized a great celebration of the event in New York, where the Order had been born, but with all the carnage and tragedy in Europe and the Far East, it was no time for celebration. The event was therefore not observed, except that *The National Jewish Monthly* published a special centennial issue. At that time, it was estimated that in its century of operation, B'nai B'rith had spent $20,000,000 on charitable institutions and community welfare programs; $10,000,000 on education, youth welfare, and citizenship work; and $5,000,000 on war relief, refugees, and the Red Cross.

President Monsky engaged Emil Ludwig, the biographer, to write a history of B'nai B'rith in connection with the centennial. But Dr. Ludwig knew absolutely nothing about the organization or about Jewish life—and cared less—and accepted the assignment solely for the large fee. As a result, the draft of his first three chapters were so unacceptable that Mr. Monsky canceled the agreement, and that was the last time the organization ever attempted the project.

The war ended the existence of B'nai B'rith on the Continent. Gone were the District Grand Lodges of Germany, Austria, Poland, Czechoslovakia, Bulgaria, and Yugoslavia. The Order remained in Great Britain and Palestine, as well as Egypt, but it was a mere holding action there.

But at home it continued to surge ahead both in size and activities. In the spring of 1943 the magic figure of 100,000 American male members was reached. The women's chapters grew, too, and the Women's Supreme Council was authorized to establish a national organization of B'nai B'rith Girls. By the beginning of 1944 there were 12,000 such girls, and the youth movement was reorganized. A B'nai B'rith Youth Organization was created, consisting of AZA and BBG, with provision for any other youth agencies that might be created. As it happened, after the war two such agencies were formed, for young people above high-school age: the BB Young Men, and the BB Young Women, but they proved cumbersome, and were combined into mixed chapters called BB

Young Adults, which have since been an integral part of the B'nai B'rith Youth Organization.

The 1944 Supreme Lodge Convention in New York was called a War Service Convention. It was obvious then that the war would be over soon, and there was much talk about the problems of returning servicemen and the changes likely to take place in Jewish life.

But most of the excitement at the convention was caused by the Zionist issue. At its January meeting the Executive Committee had voted for B'nai B'rith to remain in the American Jewish Conference (the American Jewish Committee had dropped out in protest against the Conference's stand in favor of a Jewish Commonwealth in Palestine). President Monsky was known to be an ardent Zionist, and some delegates pressed hard for B'nai B'rith to pass a resolution of its own demanding an independent Jewish state in Palestine. Several resolutions to that effect were transmitted to the resolutions committee. The non-Zionists and anti-Zionists were fearful they would be passed, because it was obvious the Zionists had enough votes. If the convention had passed a political Zionist resolution, it would have split B'nai B'rith wide open, with results that could only have been damaging, even critically so. Mr. Monsky was pressured from both sides. Once more he displayed his statesmanship. Appearing before the resolutions committee, he reiterated the Order's traditionally neutral policy, and issued this statement concerning the pro-Zionist resolutions:

> The adoption or defeat of these resolutions would be contrary to this principle. I would ask that, because in the membership of B'nai B'rith there are divergent opinions on ideological and political issues, and because B'nai B'rith recognizes the right of each member

to determine his own attitude on any such issues, B'nai
B'rith as an organization takes no position either for or
against the above-mentioned resolutions.

This statement was approved by the convention. It
satisfied the opponents of the resolutions, and their advocates were consoled by the fact that B'nai B'rith was
remaining in the American Jewish Conference, which
had come out for a Jewish State.

The convention's most colorful session took place
with 3,000 people jammed into Carnegie Hall, where the
Order's one hundredth anniversary was belatedly celebrated. Mrs. Eleanor Roosevelt read a stirring message
from the President, and B'nai B'rith's Honorary President Alfred M. Cohen dedicated a service flag in honor
of the 22,000 members who, at that time, were in the
Armed Forces.

The ADL and Hillel Commissions were reorganized
and enlarged; the new B'nai B'rith Youth and Vocational
Service Commissions were given constitutional status;
and the Constitution was amended to permit the president of the Women's Supreme Council and one representative from each Women's Grand Lodge to attend Supreme Lodge conventions, with voice but no vote. Mr.
Monsky was, of course, unanimously reelected.

The same year he was among those who laid the
groundwork for the founding of the National Community Relations Advisory Council (NCRAC). There had
been steadily mounting criticism in the American Jewish community that many organizations engaged in
fighting anti-Semitism and doing human relations work
were wastefully duplicating one another's activities, and
that there should be only one superagency in the field.
But Mr. Monsky knew that coercion was not the American way, and that all Jews did not think alike and had

different approaches to the same problems. His view prevailed, and when the NCRAC was established, it was just what its name indicated—an advisory and coordinating body of autonomous groups.

B'nai B'rith had long been interested in the United Nations, and when that agency formally organized at its 1945 conference in San Francisco, Mr. Monsky attended as a consultant to the American delegation. Together with other Jewish leaders, he played a central role in the united effort to convince UN leaders that the existing rights of the Jewish people with respect to Palestine be strictly safeguarded. This could be done only indirectly, since territorial questions were not on the agenda. But the united Jewish leadership group convinced the Trusteeship Committee to reject an Egyptian amendment which would have stripped the Jewish community in Palestine of international protection, and to pass, instead, a provision guaranteeing the rights of "any states or any peoples" living under "existing international instruments"—such as the British Mandate over Palestine.

A beginning was made, as soon as the war was over, to pick up the pieces of the shattered Order in Europe—but that was a long, difficult job. Dr. Baeck, in an article in *The National Jewish Monthly*, urged that lodges be formed again on the Continent, and even in Germany, if possible. He revealed that the B'nai B'rith property in Germany seized by the Nazis amounted to the staggering sum of 15,000,000 marks, and that B'nai B'rith should be compensated to that extent, to "serve the cause of Jewry."

B'nai B'rith could do nothing about that until the West German Government was established, in 1949, but it did plan to organize lodges again in Europe. As early as April, 1945, before the war there was quite ended, the president was authorized to spend up to $5,000 for organizational work on the Continent. A B'nai B'rith European Aid Committee had already been organized, which sent packages of food and clothing to stricken members in those parts of Europe already liberated from the Nazis, and tens of thousands of dollars were allocated to that program, which still continues, although on a reduced scale today. In April, 1945, the Executive Committee also pledged $25,000 to the building fund of the Weizmann Institute in Palestine.

Before and even during the war, the Hillel Foundations had had a program to aid refugee students who managed to reach the United States, arranging for them to live free at Jewish fraternity houses on American campuses, helping them get tuition scholarships, and making it possible for hundreds of them to graduate and become American citizens. After the war this program was continued, at a substantial cost. Another postwar effort was aimed at helping people in the Displaced Persons camps in Europe; President Monsky was a member of the Citizens' Committee on Displaced Persons.

Late in 1945, the BB Youth Organization was reorganized, with Dr. Sachar becoming its national director while retaining his post as national Hillel director. He left B'nai B'rith service in 1947 and the following year became the first president of the new Brandeis University. After an interim period, Dr. Max F. Baer, national director of the Vocational Service Bureau, while retaining that post, also became national BBYO director. In 1954, when a full-time Vocational Service director was engaged, Dr. Baer devoted full time as BBYO director, and still does.

All these actions were part of a continually expanding network of services, and although by September, 1945, there were 163,000 men in B'nai B'rith, and more than 70,000 women (who, however, pay no dues of any kind to the Supreme Lodge), it was obvious that the programs Mr. Monsky had in mind could not be supported from dues income, even supplemented by Wider Scope campaigns. He looked far into the future, and saw the need for a huge fund, the interest of which could help support the work of the Order. He therefore revived the idea of a B'nai B'rith Foundation, which the 1941 convention had approved, and he was authorized to take the necessary legal steps to create it.

The swift and steady growth of all B'nai B'rith departments continued. In 1946, Mrs. Arthur G. Laufman, a past national president of the Women's Supreme Council, became its first professional director. Another milestone was reached that year when the National Advisory Committee of the Veterans Administration Voluntary Service formally appointed B'nai B'rith, because of its work among hospitalized veterans, as a member agency, along with the American Legion, Red Cross, USO, and other organizations. During the same year B'nai B'rith was represented at the first National Conference on Citizenship and has been affiliated ever since. At about that time, the Dutch Government cited the Order—the only Jewish organization so honored—for its extensive aid to the Dutch people, in the form of food, clothing, and medical supplies. And early in 1947 B'nai B'rith organized a program to help physically handicapped people find jobs, although this caught on in only a few areas.

By the middle of 1946, with a men's membership of 190,000, the organization engaged a national membership director. There had been none since 1938—perhaps because, as more than one cynic put it, "Hitler was our Membership Director." But 10,000 of the 190,000 were still in the Armed Forces, paying no dues, and many of them, it was anticipated, would never return to active affiliation. Henry Monsky wanted a quarter million members by the 1947 Supreme Lodge convention.

But he did not live to attend that convention. On May 2, at the age of fifty-seven, while he was in New York presiding at an important session of an American Jewish Conference committee, he died suddenly, of a heart attack.

Nine days later a shocked and grieving Supreme Lodge opened its triennial meeting in Washington. Frank Goldman, of Lowell, Massachusetts, one of the three vice presidents, served as acting president. A beloved former vice president, Louis Fabricant of New York, died during the convention, which held memorial services for him and Henry Monsky, as well as for Sigmund Livingston, founder of the Anti-Defamation League, who had died the year before.

Even in the atmosphere of mourning, the delegates took several important actions. In a resolution they demanded the abrogation of the British white paper and called upon the United Nations "to facilitate the establishment of a homeland for Jewish people in Palestine." Since an effort was going to be made at the next meeting of the American Jewish Conference to convert it into a new and permanent body, the convention empowered a Committee of Sixty-Three, representing all seven American Districts and the entire Executive Committee, to determine the Order's course with reference to such a new organization.

The delegates also set up a National Finance Council to direct and coordinate all B'nai B'rith fund-raising (except that of the ADL, which raised funds jointly with the American Jewish Committee) and changed the now meaningless name of Wider Scope to B'nai B'rith National Youth Service Appeal. They urged the Executive Committee to create a bureau in Washington to promote B'nai B'rith growth in Latin America. And they amended the Constitution to give the Women's Supreme Council, under its own constitution, "jurisdiction over its District Grand Lodges and chapters."

Henry Monsky had been so dominating a personality that he had taken on the chairmanship of most of the Order's commissions—not because he relished the extra work and responsibility, but because he considered them so important that he could not bring himself to entrust their direction to anyone else. But now all that changed. Dr. Sachar succeeded him as chairman of the Hillel Commission, and J. J. Lieberman of Los Angeles succeeded him as chairman of the Youth Commission.

The convention heard reports on the growing need for a B'nai B'rith youth camp, where BBYO and Hillel conventions, meetings, and leadership training sessions could be held, and authorized the acquisition of such a camp, if funds could be found. The delegates also agreed that the first European B'nai B'rith office should be established, to rebuild the Order on the Continent. Such an office was opened in Paris by the end of 1948, headed by Saul Joftes, and during the following decade the organization was slowly revived throughout Europe.

It was announced that the men's membership stood at 194,000; the BB Women numbered 95,000; there were 165 Hillel units on campuses with 90,000 Jewish students; and there were 29,000 boys and girls in the Youth Organization. Lodges functioned in 22 countries.

Frank Goldman was elected president without opposition.

A few months after the convention, the Executive

Committee decided to create the kind of foundation Henry Monsky had wanted, and called it the B'nai B'rith–Henry Monsky Foundation.

Frank Goldman, who was born in Lowell, Massachusetts, and had been practicing law there since 1912, had long been one of Mr. Monsky's most trusted lieutenants, first as president of District No. 1 and later as a vice president of the Order. He was as dedicated a Zionist as Henry Monsky had been, but was less inhibited concerning B'nai B'rith's policy on the subject. In September, 1947, when it became known that the majority report of a United Nations Special Committee on Palestine (UNSCOP) was going to recommend the partition of the country into a Jewish and an Arab state, Mr. Goldman— with the consent of the Executive Committee—sent a wire to President Truman, stating that B'nai B'rith "appeals to you for immediate public statement supporting the principle of UNSCOP majority." This was the first time in its history that B'nai B'rith officially endorsed what was clearly an outright Zionist position. The anti-Zionists in B'nai B'rith complained, and a few resigned, but by that time American Jewish sentiment was so overwhelmingly in favor of Jewish statehood in Palestine that the opposition was meaningless.

President Goldman was in Chicago, attending the last session of the American Jewish Conference, on November 29, when news came that the UNSCOP majority report had been adopted. He and every other Jewish leader present, representing virtually all major Jewish organizations in the United States, publicly hailed the step and rejoiced at the turn of events.

At that session of the conference the delegates voted to form a new and permanent organization, with wide powers, including "the American scene," to be called the

American Jewish Assembly. But the biggest organizations refused to join it, and the following March the Committee of Sixty-Three unanimously voted against B'nai B'rith's affiliation. The new agency was still-born.

Few Jews in the 1940's had expected to see an independent Jewish state in their lifetime, and interest in the partition of Palestine crowded most other items off the Jewish agenda. In 1946 and 1947, B'nai B'rith members in New York City, acting as individuals, under the leadership of Lester Gutterman, the Order's national membership chairman, raised more than $50,000 for the Haganah, the defense organization of Palestine Jewry, which later became the nucleus of the Israeli Army.

But Jewish rejoicing over the UNSCOP vote was soon followed by grave concern. The Arab states rejected partition, and riots ensued. The important middle levels of the U. S. State Department, always bitterly opposed to Jewish statehood and sympathetic to Arab interests, succeeded in changing American policy at the United Nations, and early in 1948 the American delegate proposed that partition be shelved and replaced by a United Nations trusteeship—which would have postponed Jewish independence for perhaps a generation or more. Hundreds of thousands of Jews languishing in Europe's Displaced Persons camps, after having suffered through the Nazi nightmare, were about to lose their cherished hopes of finding peace and a new life at last, and hundreds of thousands more defied England's ban on immigration into Palestine and traveled there anyway, on overcrowded and unseaworthy ships—some of which sank, while others were intercepted by British destroyers and the anguished passengers were herded into internment camps on Cyprus. Arab attacks on Jews in Palestine killed and wounded large numbers in January and February, and for a time it seemed that the United Nations would actually reverse itself on its partition vote, largely due to American influence.

The Zionist leadership in the United States attacked the White House so bitterly for its "betrayal" that even President Truman lost patience with it. The word got out that the White House door was bolted against all Zionist leaders, and it is a fact that although many knocked, none was admitted. Meanwhile the United Nations halted all partition implementation measures. During this period, however, the president and secretary of B'nai B'rith had an audience with Mr. Truman. It had no visible effect, however, and President Goldman called on the lodges and chapters to express themselves by letters to Mr. Truman and the United Nations.

At this critical juncture, B'nai B'rith was able to make an important contribution which broke the logjam. Dr. Chaim Weizmann, internationally famous scientist and head of the World Zionist Organization, although he was over seventy and ill, came to the United States to make a personal appeal to President Truman. While he lay bedridden in a New York hotel, American Zionist leaders again tried to make an appointment for him at the White House. But President Truman refused.

It came to Frank Goldman's knowledge that one of the President's oldest and dearest friends was an Eddie Jacobson, of Kansas City, Missouri. He got in touch with A. J. Granoff of Kansas City, a prominent attorney and a past president of District No. 2. It turned out that Mr. Granoff was Mr. Jacobson's attorney, and he gladly introduced his client to the president of B'nai B'rith. Mr. Jacobson told him he was not a Zionist, and that B'nai B'rith was the only Jewish organization to which he be-

longed. He had been Harry Truman's close buddy in the
Army during World War I, had served in the same artillery unit with him in France, and after the war he and
Mr. Truman had been partners in a Kansas City haber-
dashery. He was so close to the President that all he had
to do to see him in the White House was to come to
Washington, call up, and immediately be invited to
"come on over, Eddie."

Eddie Jacobson had never abused the privilege. He
and the President merely enjoyed each other's company,
and saw each other frequently. But when Frank Goldman explained the situation, and asked Mr. Jacobson if
he would urge the President merely to grant Dr. Weizmann an appointment—without making any commit-
ment—Mr. Jacobson was reluctant. He said he knew
nothing about politics, or Palestine, or Zionism, or the
issues involved. But he agreed to try after B'nai B'rith's
president assured him he would receive a thorough
briefing on the facts.

When Eddie Jacobson walked into President Truman's office soon after, he was greeted with a big smile.
But the President became grim when his friend brought
up the subject of Dr. Weizmann. He said he was sick of
the way the Zionists had badgered and unjustly condemned him. It took all of Eddie Jacobson's friendship
and persuasive powers, but he finally induced Mr. Truman to arrange a secret meeting with the Zionist leader.
Elaborate precautions were taken to conceal Dr. Weizmann's presence in Washington from the press. He used
a suite at a Washington hotel which had been reserved
in the name of B'nai B'rith's secretary, Maurice Bisgyer,
and Dr. Weizmann entered the White House through a
rear entrance.

As anticipated, he won the President's confidence

completely. American policy at the United Nations changed again, in favor of its original action on Palestine, and on May 15, ten minutes after a Jewish State was officially proclaimed there, President Truman granted it *de facto* recognition, swiftly followed by the Soviet Union and many other nations.

And on January 31, 1949, when President Truman extended *de jure* recognition to Israel, the only invited guests in his office were Eddie Jacobson and the president and secretary of B'nai B'rith. After the ceremony, the President gave each of them one of the pens he had used.

This whole story remained untold for nearly twenty years, out of deference to both Mr. Truman and Mr. Jacobson. But in May, 1965, at the Supreme Lodge convention in Israel, when the auditorium in the new B'nai B'rith Building in Tel Aviv was dedicated to the memory of Eddie Jacobson, A. J. Granoff was there, and he read a message from Harry S. Truman:

> I always felt very comfortable in Eddie's presence
> . . . I trusted him implicitly. I never knew him to ask
> for anything that was either improper or for selfish
> motives. And when the day came when Eddie Jacobson
> was persuaded to forego his natural reluctance to peti-
> tion me, and he came to talk to me about the plight of
> the Jews and the struggles confronting the State of
> Israel, then being formed, I paid careful attention. Al-
> though my sympathies were already active and present
> in the cause of the State of Israel, it is a fact of history
> that Eddie Jacobson's contribution was of decisive im-
> portance. He deserves all the recognition that he is now
> receiving, and his name should be forever enshrined
> in the history of the Jewish people.

No sooner had Israel proclaimed its independence than the armies of five Arab nations invaded it. But even before the fighting ended, B'nai B'rith launched a campaign among its lodges and chapters to collect food, clothing, medical supplies, trucks, jeeps, and other non-military heavy equipment which the people of Israel needed desperately. So euphoric was American Jewry over Israel's independence that in less than a year B'nai B'rith was able to send ship after ship to Haifa, loaded with these supplies, which had a total value of well over $4,000,000.

The birth of modern Israel deeply stirred Jews everywhere, but one cannot dance in the streets every night. There was much for B'nai B'rith to do, and it did much. By 1949 there were 190 Hillel units, 18 metropolitan Vocational Service offices, 18 regional ADL offices, and hundreds of BBYO chapters. In the four years since 1945, the Order's program on behalf of Veterans' Hospitals had provided 2,515 pieces of equipment to those institutions—such substantial items as collapsible wheelchairs, record players, bedside radios, musical instruments, occupational therapy equipment, and many others. The B'nai B'rith Women numbered 114,000, and during 1948–49 they raised the astonishing sum of $754,000 for B'nai B'rith activities, as well as $90,000 for civic projects.

The B'nai B'rith–Henry Monsky Foundation was formally launched in the spring of 1949; it sought $2,000,-000, with which its sponsors fondly hoped they could erect a B'nai B'rith Building in Washington for the Supreme Lodge, buy a large camp, and establish a Hillel Foundation at Hebrew University in Jerusalem. In this they were overoptimistic; they raised nowhere near the quota, and the Supreme Lodge building was not constructed until 1957, and then only after an intensive fund campaign. Camp B'nai B'rith was bought in 1953, after the B'nai B'rith Home for Orphans in Erie, Pennsylvania, having closed, transferred its assets of nearly $200,000 to the Monsky Foundation. And although a Hillel Foundation was indeed opened in Jerusalem in 1950, it was financed by restitution funds from the West German Government.

Early in 1949 the lodges in France, Switzerland, Holland, Belgium, Denmark, Sweden, and England sent representatives to a conference in Paris, where a B'nai B'rith European Committee was organized, with Dr. Baeck as chairman. Out of this developed District No. 19, chartered in 1955, and consisting of the free countries on the Continent. It was numbered 19 because the numbers of the Districts that had perished were retired forever, as a gesture of respect and tribute.

In 1949, too, B'nai B'rith joined with the British Board of Jewish Deputies and the South African Board of Jewish Deputies to form the Coordinating Board of Jewish Organizations (CBJO). It soon achieved consultative status before the United Nations Economic and Social Council. In this capacity it conducted research, presented resolutions and factual documents on human welfare to ECOSOC, and helped promote public support for the United Nations.

At the end of 1949, the B'nai B'rith Women launched a campaign for $100,000 to build an institution for maladjusted children in Israel. Six years before, Henrietta Szold had approached the Palestine lodges with the suggestion that such a home be built, when thousands of Jewish children, most of them orphans and emotionally overwrought by the horrors they had experienced in Europe, were being brought to Palestine. The lodges had had no money, but they rented quarters and took in as many youngsters as possible. Later, the children were cared for in the B'nai B'rith immigrants' hostel, but that building had been damaged by Arab fire during the war for independence, and a new structure was needed, with proper facilities and trained teachers and staff. During those six years the American B'nai B'rith Women raised funds for the institution, sometimes as much as $15,000 a year, sometimes less, but now, in 1949, they determined to take over the entire project. During the 1950's they built, and still maintain, a magnificent childrens' home, staffed by experts, outside Jerusalem.

At the same time, B'nai B'rith undertook to fill a new need: providing recreation rooms, fully furnished, for Israeli war veterans, especially those in hospitals. Until B'nai B'rith brought these institutions into being, the disabled Israeli veterans had had only the crudest kind of recreational facilities.

Thus ended one of the most eventful decades in modern Jewish history, and in B'nai B'rith history, too.

18

.

1950–1953: Rise in activity, decline in size

By 1950 American Jews, even more than other Americans, were emotionally exhausted. Those over thirty-five had lived through the great economic depression, the prewar years of growing tension, World War II, the Nazi nightmare and the organized murder of six million Jews, the disheartening efforts to rescue the survivors, the campaign against the British white paper, the postwar letdown, and finally the historic re-creation of the State of Israel and the war with the Arabs that followed. How much could one absorb?

Besides, the era of unprecedented prosperity had

begun, and it was pleasant, after all the horrors and strenuous work, to relax and enjoy it. It was more fun to watch Milton Berle on TV than attend a lodge meeting. B'nai B'rith's many-sided program was fine, but let the eager beavers carry it on. Most of the members had always been mere dues-payers; they continued to pay, but they did not want to be bothered with committee work or anything else. And many even stopped paying dues. Was Israel not a state, its war of independence won? Was not organized anti-Semitism at its lowest ebb in generations? Wasn't Hitler dead? Was there not a renaissance of "religion"? Were not new congregations springing up everywhere, with synagogue memberships and religious school enrollments reaching new records? Wasn't prosperity becoming universal in America, and wasn't it a panacea for all ills?

Thus, when it was announced in 1949 that B'nai B'rith had finally reached a membership of 200,000 men in the United States and Canada, for the first time in its history, many people were surprised—especially some B'nai B'rith leaders. And no wonder—because it was not true. At one time in 1949 there were, indeed, 203,000 men's names on the roster, but investigation revealed that more than 8,000 of them in District No. 3 alone were "dead wood" and had to be pruned. In 1950 the true figure was 190,000, which, however, was impressive enough. But it began to decline.

Money was more difficult to raise, too. People had more of it than ever before, but it bought less, with taxes and prices both rising.

Succeeding events were to show that 1948 had been, in many ways, the peak year for American Jewry. Not only did it mark Israel's rebirth, but also the time when organizations were at an all-time high in membership, and neither before nor since did American Jews raise the immense sums, for all causes, that were collected and disbursed in those twelve months.

Consequently, the mood at the Nineteenth General Convention in Washington in 1950, at least among the leaders, was one of deep concern, although not pessimism. B'nai B'rith's programs represented moral commitments, and the money and manpower to meet them simply had to be found.

The convention was a social success, with UN Secretary General Trygve Lie and Vice President Alben Barkley among the guest speakers, and visitors who included the top echelon of Washington celebrities. The resolutions that were passed dealt with the leading issues of the day: demands that the UN stop the flow of Communist arms to the Arabs; that the Displaced Persons Act be liberalized; that civil-rights laws be passed and anti-Negro discrimination ended; and that decent housing be provided for all. A testimonial dinner was held in honor of Eddie Jacobson.

There was a sensation when it was announced that the two hundredth Hillel unit would be established at Hebrew University in the fall. The successful progress of the B'nai B'rith Women was recognized when they were given three seats on the Order's Executive Committee, with voice, vote, and expenses, and in addition all the officers of the Women's Supreme Council and one member from each Women's District were granted full delegate status at Supreme Lodge conventions.

A new national program took root at the convention. In 1948, led by a brilliant and dedicated young attorney, Maurice Weinstein of Charlotte, a small group of B'nai B'rith members in North Carolina organized the first B'nai B'rith Institute of Judaism. They met under the guidance of two rabbis for several days, isolated from the world, atop a privately owned mountain called Wild-acres, and studied the ancient and modern texts and wisdom of Judaism. They repeated the experiment the following summer, with a larger attendance, and were so enthusiastic over its success that Mr. Weinstein brought the project to the attention of the Supreme Lodge in 1950. The convention liked it, and asked the president to create a permanent committee to encourage Institutes throughout the Order.

This was done, and although adult Jewish education has never attracted more than a tiny percentage of the membership, it was felt to be so important, potentially, that the 1959 Supreme Lodge Convention created the Adult Jewish Education Commission, which now not only directs Institutes but a number of small study and discussion groups in lodges and chapters, as well as the publication of books, magazines, and shorter resource material for adult students. Mr. Weinstein was the first chairman.

Philip M. Klutznick ran against Frank Goldman for the presidency and lost, but everyone knew he would win the next election.

President Goldman's second term was marked by some solid achievements. The leadership of the Order refused to be panicked by the reactionary hysteria created by Senator Joseph McCarthy, and late in 1950 both the Executive Committee and the ADL, instead of passing new and frenetic resolutions denouncing communism, pointed out that as long ago as 1938 the Supreme Lodge Convention had formally denounced communism, and they reaffirmed that resolution. A year later, when the ADL conferred its America's Democratic Legacy

Award upon Senator Herbert H. Lehman, he charged in his response that "the forces gathered under the banner of the McCarthy brand of anti-Communism are among the most vicious in America today." Moreover, the ADL was able to help disprove McCarthy's charges of communism brought against a number of innocent people.

As soon as the Korean War broke out, Mr. Goldman pledged President Truman the full support of the organization. A B'nai B'rith Service Committee for Armed Forces and Veterans (SCAFV) was organized, to continue the postwar work in Veterans' Hospitals, and also to serve Armed Forces personnel. An appeal for a dollar a member brought in enough funds for many major activities, and a year after the war began Gen. George C. Marshall, Secretary of Defense, praised the Order's war efforts in a public statement. Under the SCAFV program, countless packs of cigarettes and scores of thousands of paperback books were shipped direct to the battlefronts; community farewell parties for draftees were sponsored; Buddy Bags, filled with useful items, were given the departing troops; servicemen's centers were again established at ports, as during World War II; lodges and chapters were stimulated to give blood to the Red Cross; and the programs in Veterans' Hospitals were intensified.

Soon after the 1950 Convention, Mr. Goldman went to Europe for a meeting of the Coordinating Board of Jewish Organizations. He took with him Col. Bernard Bernstein, whom he had engaged as the first director of a new B'nai B'rith UN liaison office. Later the same year B'nai B'rith launched a new "package program" for Israel: the construction of a $50,000 Rehabilitation Center at a Tel Aviv hospital for disabled Israeli war veterans; the Children's Home near Jerusalem, sponsored by the women; and the Hillel Foundation at Hebrew University.

A few weeks later Mr. Goldman headed a B'nai B'rith delegation of fifty men and women at a National Planning Conference for Israel and Jewish Rehabilitation, in Washington. More than half a million refugees had poured into Israel since 1948, and the tiny nation faced a real financial crisis. The Conference determined to help Israel get a billion dollars—through loans or grants from the United States, an intensified United Jewish Appeal drive, more private investment, and the sale of Israel Bonds if and when issued. President Goldman joined with heads of other organizations in meeting with President Truman on the loans-or-grants program. And in the spring of 1951, when Israel first issued its Bonds, their sale became so popular throughout the Order that in the following fifteen years the organization was credited with the stupendous sale of $80,000,000 worth—far more than that of any other organization, including Zionist groups.

Intensified work—in the face of a slowly declining membership—required increased income from somewhere, and in 1951 the Order created its Service Fund to support the three youth agencies—Hillel, BBYO, and Vocational Service. Each District Service Fund was assigned a quota, as well as each lodge (the women's chapters continued to raise funds in a program of their own). The lodges raised their funds in a variety of ways. Although the whole effort was voluntary and rarely resulted in fulfilled quotas, additional funds were raised, and the Service Fund technique is still used.

Two other important developments took place in 1951. Under the leadership of Dr. Nahum Goldmann, president of the Jewish Agency, a concerted movement was begun to demand financial restitution from West Germany for the Nazi theft of Jewish property. A Conference on Jewish Material Claims Against Germany was organized, with all major Jewish organizations represented. President Goldman was named to its five-man presidium. The Conference emphasized that only God could forgive the German people for their crimes against the Jews, but that it was only simple justice for Germany to return to the survivors what its Government had stolen during the 1930's and 1940's. Since the actual survivors of the death camps were relatively few, the principle was established that Germany should make restitution to the State of Israel, where so many had settled, and to organizations working for European Jewish welfare—in addition to claims made by individual survivors. As the result of the work of the Conference, Germany paid, between 1952 and 1966, more than $700,-000,000 to Israel in ships, factories, and other needed goods, and about $115,000,000 to the Conference, which allocated it to a multitude of institutions serving European Jews, both in Europe and other lands where they had fled.

Before 1951 ended, a great internal struggle began within the National Community Relations Advisory Council. The Jewish press and a number of individual leaders and organizations had been agitating against alleged "waste and duplication" in Jewish defense agencies, and demanding that the NCRAC put an end to it. The agency engaged Prof. Robert M. MacIver of Columbia University to study the problem. His report recommended that the NCRAC stop being merely "advisory" and become an "over-all" agency in the human-relations field, allocating various functions to its constituent organizations. The American Jewish Committee and the Anti-Defamation League of B'nai B'rith were the only agencies operating wholly in the field; other national Jewish organizations had in recent years added defense work to their programs, but their main emphasis was elsewhere.

The Committee and the ADL objected strenuously to the MacIver recommendations, and the running battle continued well into 1952. The two agencies, which had been in the field for nearly half a century, pointed out that the MacIver plan would actually cause more duplication and expense—since the newer agencies had little experience in the work and would have to acquire immense new resources and experienced manpower to do the job. The other NCRAC agencies, however, were adamant in insisting upon implementation of the MacIver Report, and in 1952 the Committee and the ADL withdrew from the body. Periodical efforts were made to induce them to rejoin, but it was not until 1965, when the NCRAC agreed with all the arguments it had rejected in 1952, that the ADL rejoined.

Two extraordinary emergencies in 1953 elicited help from the Order's Emergency Relief Fund. After the worst European flood in five centuries had devastated large parts of Holland, Belgium, and Great Britain, B'nai B'rith sent $20,000 to a fund for the victims. And so many refugees from communism had fled from East into West Berlin that a million-dollar fund was raised to help care for them, and B'nai B'rith contributed $5,000.

Two months later, in April, Frank Goldman became the first B'nai B'rith president ever to visit Palestine, or Israel. He conferred there with top Government officials, as well as with B'nai B'rith leaders, and visited all the Order's installations and activities.

During the same month the lodges in Latin America sent delegates to Santiago, Chile, where they formed a B'nai B'rith Latin American Committee, which in 1957 evolved into District No. 20, covering all the countries from Mexico down to Argentina.

But although the B'nai B'rith record was impressive during the early 1950's, the growing apathy of large numbers of American Jews caused the Order to shrink in size. The roster stood at 190,000 in 1950, declined to 184,000 the following year, plunged to 181,000 in 1952, and then slid to 178,000 by the time of the 1953 Supreme Lodge Convention.

19

■

1953–1959: One achievement after another

Just as the most important action of the 1938 Convention had been the election of a new president, Henry Monsky, so the most important convention action in 1953 was the unopposed election of Philip M. Klutznick. He was (and is) one of the most remarkable members in the organization.

He was the first AZA alumnus to head the Order, and its first president born in the twentieth century. Although only forty-five when elected, he had been associated with B'nai B'rith for twenty-nine years—ever since he became a charter member of AZA's second chapter in his native Kansas City, Missouri, in 1924. The following year he won the youth organization's national debating championship and was elected its second national president. A year later Sam Beber asked him to come to Omaha and be AZA's first staff executive—although the job was only part-time and the salary was a pittance—while he attended Creighton University law school. He and Sam Beber married sisters and became law partners. When Beber retired in 1941 as president of the AZA Supreme Advisory Council, Klutznick succeeded him. But before that he served for a year as president of B'nai B'rith's District No. 6.

Even as a young lawyer in Omaha he had been interested in public housing. By 1944 President Roosevelt appointed him Commissioner of the Federal Public Housing Authority, in which post President Truman continued him and gave him a citation upon his retirement in 1946. After the war Phil (as thousands of people called him then and still call him now) became president of a group of companies that built whole communities, of which the most notable was Park Forest, Illinois. The acquisition of wealth enabled him to devote most of his time to what he loved best—public service. He was nationally active in many causes, and after he retired from the presidency of B'nai B'rith, President Kennedy named him a United States Representative to the United Nations, with the rank of Ambassador.

A practical idealist, he felt that B'nai B'rith, despite its multitude of achievements, was capable of doing much, much more, and he came to its leadership champing at the bit to get started. He was the first president to give practically full time to the office, and that practice has become a job qualification ever since.

The convention changed the name of the Executive

Committee to the Board of Governors. The Central Administrative Board became the Administrative Committee, and the Preamble to the Constitution was belatedly changed to "B'nai B'rith has taken upon itself the mission of uniting persons of the Jewish faith," instead of ". . . Israelites." The national Membership Commission was replaced by a National Membership Cabinet, and the National Finance Council became the Fund Campaign Cabinet. But these were only changes in form.

More substantial was an increase in the powers of the Administrative Committee. A two-term limitation on all elected members of the Board of Governors was also voted, as well as a number of less important changes. All of them had been recommended by a Committee on Structure, headed by Phil Klutznick.

From 1947 to 1949 Klutznick had been a member of the Order's Executive Committee, and he had urged that B'nai B'rith, instead of conducting its programs on behalf of Israel in an unrelated fashion, should create one agency for them. The 1953 Convention agreed, and authorized the Board of Governors to establish a B'nai B'rith Israel Committee "for the purpose of initiating, directing, supervising, and coordinating programs, projects, and activities of the Order pertaining to Israel." Nine years later it was raised to Commission status. Morris Alexander, of Chicago, was the first chairman of the Committee and continued chairman of the Commission until he retired in 1965.

Vice President Richard Nixon was principal speaker at the convention banquet, and President Eisenhower sent a warm message of greetings. After the convention, Mr. Klutznick and a small group of other B'nai B'rith leaders called on him at the White House.

Phil Klutznick's first major project as president was

something none of his predecessors had done: he set out on a series of "grass-roots" visits to all parts of the country, meeting with members of hundreds of lodges and chapters. Later he visited B'nai B'rith in other countries —in Europe, Israel, and Latin America.

Soon after his election he reorganized the B'nai B'rith United Nations Liaison Committee, with Honorary President Frank Goldman as chairman. It became part of the program of the Order's professionally directed Department of International Affairs, which was created in Washington at the same time, and was directed by Saul Joftes.

He also turned his attention to the new adult Jewish education program. Realizing that merely giving it a name and a blessing meant little, he induced the Administrative Committee to provide a budget for professional direction, and Rabbi Harold Weisberg became the first director.

A choice corner property was bought at 17th Street and Rhode Island Avenue, on which it was planned to construct the B'nai B'rith Building as soon as funds became available. Hard on the heels of this purchase a beautiful three-hundred-acre camp was bought in the Pocono Mountains at Starlight, Pennsylvania, near the New York State line. All this took place before the end of 1953.

In November of that year, the ADL celebrated its fortieth anniversary in Washington. The highlight was a banquet tendered by the Order's Board of Governors, called "Dinner with the President." President Eisenhower had dinner with the Board, the ADL Commission, and a thousand guests, and spent the evening with them. The ADL gave him its America's Democratic Legacy Award; the brightest stars of stage and screen entertained, and the program was seen by forty million people via television.

Early in 1954, on the recommendation of the Committee for Israel, a new project was launched—a B'nai B'rith Martyrs' Forest in Israel. The plan was to plant a half million trees in memory of the B'nai B'rith men and women who had perished in Nazi Europe. Lodges, chapters, and individuals bought the trees at $1.50 each (later at $2), and they were planted by the Jewish National Fund, which also erected a cavelike sanctuary, hewn out of solid rock, in which the names of the dead were listed. The half million trees were all planted by the time the Supreme Lodge held its 1965 Convention in Israel, and it was voted to plant another half million.

In 1954, the failure of "denazification" in Germany, and ominous reports that neo-Nazi groups were forming there, led the Bonn Government to invite the ADL to send a delegation of its staff experts, at Germany's expense, on a four-week study tour of the country, under the America Exchange Program. It was Germany's first invitation to a Jewish defense agency, and the ADL submitted a detailed series of recommendations to Bonn after the study was completed.

Another important development of the year was the formation of a Conference of Presidents of Major American Jewish Organizations, known popularly as the Presidents' Conference. It met informally and limited its scope to matters concerning Israel and how it might be helpful. Its first major action was to send a delegation, headed by President Klutznick, to confer with Secretary of State John Foster Dulles and urge the United States not to send arms to the Arabs, as was being contemplated, until they ended their open threats to destroy Israel. Since then the Presidents' Conference has broadened its scope and employed a more formal technique of voluntary unity in American Jewish organizational life. Mr. Klutznick was elected its first chairman.

In June, 1954, Camp B'nai B'rith opened, sponsored by the Monsky Foundation, and several thousand youths and adults held meetings there. In addition, a regular camping season was enjoyed by hundreds of younger children. Several years later the administration of Camp B'nai B'rith was transferred to the BB Youth Organization.

In August the camp was formally dedicated during a session there of the Administrative Committee. The United States Supreme Court had rendered its decision outlawing segregation in public schools in May, and the Committee unanimously urged all members of the Order to support that decision.

This support of integration, plus the fact that the ADL had been "a friend of the Court" during the case, caused a sharp reaction in some of the Southern lodges, from which hundreds of members resigned. President Klutznick made a special trip to meet with the leadership in the South and explain that B'nai B'rith policy was based on the ethics and morality of the Jewish tradition of justice. But many members in the South found themselves "in the middle," being pressured from one side by the white reactionary forces, and on the other side by threatened Negro boycotts—to say nothing of their own consciences. It is to their credit that the great majority of Southern members remained in the Order.

In Europe that year B'nai B'rith spread for the first time into Ireland and Italy when lodges were chartered in Dublin and Milan.

In the summer of 1955 District No. 19 was chartered at a solemn ceremony in Basel. Representatives of lodges were present from Belgium, Denmark, France, Greece, Holland, Italy, Luxembourg, Norway, Sweden, and Switzerland. Although only a shadow of prewar B'nai B'rith in Europe, the new District firmly planted the Order's banner on the Continent.

And in November of that year the B'nai B'rith Women of America dedicated their children's home at Beit V'gan, a Jerusalem suburb. It consisted of three splendidly equipped buildings, and the cost, instead of the $100,000 originally contemplated, had risen to $250,000. But the women pledged the entire amount, and in addition they undertook the maintenance.

Under President Klutznick's dynamic leadership the entire Order had been given a lift and was humming with activity. When he was reelected at the 1956 Supreme Lodge Convention in Washington, the membership had, during his three-year term, climbed from 178,-000 to 190,000, in spite of a still-spreading apathy in Jewish life generally.

During the convention the cornerstone was laid for the B'nai B'rith Building. The B'nai B'rith Women, who had pledged $300,000 to the building fund, announced they were contributing, in addition, $40,000 for a Four Freedoms Library, as part of the structure, in memory of President Franklin D. Roosevelt. The Constitution was amended to constitute the B'nai B'rith Women as a national organization, under the authority of the Supreme Lodge, but—for the first time—with jurisdiction over the Women's Districts and local chapters. The title, Women's Supreme Council, was dropped, and B'nai B'rith Women became the official title.

Secretary of State Dulles was principal speaker at the convention banquet, and again hundreds of the nation's leaders attended a B'nai B'rith affair. At the business sessions the delegates voted to limit the president of the Order to two terms, beginning then. This meant that Mr. Klutznick could have been elected again in 1959, but he publicly announced he favored the two-term limitation, and would not be a candidate in 1959. The office of treasurer was similarly limited, but later its traditional occupant, Sidney G. Kusworm, was elected for life. Vice presidents were also limited to two terms, retroactive to 1953. The presidents of overseas Districts were made members of the Board of Governors and vice presidents of the Order. The title of secretary was changed to executive vice president. Finally, the name of the Vocational Service Bureau was shortened by eliminating the word Bureau.

The convention was scarcely over when, in June, Morocco suddenly announced it would no longer permit the mass emigration of Jews. This caused a serious crisis, because the Jewish situation in the country was deteriorating, and most of the Jews yearned to settle in Israel. Mr. Klutznick immediately flew to Morocco, although there was a dearth of authentic firsthand information on the situation, and few if any contacts there. He and other outside Jewish leaders were able to be of some help, and later the ban was eased.

But the experience emphasized, to Phil Klutznick, the importance of international work on behalf of Jews beleaguered anywhere. Two years later B'nai B'rith joined with representative Jewish organizations in the United States, Canada, South America, Great Britain, France, Argentina, Australia, and South Africa, as well as with the World Jewish Congress, to form a new body called the Conference of Jewish Organizations (COJO), which today is strengthening its structure and techniques for coping with Jewish problems globally.

The most severe crisis since 1948 occurred, of course, in October, 1956, after Israel had suffered numberless invasions by murderous bands of *fedayeen*, trained in Egypt, while the paralyzed United Nations did nothing. Israel then invaded the Sinai Peninsula and wiped out all the marauders' nests and training centers. With England and France attacking Egypt in an effort to seize the Suez Canal, a general war seemed possible.

A month later it was reported that Egypt was imprisoning, deporting, and terrorizing its own Jewish citizens. B'nai B'rith participated in an emergency conference in New York of three hundred delegates of major Jewish groups, who appealed to President Eisenhower to instruct the United States Ambassador in Egypt to express "our country's shock" at these atrocities. At the same time B'nai B'rith asked its lodges in all metropolitan areas to join with other groups in local protest meetings.

Early in 1957, when the United Nations was discussing the application of sanctions against Israel for its Sinai attack, without even mentioning its cause, the Order's Administrative Committee passed a resolution declaring that such a UN action "would fly in the face of our own American conceptions of morality and national interest."

As the result of the "second round" of war between Israel and Egypt, B'nai B'rith made another, and greater, contribution to Israel's Vaad Lemaan Hechayal, which is comparable to the USO. The B'nai B'rith Committee for Israel organized a nationwide campaign which resulted in a flood of items, from toothpaste to station wagons, and from wristwatches to bed sheets. Carloads of such commodities were sent to Israel.

At the end of 1956 the Vocational Service undertook its third decennial census of Jewish college students, finding approximately 200,000 of them in American and Canadian universities. It was also announced that Hillel Foundation scholarships totaling $20,000 a year were available.

B'nai B'rith's most important happening in 1957 occurred in September, when the Supreme Lodge moved into its own building in Washington. The B'nai B'rith Women, whose headquarters had been in Chicago, moved in as well, and the $1,600,000 structure housed the national offices of all B'nai B'rith agencies except the ADL, which remained in New York. The dedication, held in November, was impressive, with Vice President Richard Nixon unlocking the front door and Mrs. Eleanor Roosevelt dedicating the Four Freedoms Library of the BB Women and unveiling a bronze bust of her husband. The building contained an Exhibit Hall, named for Mr. and Mrs. Klutznick, and containing displays of Jewish literary, artistic, patriotic, and other contributions to democracy and mankind. The Exhibit Hall is supervised by a B'nai B'rith Historical Committee, and Robert Shosteck is its first curator.

In April, 1958, Congress passed the first Civil Rights bill in eighty years. The ADL, which for years had been in the forefront of the civil rights struggle, presented its America's Democratic Legacy Award to the entire Eighty-fifth Congress at a "Dinner with Congress."

Later in 1958 the Board of Governors took the first steps to form a B'nai B'rith Foundation of the United States to raise funds for the Order's youth programs through large contributions from individuals. It actually came into being in 1959, with Myron E. Herzog of Chicago as chairman. Another late-1958 action was a restitution claim for $2,500,000 made by B'nai B'rith against West Germany, for portable assets seized by the Nazis when they forcibly destroyed B'nai B'rith in Germany in 1937.

As early as November, 1957, President Klutznick had suggested the possibility of holding the 1959 Supreme Lodge Convention in Israel. This was a bold and visionary proposal. No major Jewish organization had yet held a convention in the new Jewish State, and none was scheduled. The idea filled some leaders of the Order with exaltation, others, with grave misgivings: the travel expenses were too formidable; it would give the public the wrong impression about the Order; only the wealthy members could afford to attend, etc. But Phil Klutznick overcame all objections; a group all-expense fee that most members could afford was worked out, and in May the Order held its Twenty-second General Convention in Jerusalem.

Some thirteen hundred delegates and their wives and many visitors flew to Israel, chiefly from the United States, but also from England, the Continent, South America, and Australia. Israel had never seen anything like it. The visitors toured the country before and after the convention sessions, and the entire project was a two million dollar affair, which had a far-reaching impact.

The convention was addressed by Israel's President Itzhak Ben-Zvi, Prime Minister David Ben-Gurion, and other national leaders. Scholars and experts on various phases of Jewish life discussed contemporary Jewish problems, with the audience participating, at special sessions. The most spectacular was the evening meeting in the Hebrew University amphitheater. All three thousand seats were filled to hear an address by Premier Ben-Gurion. It was announced that the B'nai B'rith Building in Washington was debt-free, and the mortgage was ceremonially burned. All lights were extinguished, and the vast audience, which had been supplied with candles as they filed in, lit them, and three thousand flames flickered in the dark velvet night.

When the lights came on again, the Order's venerable "Dean" of the Board of Governors, Sidney G. Kusworm, on behalf of B'nai B'rith, presented a specially made Sefer Torah to President Klutznick as a gift. The evening ended on a note on high inspiration.

During the business sessions Mr. Klutznick received an ovation when he announced that West Germany had agreed to the Order's claim for German B'nai B'rith property and had made a $2,400,000 settlement, of which half had just been deposited to B'nai B'rith's account in a West Berlin bank. The other half was to be paid later. Mr. Klutznick also announced that the former B'nai B'rith Building in the heart of Berlin, which had once housed the headquarters of the German District Grand Lodge, had been sold for $280,000. It was decided that the larger fund would be allocated for projects to help reestablish the shattered communal lives of former German B'nai B'rith members living in Israel, Europe, and South America. The many lodges in Tel Aviv greatly needed a building, and it was agreed to use the $280,000 for that purpose.

Another inspiring session was held when the B'nai B'rith Martyrs' Forest was formally dedicated.

But in addition to the pageantry and emotion of the special events, the business sessions yielded an abundant harvest of important actions. The Committee on International Affairs was upgraded to a B'nai B'rith International Council, with responsibility for executing the Order's policies and operations in international work, UN relationships, and related activities. Its first charge was to allocate the $1,200,000 from Germany.

The Adult Jewish Education Committee was promoted to a Commission, and a one-dollar per-capita assessment was levied on each member, with half going to the Adult Jewish Education Commission and the other half to the International Council.

A plan was adopted to make group life insurance available, on a completely voluntary basis, to all B'nai B'rith men and women (in later years major medical and income protection coverage were added, under a B'nai B'rith Insurance Department, directed by Carl Weinstein, and with Dr. William A. Wexler heading its policy committee).

Philip Klutznick was elected an honorary president, after a six-year tenure crowned with major achievements. Membership had grown, during that period, from 178,000 to 196,000 men, and the B'nai B'rith Women numbered 130,000. With the creation of an International Council, the long chain of B'nai B'rith institutions had been substantially strengthened, and no new links were foreseen. The Order was at the peak of its strength, prestige, and service.

When Label A. Katz of New Orleans defeated Herman Fineberg of Pittsburgh to succeed Phil Klutznick as president, he knew how large were the shoes he was being called on to fill.

20

.

The 1960's, and new challenges

With the beginning of the 1960's, the effects of the new era in Jewish life which began after World War II became more noticeable. This is not the place for a detailed study of the sociological changes that were occurring in the Western World and their impact on American Jewish life. Suffice it to say that in prewar America the Jewish community was largely foreign-born; in postwar America, predominantly native-born. Formerly working class, the majority was now middle class and lived in suburbia. The "new Jew"—a third- or fourth-generation American—was becoming more and more a college graduate, a professional man, scientist, government official, organization man—and less "visible" than his forebears. His grandparents had been far from the devout and saintly scholars so often depicted in fiction, but they had been deeply influenced by the values of the East European small towns of their origin. The young people did not hesitate to identify themselves as Jews (were not practically all Americans expected to be either Catholics, Protestants, or Jews?), but it was all too often only an empty identification, devoid of Jewish content.

Would such men and women join B'nai B'rith, or be interested in what it was doing? They joined synagogues in large numbers, but few attended services, except on the High Holy Days. They all wanted their children to attend religious schools—until they were confirmed or till Bar Mitzvah, after which they lost all interest in the youngsters' Jewish education. But in the American Jewish community of more than five million, there were enough adults of all ages who joined B'nai B'rith to cause it to continue its slow but steady growth after 1959, although the membership of most other Jewish organizations declined.

Label Katz was only forty when he became president. Like his predecessor, he had been a member of AZA, and had been associated with B'nai B'rith ever since. He had a law degree but after several years of practice had branched out into housing rehabilitation and investments. He had had an intensive Jewish education, and was the first president who could read and speak Hebrew fluently. He became a leader in the United Jewish Appeal, the Federations, and other leading American Jewish agencies. He headed District No. 7 and later became national chairman of the B'nai B'rith Youth Commission.

Partly because he was so aware of the watering-down of Jewish consciousness in so many American Jews, and partly because his own Jewish background was so rich and fulfilling, he was determined to use his new office to stimulate greater interest in Jewish education. He was passionately devoted to the welfare of Israel, and like his predecessor he believed in the United Nations as a peace agency. He was also convinced that a steady pressure of public opinion could gradually force the Soviet Union to end or lessen the special discrimination suffered by Soviet Jews. These were among his primary concerns as president of the Order, but he was soon engulfed in its plenitude of agencies, all of which required attention The B'nai B'rith family of activities was now so large that new ones could hardly even be considered. What was needed, above all, was a consolidation of the growth of the past few years and a steadily rising income to support all the departmental budgets. To these ends Mr. Katz devoted himself with such energy that by the end of his two terms his health was seriously impaired.

During his first year in office a director was engaged for the new B'nai B'rith Foundation of the United States, and Mr. Katz traveled through all Districts preaching the gospel of increased income for the Order's Service Fund. In addition to the more than 200 Hillel units, requests for Hillel service had piled up from another 150 universities, but they could not be granted for lack of funds. The BB Youth Organization faced a somewhat similar problem. It refused to allow the proliferation of unsupervised chapters, but insisted that all be guided by trained professionals with high standards. But since the same lack of funds prevented any substantial staff expansion, thousands of youngsters who applied for admission to the crowded existing chapters or who wanted to form new ones had to be turned away, and the waiting lists lengthened.

It took years for the B'nai B'rith Foundation to get off the ground, and President Katz had his hands full trying to stimulate larger fund-raising efforts by the lodges which, for the most part, had done little of it in the past and often balked at accepting what seemed to them impossible quotas.

With an increased budget, the Adult Jewish Education Department engaged in more research and programming, increasing the number of summer institutes, expanding the number of local study groups, and publishing material for their use. One such text was a five-volume set of books on great personalities and ideas of the Jewish tradition, written by competent scholars and sold by the thousands. The first volume appeared in November, 1959. The Department also began publishing a quarterly magazine, *Jewish Heritage*, for the study groups and individuals.

Throughout his two terms, President Katz was active in international affairs. In January, 1960, he had an audience in Rome with Pope John XXIII, to discuss Catholic-Jewish relations. Shortly before, synagogues throughout Europe and North America had been smeared with swastikas and anti-Jewish threats, and the Pope condemned anti-Semitism in ringing words. From Rome, Mr. Katz went to Tel Aviv, where he dedicated the cornerstone of the B'nai B'rith Building under construction, and discussed the Order's Israel programs with some of the nation's leaders. On his way home he stopped in Amsterdam for the organizing meeting of the B'nai B'rith International Council, and met with Queen Juliana and Prince Bernhard.

When Phil Klutznick left office as chairman of the

Council, Label Katz succeeded him. About that time, American Jewry was aroused by reports that Saudi Arabia was discriminating against those American troops stationed at an American air base there who happened to be Jewish. President Katz made representations to the State Department and others, and received the strong support of Vice President Nixon. The charges were later found to be exaggerated, and the problem was overcome.

During the same summer he attended a meeting of the Conference of Jewish Organizations in Paris, where he strongly backed the proposal that a world conference on Jewish education be held. Then he flew to Israel, where, as head of the Presidents' Conference, he met with Prime Minister Ben-Gurion on the subject of bringing about a more mature relationship between Israel and American Jewry. A few weeks later he was in Paris for a one-day conference on the problems faced by Soviet Jewry.

In the autumn of 1960 the Order's International Council submitted three important documents on which it had done research to agencies of the United Nations. One was on emigration practices of the Soviet Union and other countries, and how those practices affected the Jewish people of those lands. The second dealt with a study of the "swastika epidemic," and the third concerned the rules on religious rights laid down by the UN Subcommission on Prevention of Discrimination. The following February, President Katz, representing COJO, appeared before that subcommission to present detailed evidence of anti-Jewish discrimination in various parts of the world.

If all this seems dull and futile, it is because the results were usually not immediately apparent. But on other occasions this kind of international work was more lively. Early in 1961, for example, Mr. Katz met with State Department officials and also with the Moroccan Ambassador in Washington, to plead for the right of Jews to either stay in Morocco unmolested, or to leave, as they wished—since the ban on emigration was still in effect. At one point in the interview the Ambassador impatiently remarked that Jews were always zealous about the welfare of other Jews but were not concerned with the fate of non-Jews. This gave Mr. Katz the opportunity to tell the Ambassador something about the B'nai B'rith program and history: how it raised millions of dollars for the relief of people of all faiths when they were victims of catastrophes; the traditional nonsectarian policies of B'nai B'rith hospitals; the completely nonsectarian nature of its World War II program and most of its local civic work; and how it stood in the forefront of the struggle for civil and economic rights for Negroes, Puerto Ricans, and others. The Ambassador was visibly impressed, his attitude changed, and he forwarded Mr. Katz's appeal, by cable, to his Government. It cannot be known whether it had any effect, but a few weeks later King Mohammed V revoked the ban on Jewish emigration, and most of the Jews, in time, were able to settle in Israel. Of course, B'nai B'rith was only one of several Jewish organizations that worked for that same cause.

In 1960 and 1961 two B'nai B'rith agencies inaugurated new programs of considerable potential value. The ADL financed a half-million-dollar five-year study of anti-Semitism in the United States, which was undertaken by the University of California Research Institute. Hillel Foundation leaders tackled a very different problem. Not only was the indifference, and sometimes hostility, of the Jewish college student toward his own heritage a serious development, but it was exacerbated by many Jewish faculty members, who were either antireligious or without interest in Judaism. So Hillel organized a series of seminars for such faculty people, at which off-campus intellectuals discussed Jewish issues on a high level. Today there is a growing body of Jewish professors who pass on to Jewish students some of their own interest in the Jewish heritage.

In the summer of 1961 President Katz and Executive Vice President Bisgyer visited the Soviet Union. They attended synagogue services in Moscow and Kiev, talked to a number of Jews in both cities, and had a conference with the First Deputy Minister of Culture. They learned something at firsthand of the fears and yearnings of many Soviet Jews, and something of the official techniques of pretending that all was well with Soviet Jewry. From that time on, Mr. Katz devoted a goodly portion of his energies to the issue.

Of course B'nai B'rith's international concerns were not limited to Russia. The International Council opened offices in Israel, Europe, and Latin America, and in 1962 it was granted consultative status with the UN Educational, Scientific, and Cultural Organization (UNESCO), as well as with the Organization of American States.

Label Katz was unanimously reelected president at the Twenty-third General Convention in Washington, in May, 1962. Membership had remained on a plateau during the triennial period, still a few thousand short of 200,000, but the Order's prestige had gained new levels. The delegates authorized the institution of District Grand Lodge No. 21 in Australia–New Zealand; combined the Commission on Citizenship and Civic Affairs with the Service Committee for Armed Forces and Veterans into a single Commission on Citizenship, Veterans and Community Affairs; elevated the Committee for Israel to Commission status; and added to that agency's program the establishment of high-school scholarships for needy Israeli teen-agers.

They also voted that "B'nai B'rith shall continue its established policy of participating in consultative and coordinating assemblies created within the Jewish community for the purpose of advancing cooperative activity and a spirit of voluntary unity among independent Jewish organizations." This was like an echo of the ancient Preamble to the Order's Constitution: "B'nai B'rith has taken upon itself the mission of uniting Jews . . ."

There was another echo, too. Probably because the membership was at a standstill, a delegate proposed that non-Jews be admitted—the very issue that had broken up B'nai B'rith's third lodge, in Baltimore, in the 1850's. It was overwhelmingly defeated.

During the convention sessions Mr. Katz and other organization leaders called on President John F. Kennedy, presented him with an ornamental silver wall plaque containing traditional Jewish symbols, and discussed with him such subjects as civil rights, the status of Soviet Jewry, and Middle East affairs.

The convention devoted a lot of time to the agonizing question of how to meet its expanding budget. The fact is, B'nai B'rith was experiencing the price of success, namely, relentless pressure for more and more success. And its very bigness raised vast and intricate problems of internal communication. Its bewildering network of agencies and activities, professional and lay leaders, scores of area councils and Districts, hundreds of lodges, commissions and committees, worldwide relationships, membership in "roof organizations," public relations and financial problems—all this made it seem like a kind of octopus, none of whose many tentacles knew what the others were doing. President Katz was no more able to solve this perhaps insoluble problem than any of his predecessors, involved as he was more in international than internal affairs.

In the months following the 1962 Convention ominous developments took place in the Algerian struggle against France. The Jews were caught in the middle between rebel and "loyalist" factions. In Latin America former Nazis from Germany, and a few Arab League agents, were stirring up violent anti-Semitism. The situation in Argentina was the worst of all, and President Katz conferred in Washington with the Argentine Ambassador and presented him with evidence of one hundred cases of anti-Jewish violence in his country within the previous year, without arrests.

During the summer Mr. Katz made a world trip. He conferred on common problems with heads of Jewish organizations in England, attended a World Conference on Jewish Education in Israel, met briefly with Prime Minister Nehru in India to discuss matters pertaining to Israel and Near East issues, and in Australia he installed the new District No. 21. During his stay in Israel he announced B'nai B'rith would contribute $150,000 to build a B'nai B'rith Library for the planned Desert Educational Institute at Sde Boker, home of Premier Ben-Gurion, with the library serving as the nucleus of a future College of the Negev.

But on his return home a new wave of anti-Jewish terrorism swept through Buenos Aires and other Argentine cities. Jews were beaten on the streets, synagogues and Jewish-owned shops were bombed, and Jewish institutions were desecrated. Mr. Katz flew to Buenos Aires and was received by the nation's President, who assured him the Government intended to outlaw all political movements that promoted racial or religious discord. This was indeed done, and for a time the furore died down, but the peace was only temporary.

Two factual monographs on the 1959–60 "swastika epidemic" prepared by the Order's International Council office at the United Nations served as the basis for strong General Assembly resolutions asking member governments to fight bigotry. Early in 1963 President Katz, representing COJO, spoke at a UN subcommission in favor of the right of all individuals to emigrate from any country. He was promptly attacked by the Soviet delegate, who evidently felt that the shoe fit, but the subcommission adopted a report in favor of such a right.

Soon after, Mr. Katz received documentary evidence of the publication of several books of the most viciously anti-Jewish character in the Soviet Union, and exposed their existence through the press—at the very time when Soviet authorities were denying that anti-Semitism existed in their country.

In the first part of 1963, President Katz met in Rome with Augustin Cardinal Bea, who played so large a part in the passage by the Ecumenical Council of the schema attacking anti-Semitism. Throughout the Council's years of sessions, ADL experts, on request, advised Vatican leaders of contemporary attitudes of Jews on many subjects.

During the same year the International Council and the ADL joined with other nongovernmental agencies in helping the U. S. Mission to the UN attack the problem of discrimination which made it so difficult for African delegates to find decent housing in New York, and the B'nai B'rith Metropolitan Council formed a hospitality committee to help make leading UN personnel feel at home by taking them on tours of industrial and other points of interest they wanted to see.

After more than twenty years of joint fund-raising, the ADL and the American Jewish Committee ended the arrangement over a policy disagreement, and beginning in 1963 each began to raise its money separately. Interestingly enough, each raised more funds that way.

The ADL celebrated its fiftieth anniversary early in 1963 with one of its most notable affairs. President Kennedy was guest of honor and was given the same award that had been presented to President Eisenhower ten years before. His talk, and some professional entertainment, were nationally telecast. And one of the entertainment industry's outstanding personalities—movie producer, author and playwright, Dore Schary—was elected national chairman of the ADL.

A few months later B'nai B'rith bought the old American Red Cross headquarters in New York and remodeled it for use as a B'nai B'rith Building, to house the national ADL offices as well as District No. 1 headquarters and offices for the many other B'nai B'rith branch agencies in the metropolitan area.

In October, 1963, the Order began a year-long celebration of its 120th anniversary. Because Moses lived to be 120, it has long been a Jewish tradition, on birthdays, to wish individuals a life of the same length. In B'nai B'rith's case, however, the anniversary marked the launching point of a "second 120 years," and consequently as the occasion for special membership and fund-raising campaigns. It so happened that 1963 also witnessed the 75th anniversary of the Order's existence in Israel; the 50th anniversary of the ADL; the 40th birthday of the Hillel Foundations; and the 25th year of

B'nai B'rith Vocational Service—and all were included in the festival year of celebration.

But the joyous mood was changed to sorrow when President Kennedy was assassinated in November. Some of the Order's anniversary programs were postponed. Label Katz issued a statement expressing B'nai B'rith's grief over the tragedy. At the same time he sent Lyndon B. Johnson a wire pledging the Order's wholehearted support. The new President had twice attended national B'nai B'rith meetings, and in April, 1963, as Vice President, he had received the ADL's Human Rights Award.

The year 1964 was Mr. Katz's last as president of B'nai B'rith, and he intensified the work he considered most important. He again urged the lodges to raise their fund-raising goals, and many did. Early in the spring he returned to Rome for an audience with Pope Paul VI at which, with the second session of the Ecumenical Council looming ahead, he discussed Catholic-Jewish relationships and B'nai B'rith's interest in the Church's declarations on anti-Semitism and religious freedom for all.

For some time he and the heads of twenty-three other major Jewish organizations had been quietly organizing an American Jewish Conference on Soviet Jewry, to focus public attention more strongly on the problem of anti-Jewish discrimination in the USSR. In April the Conference held its first meeting, in Washington, and worked out a program which could be implemented in local communities throughout the country. In the summer of 1965 the Conference staged a protest demonstration which brought ten thousand people to Washington, probably more than half of them members of B'nai B'rith.

During 1964 the B'nai B'rith Youth Organization observed its fortieth anniversary, and District No. 22 was chartered. Carved out of District No. 1, it consists of eastern Canada and was the first new District in North America to be chartered since the origin of District No. 7 in 1873.

A number of important events took place in 1965. Maurice Bisgyer, executive vice president for nearly twenty-seven years—the longest service in that post in the organization's history—retired on January 1.

The centennial of B'nai B'rith's relationship with Palestine or Israel was celebrated throughout the year. That relationship began with the large contribution the Order had made to help cholera victims in 1865.

In February, B'nai B'rith and its ADL rejoined the National Community Relations Advisory Council. The ADL Commission met that month in Washington and presented its America's Democratic Legacy Award to President Johnson, who, with Mrs. Johnson and a host of national figures, attended the ADL's annual banquet.

In April, B'nai B'rith finally reached—and passed—the long-sought membership figure of 200,000 men.

In May, Rabbi Jay Kaufman became executive vice president of the Order, just a few weeks before the Twenty-fourth General Convention. For sixteen years he had been a top executive with the Union of American Hebrew Congregations and had represented that body at many national conferences. At the same time the office of associate executive vice president was established, with Dr. Sidney Nelson as incumbent.

The outstanding event of the year, of course, was the Supreme Lodge convention, which was held in Israel again, late in May. This time it took place principally in Tel Aviv, although it opened in Jerusalem. Like the meeting held there in 1959, it brought well over thirteen hundred delegates and visitors to the country and included tours through Israel and Europe.

The auditorium of the new B'nai B'rith Building in Tel Aviv was dedicated in memory of Eddie Jacobson, and the B'nai B'rith Library at Sde Boker was formally dedicated, as was a graceful stone arch at the entrance to the B'nai B'rith Martyrs' Forest.

The emotional peak of the convention was reached at an evening meeting in the two-thousand-year-old amphitheater at Caesarea, built by King Herod and recently excavated by archeologists. There Israel's Prime Minister Levi Eshcol delivered the principal address, and Label Katz, on his last evening as president of the Order, was paid a tribute.

The convention voted to increase the number of future delegates by reducing the number of members each one represents from eight hundred to six hundred, and by giving each Women's District two instead of one. The size of all Commissions, except that of the ADL, was also increased. The office of honorary executive vice president was authorized, and bestowed upon Mr. Bisgyer. And the often-changed name of the Order's citizenship and veterans' program was changed again, to Commission on Community and Veterans' Services.

Dr. William A. Wexler was elected president of the Order after a contest with Judge David A. Coleman of Los Angeles. Dr. Wexler was born in Toledo, Ohio, in 1913, but has been practicing optometry in Savannah, Georgia, since the 1930's.

A member of B'nai B'rith all that time, he probably served in more high posts in the Order than any of his predecessors before their election. He was president of his lodge in Savannah; president of the Georgia B'nai B'rith Association; president of District No. 5; honorary vice chairman of the ADL's Southern regional board; a national vice president of the Order; a member of its International Council; a member of the National ADL Commission; chairman of the Order's Insurance Committee; vice chairman of the Commission on Israel; a member of the National Vocational Service Commission; and chairman of the National Membership Cabinet, which had just triumphantly announced that membership had surged past the 200,000 mark for the first time in B'nai B'rith history.

But his activity in other causes was also noteworthy. The list is too long to record, but it involved, among other things, service as an alderman of his city, leadership in a number of fraternal orders and civic groups, the presidency of his local Jewish community center and of the Southern region of the Jewish Welfare Federation, membership on the National Campaign Cabinet of the United Jewish Appeal and the National Council of the Joint Distribution Committee, and many other causes.

Life in the South had not dulled his devotion to liberal principles of justice as they apply to all people. Before and after his election to the presidency he spoke out forthrightly on behalf of civil rights for Negroes at the same time he was fighting against the discrimination suffered by Jews and others. But he did more than merely talk. Two years before he became president of the Order he put up his own home as bail for a young man from the North, a Christian and a perfect stranger, who had been arrested in Savannah while helping Negroes there to register and vote. The judge had set an exorbitant bail. The young man's father was over-whelmed by Dr. Wexler's action, and wrote him of his gratitude in memorable terms.

All this experience—plus glowing health, a dynamic nature, and a dedication to B'nai B'rith's traditional covenant to serve the Jewish people and humanity—he brought to his new position.

He had a lot going for him, and a lot going against him. B'nai B'rith was at a new high level in size and activity. Functioning in forty-three countries around the world, coordinated by an International Council, with official status at the United Nations and other international agencies, its prestige had never been greater. It had a membership of 205,000 men in some 1,350 lodges, and 130,000 women in more than 900 chapters, and there were close to 50,000 young people in 1,600 BBYO chapters. Its 260 Hillel units were operating on that many college campuses, with a total of some 350,-000 Jewish students. Its 23 Vocational Service offices were giving group and individual career counseling annually to more than 75,000 youngsters in metropolitan areas (and special advice to their parents), and its Anti-Defamation League was generally recognized as the leading "defense" and human-relations agency in American Jewish life, with thirty regional offices working closely with the thousands of lodges and chapters.

B'nai B'rith's Adult Jewish Education program had had nearly twenty years of experience, and the Order's beautiful camp in Pennsylvania was the scene of many adult meetings and youth conventions every year. Its official organ, *The National Jewish Monthly*, was the oldest Jewish magazine in America, read by about a half million adults. Its Commission on Israel was involved in a dozen projects of importance to the Jewish State,

and in 1966 launched a new one authorized by the 1965
Supreme Lodge convention—a B'nai B'rith Israel Technical Corps, which recruited thousands of American and
Canadian Jewish technicians and skilled workers to
work in Israel, where they were sorely needed, for several years or permanently. The B'nai B'rith Community
and Veterans Services Department stimulated hundreds
of programs and activities in lodges throughout the
country on behalf of civic needs and hospitalized veterans. Through its Insurance Department it was able, by
mass purchasing power, to furnish protection for tens of
thousands of its members on a voluntary basis and at
the same time derive a substantial income for the Order's activities.

Through its membership in the Presidents' Conference, COJO, the Conference on Soviet Jewry, the Claims
Conference Against Germany, the World Conference on
Jewish Education, and the NCRAC, it was acting in
unity with other leading Jewish bodies in making major
contributions to the general Jewish welfare. Its voice on
behalf of the persecuted among its own and other people
had been heard for nearly a century and a quarter and
was well known and respected in influential circles at
home and abroad.

And its Washington building was the symbol of its
success and stability as well as the home of an increasingly respected Hall of Exhibits of Jewish contributions
to humanity and of a growing Four Freedoms Library.

But this team of successful agencies was not in an
open field and running with the ball. Between it and the
goal posts loomed some ominous adversaries.

One was the increasing difficulty of stimulating large
numbers of Jews to become organizationally active in a
time of unparalleled prosperity and an atmosphere of

unlimited freedom, growing social integration, and decreasing organized anti-Semitism. Another was the mounting cost of everything the Order was doing. A third was the weight of tradition in an agency as old as B'nai B'rith. Patterns had been set in many areas, vested interests flourished, leaders were often loyal only to the agency in which they were specially interested rather than to the organization as a whole.

Many questions were arising: Was the lodge still useful as a form of organization? Could the youth agencies do the required job with their limited resources in the face of the population and college explosions? Had any of the old-line agencies outlived their usefulness? Were new agencies needed? Had the changing nature of the American Jewish community been really confronted, and basic adjustments made accordingly? And perhaps most important of all, would the upcoming younger generation give Jewish life its loyalty and support to the same extent the older ones had?

21

■

Past, present, and future

Methuselah's only claim to fame is that he lived so long. The same cannot be said of B'nai B'rith. Its record speaks for itself. Looking back, is a pattern discernible? Looking ahead, what are the prospects?

From the very beginning, the pattern is clear. It is stated in the first phrases of the Constitution's Preamble, dating all the way back to that autumn day in 1843, when Henry Jones read aloud to the assembled founders the work of his pen: "B'nai B'rith has taken upon itself the mission of uniting Israelites in the work of promoting their highest interests and those of humanity."

Thus, the unity of the Jewish people has always been the basic goal—not as an end in itself but as the best means for creative Jewish survival, which is itself a contribution to mankind. In every generation there have been Jews who, influenced by their foreign birth and Old World conditioning, have sought to graft upon the American Jewish community some of the characteristics of the old East European kehillah, with its rigid control over individuals and the group. But that is not the American way, nor the B'nai B'rith way. It was remarkable that the twelve founders of the Order, although born abroad and living here less than a score of years before 1843, should have imbibed this American spirit to such a degree.

But does American Jewry of the 1960's need unity? Surely its different segments bear no resemblance to the feuding, brawling Jewish community of 1843? Today they are practically all native-born, and increasingly of the third and fourth generation. They have no memories of Old World kehilloth, pogroms, feuds, superstitions, insecurities, lack of secular education, and all the other factors that influenced their forebears.

But today they are divided along other lines. Some want to be invisible Jews; others are chauvinists. Many want to be active in Jewish life; many more prefer to pay all their Jewish obligations by check. There are those who give neither money nor time—not to mention those who, as in every generation since Moses, quietly drift away from their Jewish identification altogether. There are some who are militantly traditional, others who are militantly liberal, and still others who are neither traditional, liberal, nor militant about anything. There are Jews who believe in the peoplehood of Israel, and others to whom Jewishness is solely a matter of religious affiliation.

In spite of these differences—and there are many others—all except those who have drifted away have their Jewishness in common, however it is defined. They want to remain Jewish, for one reason or another. But they have different approaches to common problems.

B'nai B'rith's great contribution a century and a quarter ago, and today, is that it has always succeeded in uniting dissident factions in programs on which they could agree. In the 1840's Germans and non-Germans— and even Germans among themselves—differed violently in many ways, but in B'nai B'rith they united in caring for the widow and orphan. In the 1850's they worked together against the discrimination practiced against Jews in Switzerland. In the ensuing decades these disunited elements united, in the B'nai B'rith lodge room, to help victims of natural catastrophes, to maintain libraries, to establish vocational schools and adult lectures, to fight anti-Semitism, to protest foreign and domestic injustices based on widely differing ideologies, to work as a unit during American wars and other emergencies, to provide facilities for Jewish youth to regain their Jewish heritage, to cooperate in a thousand ways in local community work, even to overcome their differences on the most controversial issue of three generations and help father and then support the State of Israel.

With all due respect, no other Jewish organization of any kind has done that.

And B'nai B'rith has been able to do it only because of another facet of its nature—its flexibility. It has never had a set program. For decades, in the beginning, its leaders spoke constantly of its "higher objects," but they differed as to what they meant by that nebulous term. B'nai B'rith cannot be called a philanthropic organization, nor a fraternal one, nor one concerned with public affairs. It is not limited to community activites, fighting anti-Semitism, promoting education, sponsoring youth work, advancing the welfare of the Jewish State, or any of a score of other categories, although it encompasses all of them. That is why, for want of a better description, it is generally known as a Jewish service organization.

But there are no other Jewish service organizations, and the many great non-Jewish ones are, by definition, totally different—they don't have to cope with "the Jewish problem" on top of everything else.

Yet it has always been precisely that "Jewish problem" which has been central to B'nai B'rith's *raison d'être* and appeal. That is why, in every generation, it beat down efforts to make it nonsectarian. Its members have always disagreed concerning the nature of Judaism, but they never disagreed about being Jews. They always differed about how to solve Jewish problems, but they never doubted the problems existed, and had to be solved. Some of them, in more recent times, joined the Order solely to get a place on the crowded bowling alleys as members of a lodge team, and then became interested in one or another of the organization's substantive activities. Some joined only because of the work of the Anti-Defamation League and never developed an interest in anything else. Others came into the Order because of some local lodge project that appealed to them, or because they had friends who were members, or because they were strangers in town and longed for Jewish fellowship, or because, although they hadn't the slightest idea of what B'nai B'rith was doing, they felt it was a "good cause" and deserved their support. Whatever the reason, however tenuous the connection, the Jewishness of the organization was always a greater or lesser factor.

It was that way in 1843, and has been ever since. Much has been said about "the new American Jew," and there is no doubt that there is a great difference between today's young Jewish atomic scientist, with his degrees from Harvard and M.I.T.—and his grandfather from Poland or Russia who came to New York early in the century. But not all Jewish young men are atomic scientists, or even intellectuals. A great many of today's Jewish college graduates are confused about the meaning of their Jewish identity, and to some it plays little or no part in their lives. But many—perhaps the majority—are not fundamentally different from their parents—or won't be after they've become parents themselves.

B'nai B'rith today, from Toronto to Texas, has scores of thousands of such young members, as well as their elders. In countless cases those same elders were part of the rebellious generation of Jewish youth of the 1920's and 1930's.

The fact remains that there are still needs in the Jewish community which have to be met. Some young Jews have lived for thirty years without being personally affected by anti-Semitism and tend to believe it no longer exists—but it does. The five-year research program at the University of California, sponsored by the ADL, has revealed so much data on this subject—much of it ominous—that a whole series of books is being published to report the results.

Many Jewish communities in lands overseas, where democracy is a new, and only weakly grafted, phenomenon, face darkly uncertain futures. The problems of the State of Israel are many and knotty, despite its remarkable progress. Jewish education in the United States, on which some $100,000,000 a year is spent, has been described as "a mile wide and an inch deep," and few previous generations in Jewish history have been so ignorant of the Jewish heritage as the present one, although American Jewry has produced many outstanding native-born Jewish scholars and teachers. Intermarriage seems to be increasing, with a consequent loss to the Jewish people of some of the participants and especially their children. Many Jews, instead of assimilating the finest American traditions and practices, assimilate the worst, along with their conforming neighbors.

These are only some of the issues on the agenda of Jewish life today. B'nai B'rith grappled with other difficult ones in past eras, and is now addressing itself to the new ones, which in many ways are more difficult than those of yore. This is a massive and complicated challenge that will require manpower, womanpower, money, brains, time, energy, dedication, and statesmanlike leadership. But B'nai B'rith at least has the flexibility and experience to undertake the task. In the past, it never acted merely to be doing something, but only because there were needs to which it responded. And after the need had been filled, the Order quietly ended its program, as it ended its war service after the war, as it liquidated its Mexican Bureau in 1930, and as it withdrew from the sole sponsorship of hospitals, orphanages, and homes for the aged when times changed. On the other hand, the magnitude of some current problems is such that B'nai B'rith recognizes the importance of more cooperation with other agencies, not merely during emergencies, as in the past, but on a continuing basis.

Jews have always looked objectively at the world, and have seen wars, revolutions, pogroms, starvation, disease, cruelty, injustice, and horrors of all kinds—as well as kindness, decency, love, and man's infinite capacity to raise the level of his existence and his relationship with his fellows. As a result, they have always been optimists when it comes to man's fate, but at the same time they are convinced the Messiah is yet to appear.

They know, too, that Messianic times, if they ever do arrive, will come not by a miracle but through man's will and work. That is why the old B'nai B'rith ritual contained the injunction "to watch and wait, to work and strive." B'nai B'rith is only a tiny fraction of mankind, but it has many natural allies in spirit—among the Jewish people and among all people who are committed to human progress.

Thus, although a torrent of questions and problems descended upon the Order during the 1960's, Dr. Wexler, as he got his new administration well under way, was fully aware of them, which is the first step toward overcoming them. He knew how important all the questions were, and he decided to seek the answers, through studies and surveys of every operation of the Order. That will take time, but since he will undoubtedly be elected, like all his predecessors, to a second term, in 1968, it means he will lead B'nai B'rith into the 1970's, when the right answers will have become indispensable.

It is foolhardy to predict the future. But B'nai B'rith found the right answers for the crisis that brought it into being and for all the revolutionary changes that have occurred since. Why not once more?

A final word

The story of B'nai B'rith had a beginning, but it has no end. Or, more accurately, it has no end that can be fore-seen. It is unique among the multitude of Jewish organi-zations in the world, not only in its historical develop-ment and achievements but in the universality of its appeal to the Jewish people.

The honorary president of the Order, Philip M. Klutz-nick, put it succinctly when *The National Jewish Monthly* asked him why he belongs to the organization. This was his reply:

B'nai B'rith is singular in its family composition, with a division or an activity for men, women, and children; it is comprehensive in its concern with the totality of human experience; it is sensitive to the differences that divide people, yet persistent in its search for areas of agreement; and above all, it is available as a movement for all Americans of the Jewish faith. In B'nai B'rith is to be found the synthesis of the American Jewish search for the genuine compatibility of a great Jewish heritage with the inspirational qualities of the American dream itself.

Index

Aid (Contd.)

202; Jews in Constantinople, 154; Palestinians in Egypt, 154; refugees from Communism, 256; Rumanian District, 154; starving in Near East, 154; to immigrants, 89, 110

Alexander II, Czar, 89

Alexander, Morris, 260

Alfred M. Cohen Colony, 224

Algerian situation, 279

Alliance Israelite Universelle, 67, 90

American Committee for Ameliorating the Condition of Russian Refugees, 110

American fascist groups, 200

American Hebrew, 96

American Israelite, 96

American Presbyterian Union, 31

Americanism Commission, 224, 229

Americanism Committee, 215

Americanization Department, 166, 175, 184

American Jewish Assembly, 242

American Jewish Committee, 137, 139, 149, 157, 160, 164, 171, 191, 196, 199, 202, 214, 218, 223, 234, 239, 256, 281

American Jewish Congress, 231, 232, 234, 235, 239, 241

American Jewish Conference on Soviet Jewry, 282

American Jewish Congress, 157, 163, 164, 191, 195, 199, 201, 202, 214, 218

American Legion, xviii, 238

American Red Cross, xvii,

222, 226, 228, 229, 238, 253

Anspacher, Henry, 16

Anti-Catholicism, 7

Anti-Defamation League, viii, 140, 150, 165, 166, 170, 175, 181, 184, 185, 187, 189, 193, 194, 200, 201, 205, 206, 213 *et seq.*, 223, 235, 239, 246, 252, 253, 256, 261 *et seq.*, 267, 276, 280, 281, 286, 292, 293; origin, 140

Anti-Nazi boycott, 201, 221

Anti-Semitism, 139, 150, 170, 206

Apathy in B'nai B'rith, 93

Arab anti-Jewish riots, 210

Arab League, 279

Ararat Lodge, 72

Arbeitsgemeinschaft, 185, 202

Argentina, 279

Arms sent to Russian Jews, 135

Arthritic Hospital in Hot Springs, Ark., 130, 139

Ashkenazim, 5

Ashkenazim and Sephardim, 100, 109

Associated Press, viii, 140

Atlanta Jewish Orphan Home, 103

Auerbach, Dr. Israel, 174

Australia-New Zealand District founded, 277

Austria, 6

Austria-Hungary District Grand Lodge founded, 114

Austrian District Grand Lodge, 102, 165

Auxiliary lodges, 115

AZA, 183, 184, 187, 188, 193, 194, 205, 207, 212, 217,

B'nai B'rith (Contd.)

pean office, 240; fiftieth anniversary, 109, 111; first contested election for presidency, 185; first court cases, 25 *et seq.;* first magazine, 99; first endorsement of a Zionist position, 241; first joint fund-raising with others, 191; first letter from an U.S. president, 111; first meeting, 18; first structure, 21; first uniform age minimum set, 156; first women's group, 115; Foundation, 224, 238; Foundation of the U.S., 267, 273, 274; fund for European Jewish relief, 152; fund-raising difficulties, 200, 201; garden community in Jerusalem, 173; Girls, 204, 217, 225, 233; golden anniversary, 109, 111; Historical Committee, 267; history, xvii, 83, 99, 146, 155, 174, 223; Home for Orphans in Erie, Pa., 247; Immigration Commission, 154; Infirmary dedicated at National Jewish Hospital, 186; in Germany, 100; in Latin America, 240; in international affairs, 274; in New York, 213; Institute of Judaism, 251; Insurance Department, 270, 287; International Council, 269, 270, 274, 275, 277, 280, 286; international work, 265, 277; in the South, 77, 78; Israel Technical Corps, 287; joins first American Jewish Congress, 159; Latin American Committee, 257; libraries, 92; Library at Sde Boker, 279, 284; Martyrs' Forest in Israel, 262, 269, 284; Medal, 149; Metropolitan Council, 280; Mexican Bureau, 172, 174, 181, 184, 187, 194, 294, founded, 171; Monsky Foundation, 263; motto, 20; name is shortened, 190; National Boycott Committee, 221; National Defense Committee, 222; National Finance Council, 239; National Youth Service Appeal, 240; observes 120th anniversary, 281; organizes American Soldiers and Sailors Welfare League, 161; orphanage, 91; plans for Peace Conference, 153; professional fund-raising, origin of, 181; program aids Israel, 246; proposes Board of Deputies, 196; protests British White Paper, 213; rebuilds in Europe, 237; Rehabilitation Center in Tel Aviv, 253; research fellowship at Hebrew University, 174; restored to Canada, 155; self-effacement in Civil War, 58; secrecy in, 98, 122, 146, 166; self-criticism in, 93; Service Committee for Armed Forces and Veterans, 253; Service Fund, 254, 273; seventieth anniversary, 150; Social Service Bureau, 154, 155; origin, 181; supports Jewish colonization of